MONSTER MOTORS

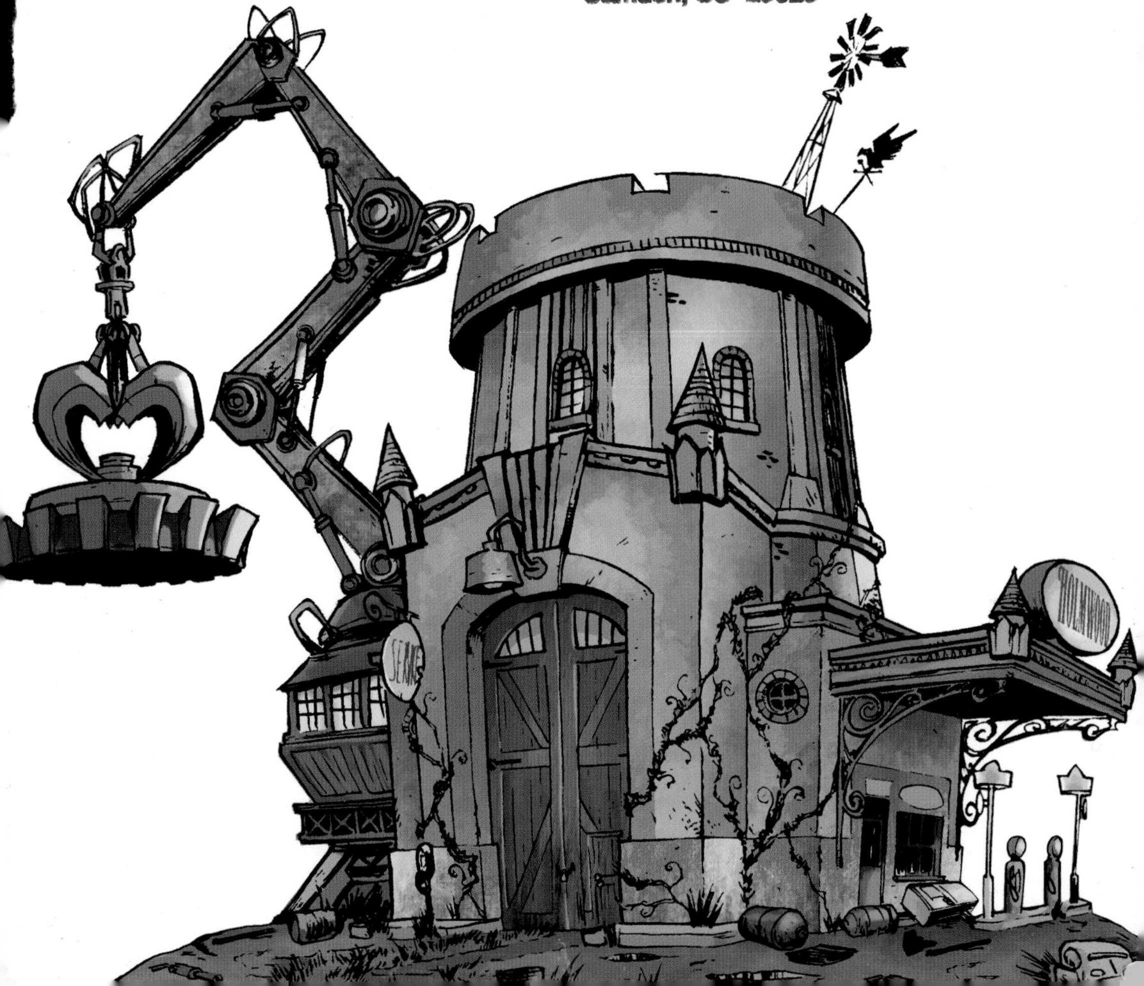

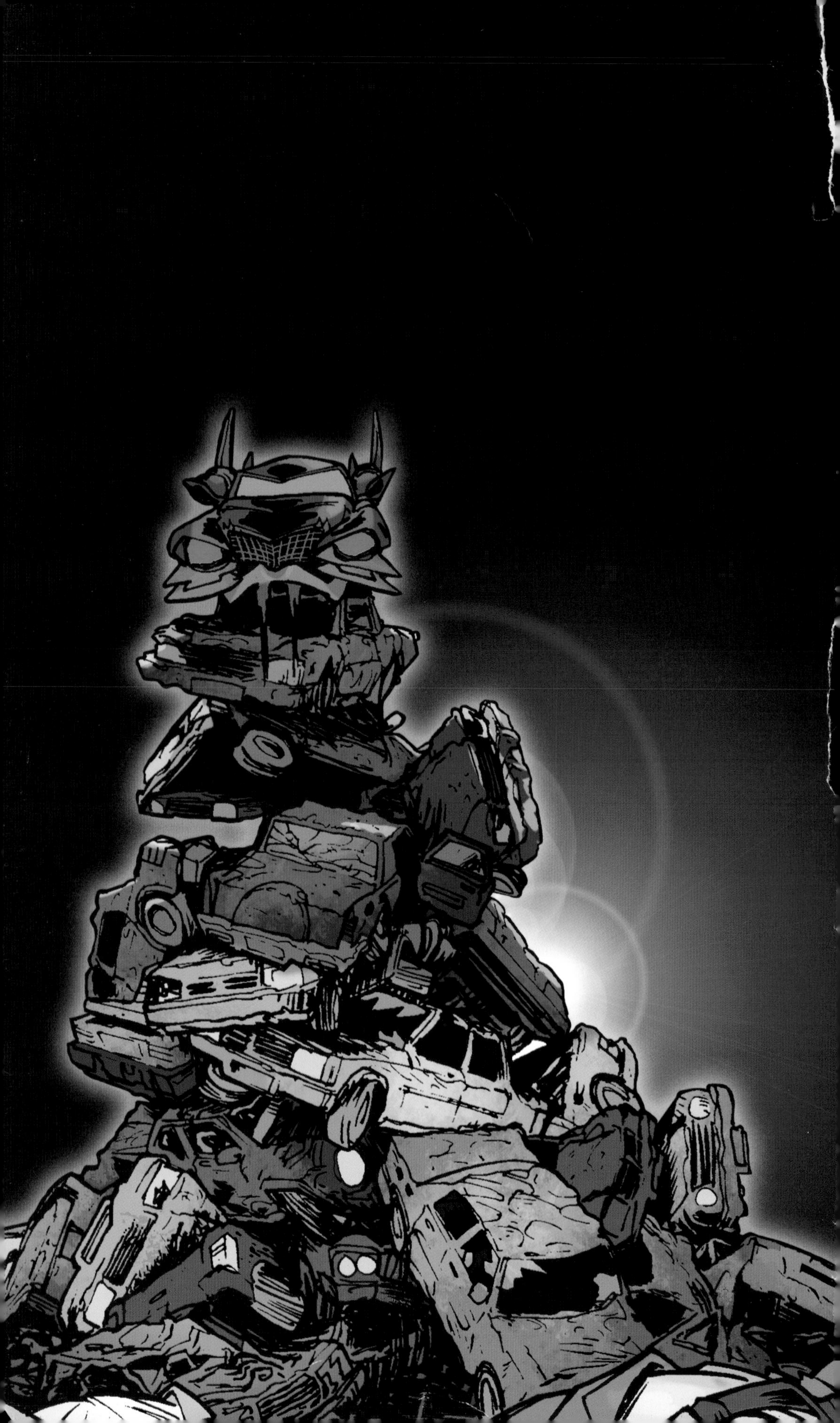

MONSTER MOTORS

CREATED AND WRITTEN BY
Brian Lynch

ILLUSTRATED BY
Nick Roche

COLORED BY
Leonard O'Grady

LETTERED BY
Tom B. Long

SERIES EDITED BY
Chris Ryall

EDITORIAL ASSISTANCE BY
Michael Benedetto

ALL COVERS BY
Nick Roche

ALL COVER COLORS BY
Leonard O'Grady

COLLECTION EDITS BY
Justin Eisinger AND **Alonzo Simon**

COLLECTION DESIGN BY
Rich Sheinaus/Gotham

SPECIAL THANKS TO
Chris Meledandri, Adriana Alberghetti, Carrie Beck, Eoin Colfer, Joan Cassese, Jeffrey Frankel, Catherine Howard, Stephen Mooney, Gary Schneider, Dan Schoening, Scott Whitehead and Anne-Marie Roche

IDW

Become our fan on Facebook   **facebook.com/idwpublishing**
Follow us on Twitter   @**idwpublishing**
Check us out on YouTube   **youtube.com/idwpublishing**
Tumblr   **http://tumblr.idwpublishing.com/**
Instagram   **instagram.com/idwpublishing**

978-1-63140-337-8   18 17 16 15   1 2 3 4

Originally published as MONSTER MOTORS and MONSTER MOTORS: THE CURSE OF MINIVAN HELSING issues #1–2.

Ted Adams, CEO & Publisher
Greg Goldstein, President & COO
Robbie Robbins, EVP/Sr. Graphic Artist
Chris Ryall, Chief Creative Officer/Editor-in-Chief
Matthew Ruzicka, CPA, Chief Financial Officer
Alan Payne, VP of Sales
Dirk Wood, VP of Marketing
Lorelei Bunjes, VP of Digital Services

IDW founded by Ted Adams, Alex Garner, Kris Oprisko, and Robbie Robbins

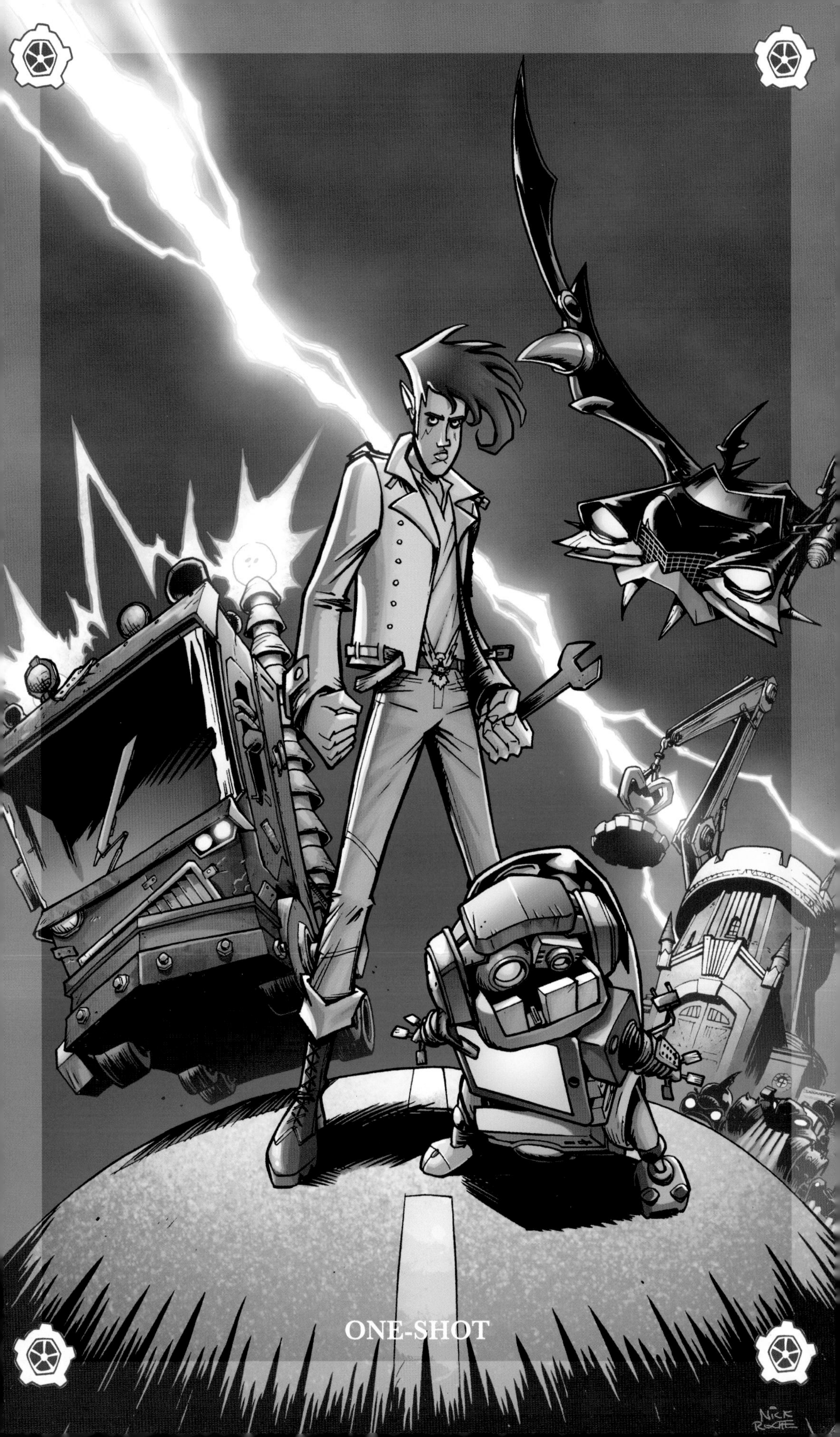
ONE-SHOT
NICK ROCHE

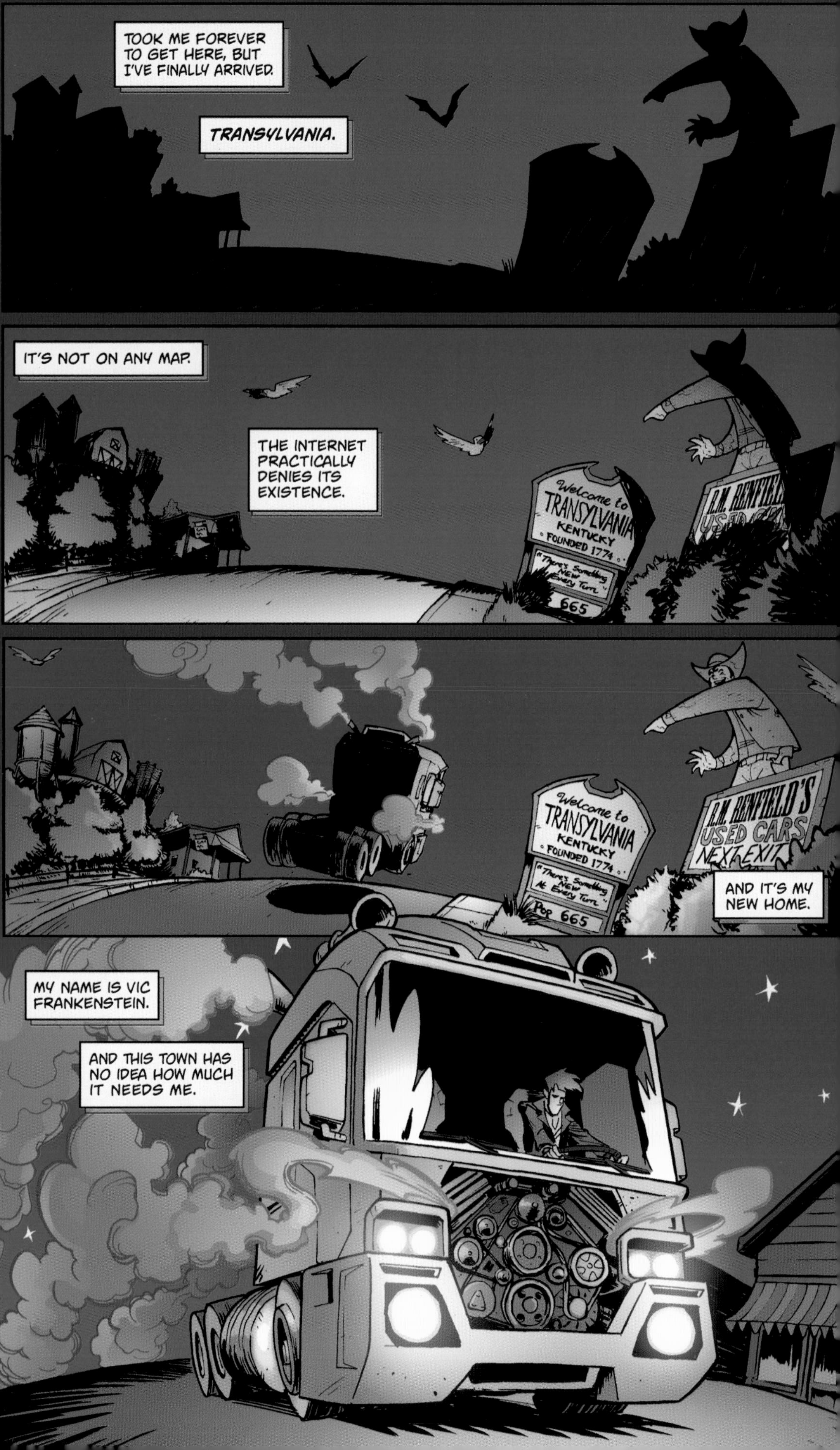
TOOK ME FOREVER TO GET HERE, BUT I'VE FINALLY ARRIVED.
TRANSYLVANIA.
IT'S NOT ON ANY MAP.
THE INTERNET PRACTICALLY DENIES ITS EXISTENCE.
Welcome to TRANSYLVANIA KENTUCKY FOUNDED 1774
"There's Something New At Every Turn."
Pop 665
R.M. RENFIELD'S USED CARS NEXT EXIT
AND IT'S MY NEW HOME.
MY NAME IS VIC FRANKENSTEIN.
AND THIS TOWN HAS NO IDEA HOW MUCH IT NEEDS ME.

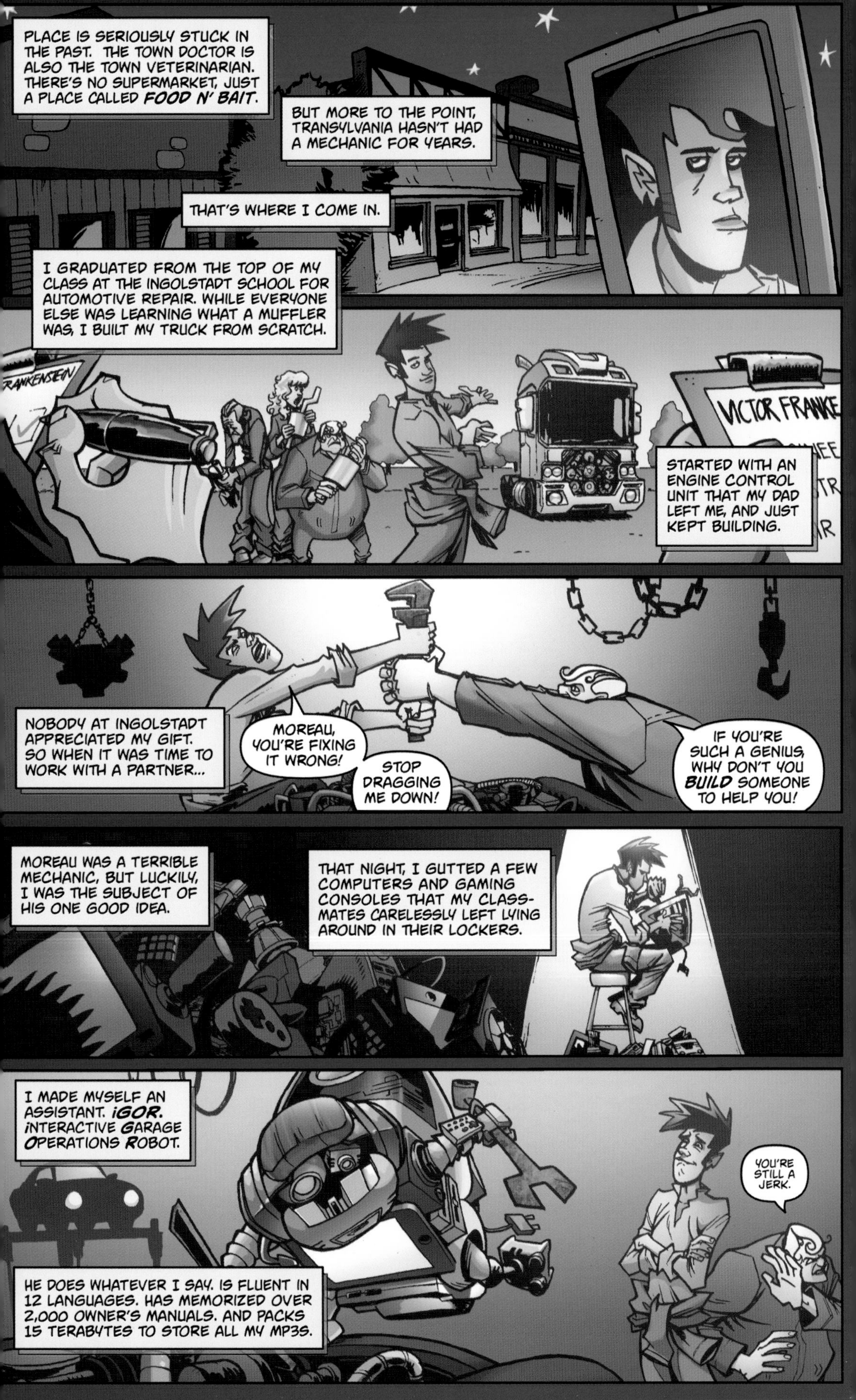
PLACE IS SERIOUSLY STUCK IN THE PAST. THE TOWN DOCTOR IS ALSO THE TOWN VETERINARIAN. THERE'S NO SUPERMARKET, JUST A PLACE CALLED *FOOD N' BAIT*.
BUT MORE TO THE POINT, TRANSYLVANIA HASN'T HAD A MECHANIC FOR YEARS.
THAT'S WHERE I COME IN.
I GRADUATED FROM THE TOP OF MY CLASS AT THE INGOLSTADT SCHOOL FOR AUTOMOTIVE REPAIR. WHILE EVERYONE ELSE WAS LEARNING WHAT A MUFFLER WAS, I BUILT MY TRUCK FROM SCRATCH.
STARTED WITH AN ENGINE CONTROL UNIT THAT MY DAD LEFT ME, AND JUST KEPT BUILDING.
NOBODY AT INGOLSTADT APPRECIATED MY GIFT. SO WHEN IT WAS TIME TO WORK WITH A PARTNER...
MOREAU, YOU'RE FIXING IT WRONG!
STOP DRAGGING ME DOWN!
IF YOU'RE SUCH A GENIUS, WHY DON'T YOU *BUILD* SOMEONE TO HELP YOU!
MOREAU WAS A TERRIBLE MECHANIC, BUT LUCKILY, I WAS THE SUBJECT OF HIS ONE GOOD IDEA.
THAT NIGHT, I GUTTED A FEW COMPUTERS AND GAMING CONSOLES THAT MY CLASSMATES CARELESSLY LEFT LYING AROUND IN THEIR LOCKERS.
I MADE MYSELF AN ASSISTANT. *iGOR*. *i*NTERACTIVE *G*ARAGE *O*PERATIONS *R*OBOT.
YOU'RE STILL A JERK.
HE DOES WHATEVER I SAY. IS FLUENT IN 12 LANGUAGES. HAS MEMORIZED OVER 2,000 OWNER'S MANUALS. AND PACKS 15 TERABYTES TO STORE ALL MY MP3S.

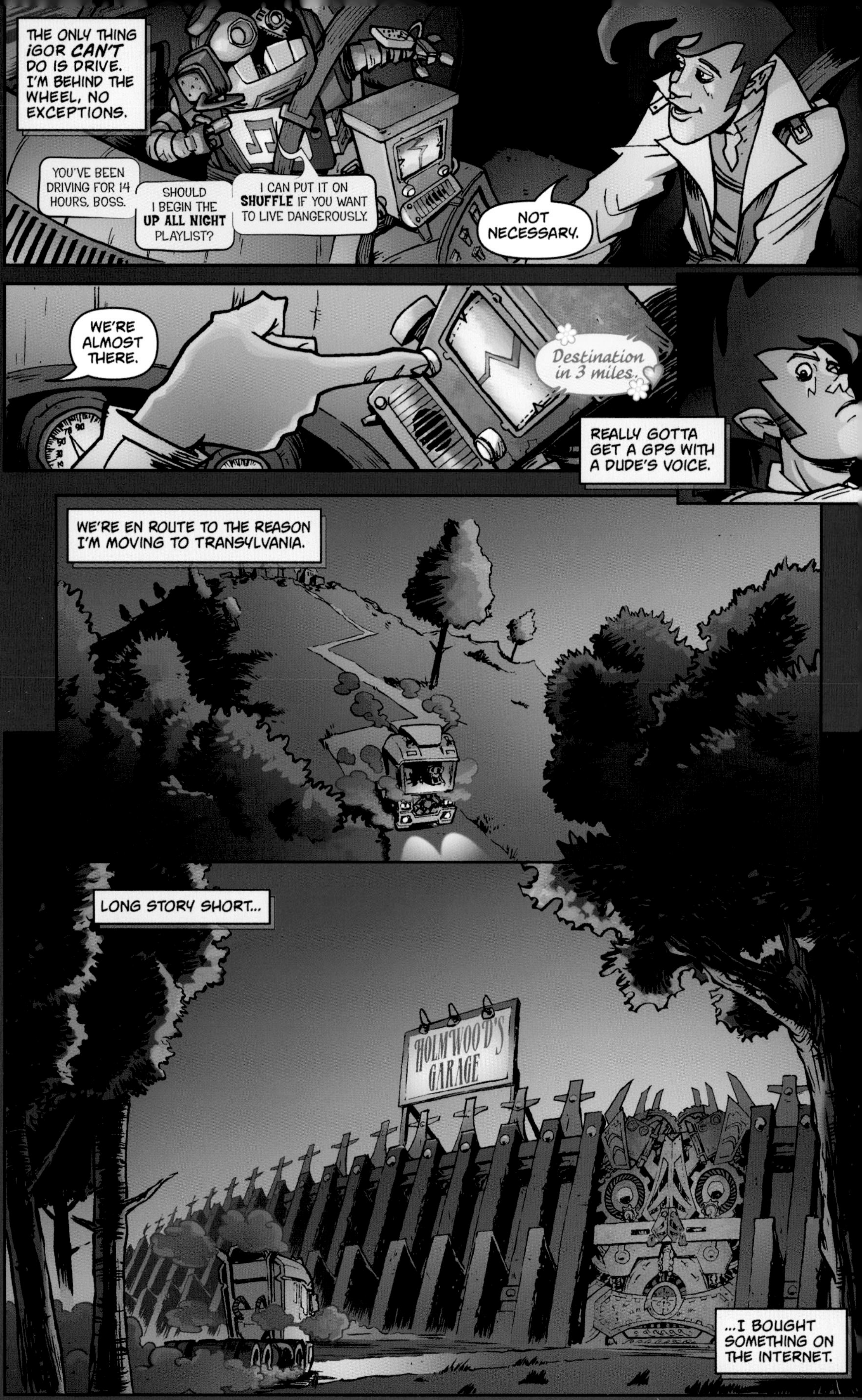
THE ONLY THING IGOR CAN'T DO IS DRIVE. I'M BEHIND THE WHEEL, NO EXCEPTIONS.
YOU'VE BEEN DRIVING FOR 14 HOURS, BOSS.
SHOULD I BEGIN THE UP ALL NIGHT PLAYLIST?
I CAN PUT IT ON SHUFFLE IF YOU WANT TO LIVE DANGEROUSLY.
NOT NECESSARY.
WE'RE ALMOST THERE.
Destination in 3 miles.
REALLY GOTTA GET A GPS WITH A DUDE'S VOICE.
WE'RE EN ROUTE TO THE REASON I'M MOVING TO TRANSYLVANIA.
LONG STORY SHORT...
HOLMWOOD'S GARAGE
...I BOUGHT SOMETHING ON THE INTERNET.

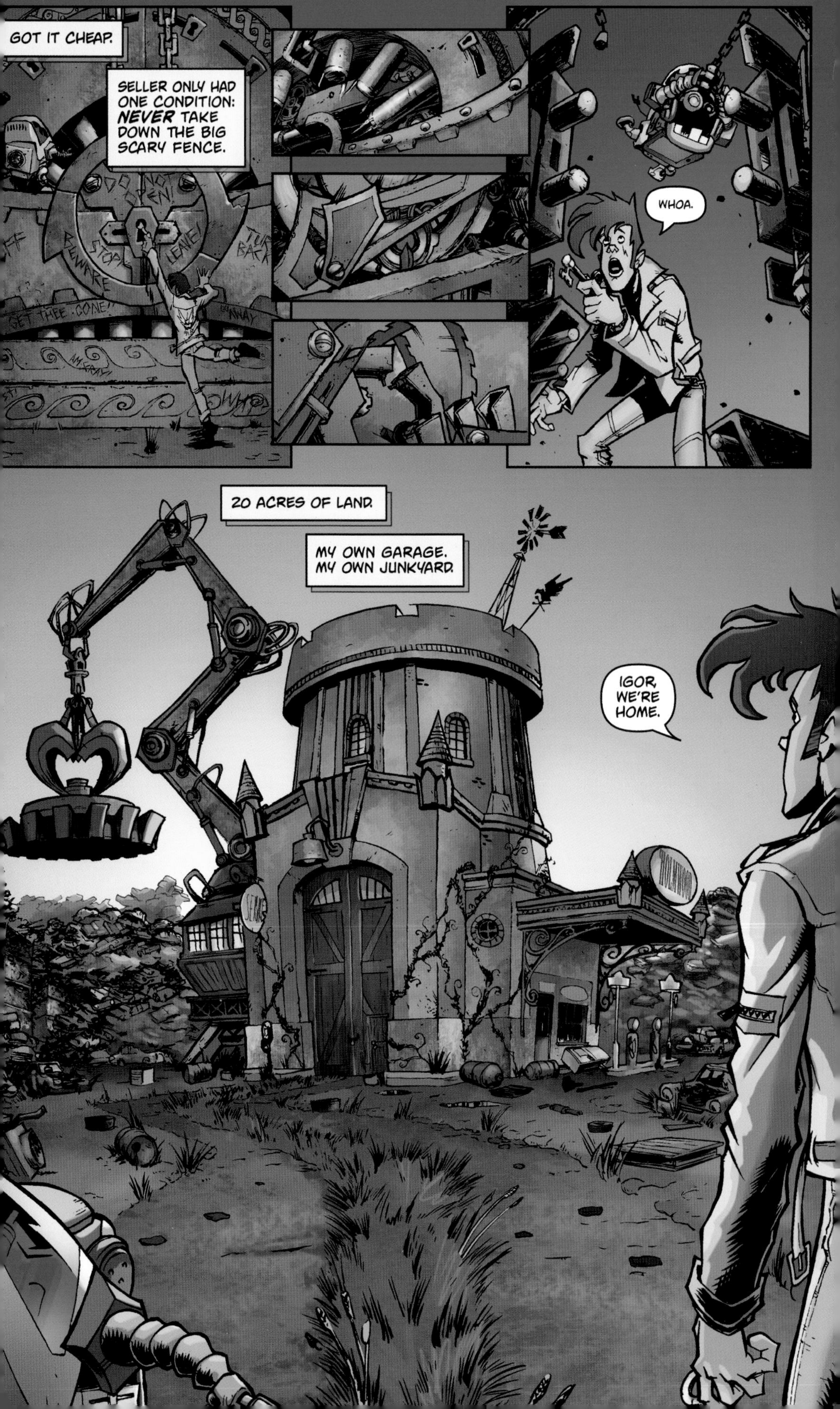
GOT IT CHEAP.
SELLER ONLY HAD ONE CONDITION: ***NEVER*** TAKE DOWN THE BIG SCARY FENCE.
DO NOT OPEN!
STOP!
LEAVE!
BEWARE
TURN BACK
GET THEE GONE!
RUN AWAY
WHOA.
20 ACRES OF LAND.
MY OWN GARAGE. MY OWN JUNKYARD.
IGOR, WE'RE HOME.

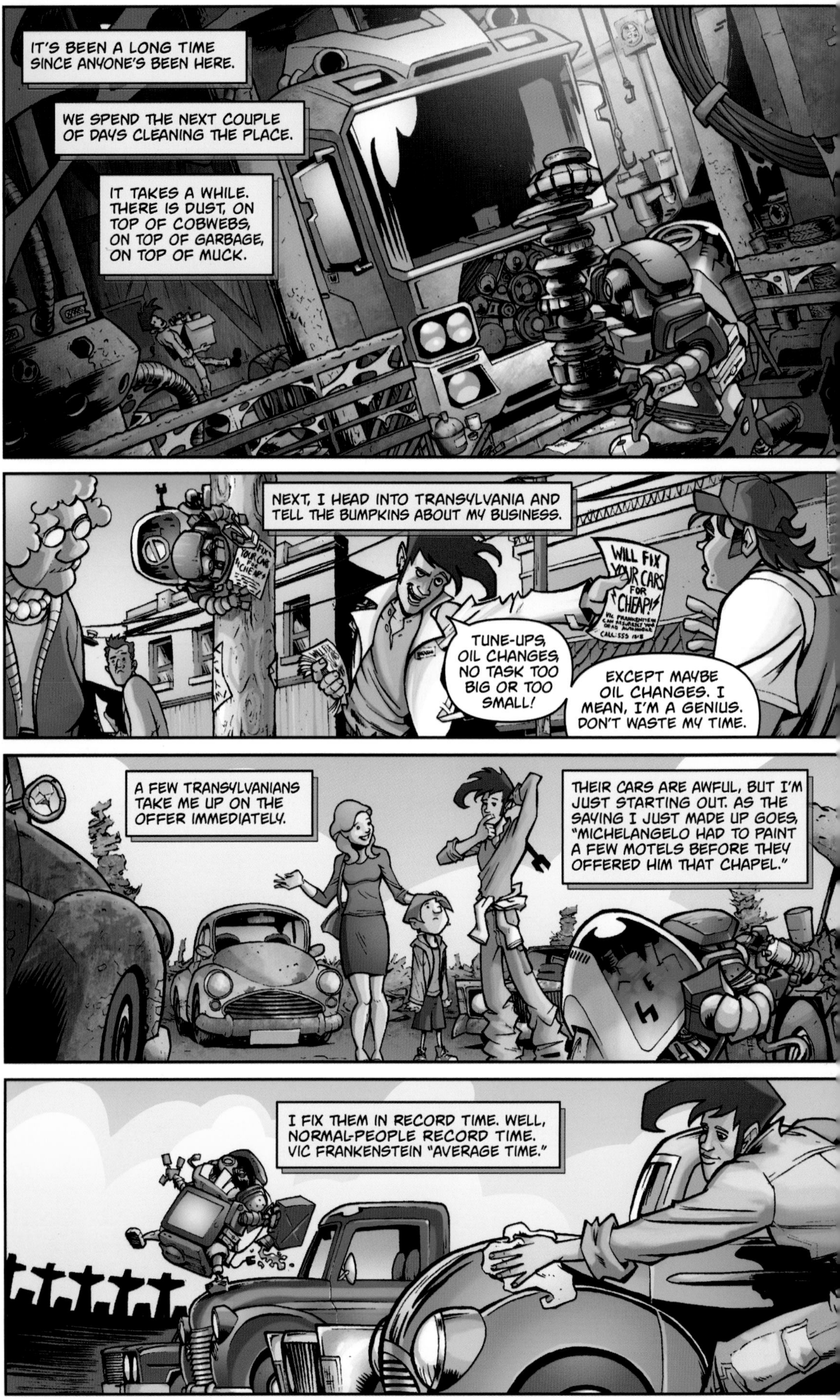
IT'S BEEN A LONG TIME SINCE ANYONE'S BEEN HERE.
WE SPEND THE NEXT COUPLE OF DAYS CLEANING THE PLACE.
IT TAKES A WHILE. THERE IS DUST, ON TOP OF COBWEBS, ON TOP OF GARBAGE, ON TOP OF MUCK.
NEXT, I HEAD INTO TRANSYLVANIA AND TELL THE BUMPKINS ABOUT MY BUSINESS.
WILL FIX YOUR CARS FOR CHEAP!
TUNE-UPS, OIL CHANGES, NO TASK TOO BIG OR TOO SMALL!
EXCEPT MAYBE OIL CHANGES. I MEAN, I'M A GENIUS. DON'T WASTE MY TIME.
A FEW TRANSYLVANIANS TAKE ME UP ON THE OFFER IMMEDIATELY.
THEIR CARS ARE AWFUL, BUT I'M JUST STARTING OUT. AS THE SAYING I JUST MADE UP GOES, "MICHELANGELO HAD TO PAINT A FEW MOTELS BEFORE THEY OFFERED HIM THAT CHAPEL."
I FIX THEM IN RECORD TIME. WELL, NORMAL-PEOPLE RECORD TIME. VIC FRANKENSTEIN "AVERAGE TIME."

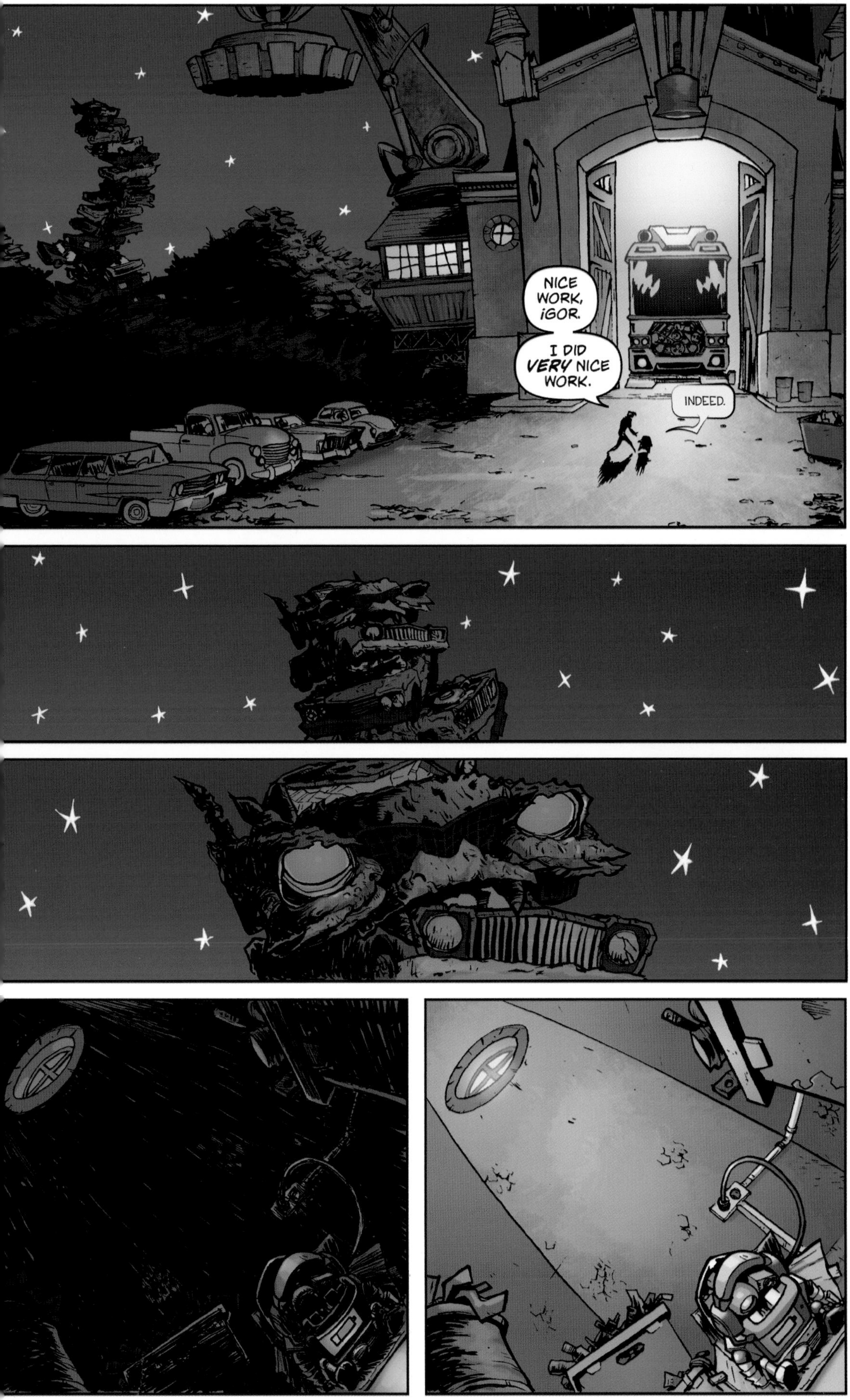
NICE WORK, iGOR.
I DID VERY NICE WORK.
INDEED.

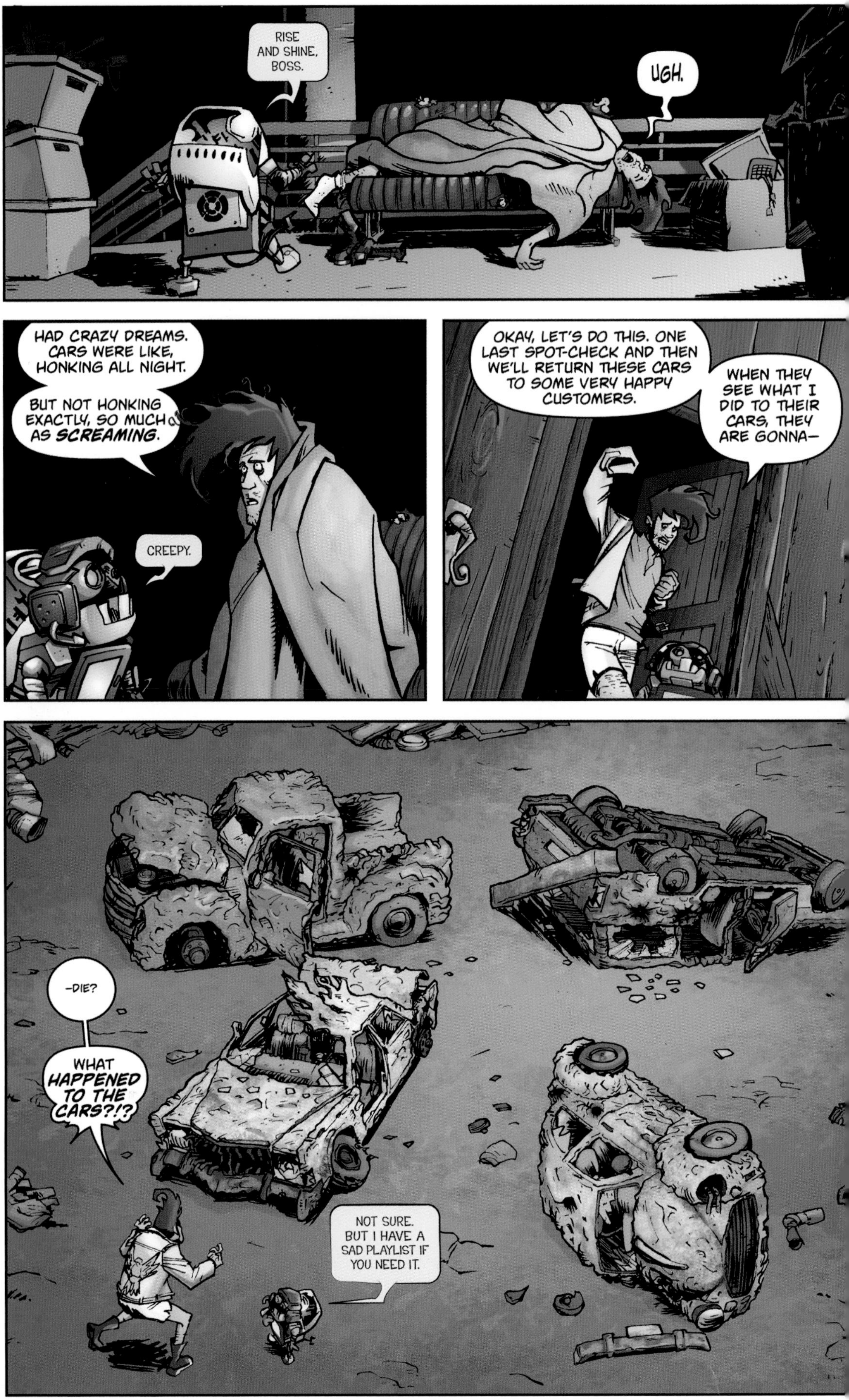
RISE AND SHINE, BOSS.
UGH.
HAD CRAZY DREAMS. CARS WERE LIKE, HONKING ALL NIGHT.
BUT NOT HONKING EXACTLY, SO MUCH AS SCREAMING.
CREEPY.
OKAY, LET'S DO THIS. ONE LAST SPOT-CHECK AND THEN WE'LL RETURN THESE CARS TO SOME VERY HAPPY CUSTOMERS.
WHEN THEY SEE WHAT I DID TO THEIR CARS, THEY ARE GONNA—
—DIE?
WHAT HAPPENED TO THE CARS?!?
NOT SURE. BUT I HAVE A SAD PLAYLIST IF YOU NEED IT.

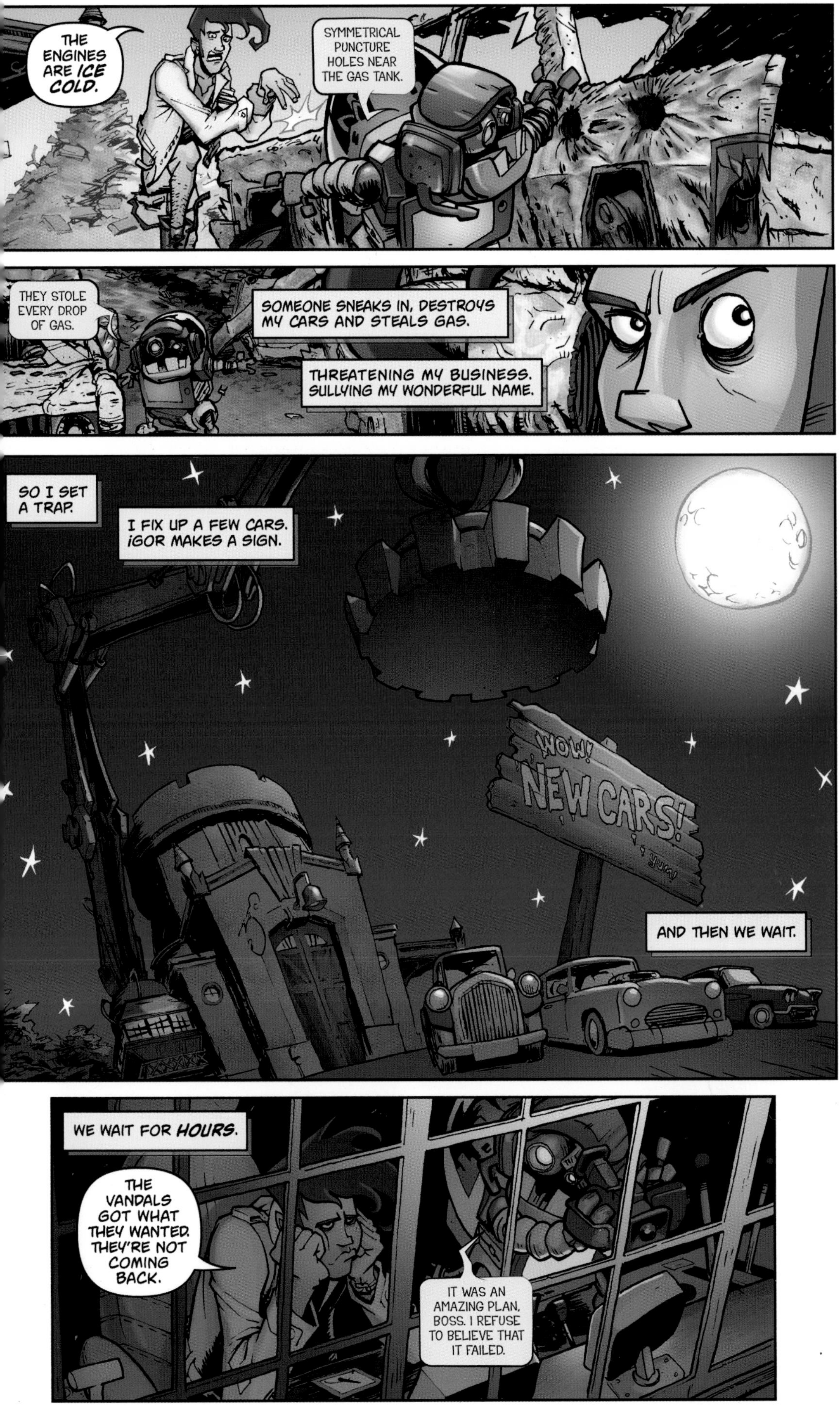
THE ENGINES ARE *ICE COLD.*
SYMMETRICAL PUNCTURE HOLES NEAR THE GAS TANK.
THEY STOLE EVERY DROP OF GAS.
SOMEONE SNEAKS IN, DESTROYS MY CARS AND STEALS GAS.
THREATENING MY BUSINESS. SULLYING MY WONDERFUL NAME.
SO I SET A TRAP.
I FIX UP A FEW CARS. iGOR MAKES A SIGN.
WOW! NEW CARS!
yum!
AND THEN WE WAIT.
WE WAIT FOR ***HOURS***.
THE VANDALS GOT WHAT THEY WANTED. THEY'RE NOT COMING BACK.
IT WAS AN AMAZING PLAN, BOSS. I REFUSE TO BELIEVE THAT IT FAILED.

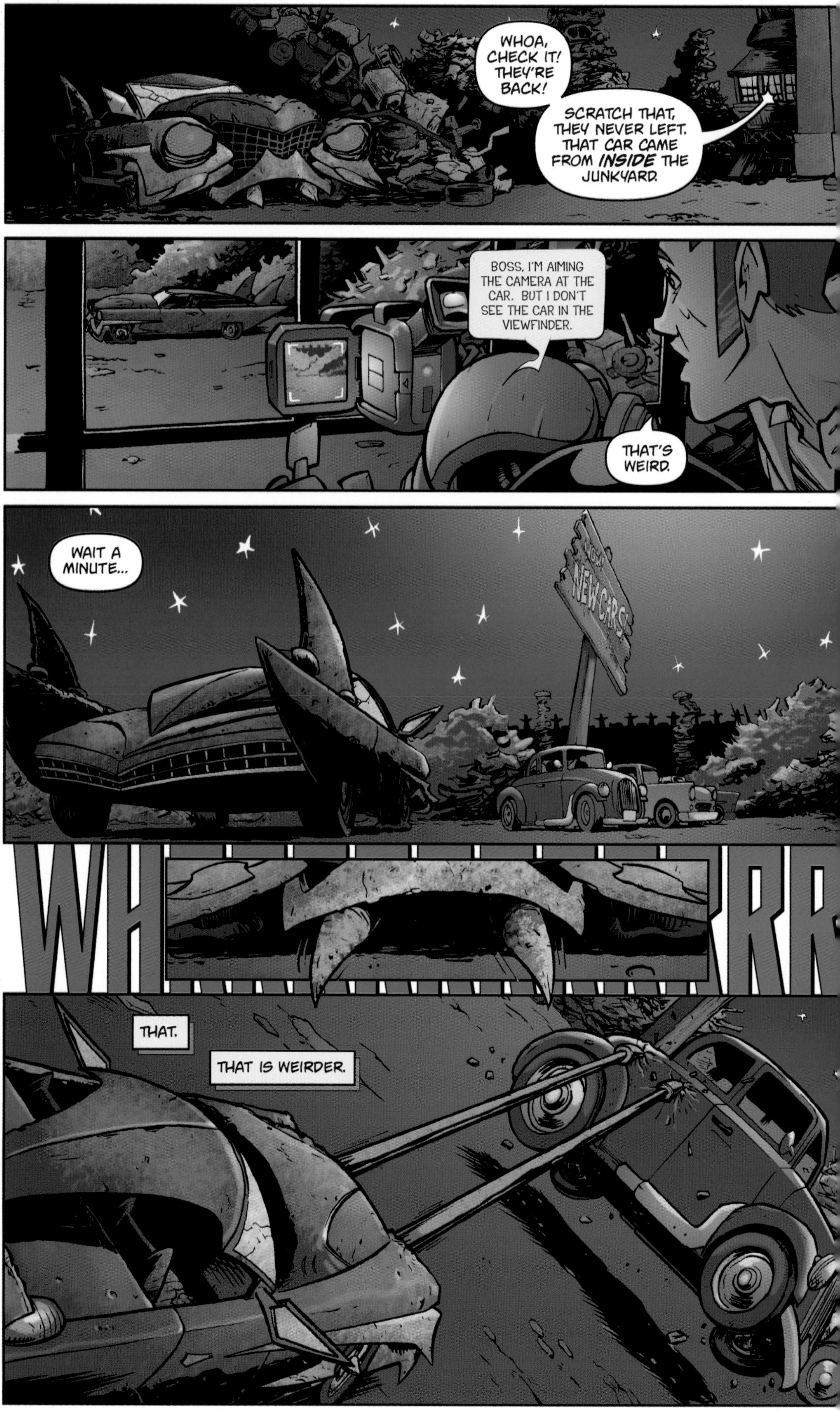

WHOA, CHECK IT! THEY'RE BACK!
SCRATCH THAT, THEY NEVER LEFT. THAT CAR CAME FROM *INSIDE* THE JUNKYARD.
BOSS, I'M AIMING THE CAMERA AT THE CAR. BUT I DON'T SEE THE CAR IN THE VIEWFINDER.
THAT'S WEIRD.
WAIT A MINUTE...
NEW CARS!
THAT.
THAT IS WEIRDER.

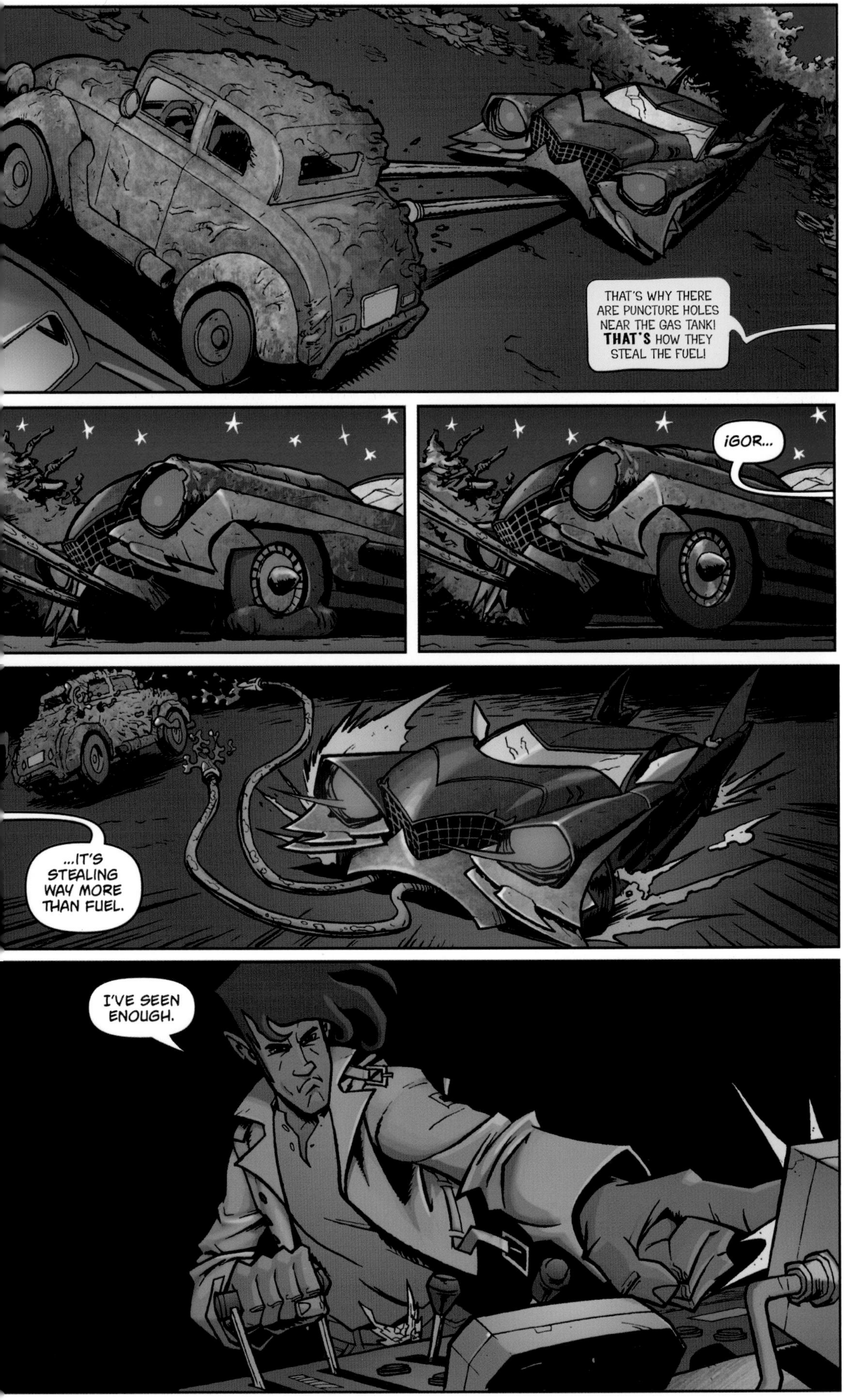
THAT'S WHY THERE ARE PUNCTURE HOLES NEAR THE GAS TANK! **THAT'S** HOW THEY STEAL THE FUEL!
¡GOR...
...IT'S STEALING WAY MORE THAN FUEL.
I'VE SEEN ENOUGH.

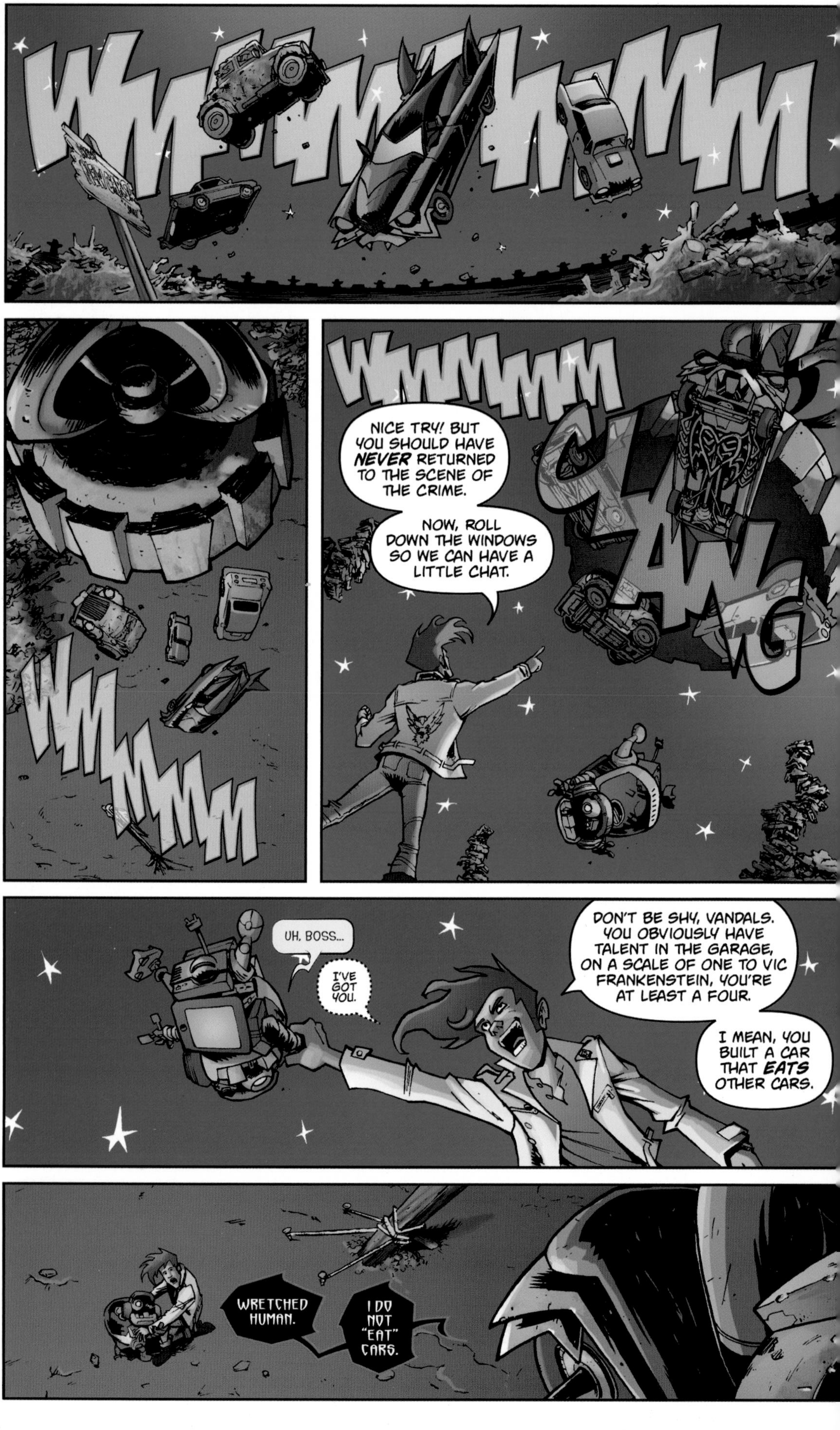
WMMMMMMMM
WMMMMMMM
WMMMMMMM
NICE TRY! BUT YOU SHOULD HAVE NEVER RETURNED TO THE SCENE OF THE CRIME.
NOW, ROLL DOWN THE WINDOWS SO WE CAN HAVE A LITTLE CHAT.
CLANG
UH, BOSS...
I'VE GOT YOU.
DON'T BE SHY, VANDALS. YOU OBVIOUSLY HAVE TALENT IN THE GARAGE, ON A SCALE OF ONE TO VIC FRANKENSTEIN, YOU'RE AT LEAST A FOUR.
I MEAN, YOU BUILT A CAR THAT EATS OTHER CARS.
WRETCHED HUMAN.
I DO NOT "EAT" CARS.

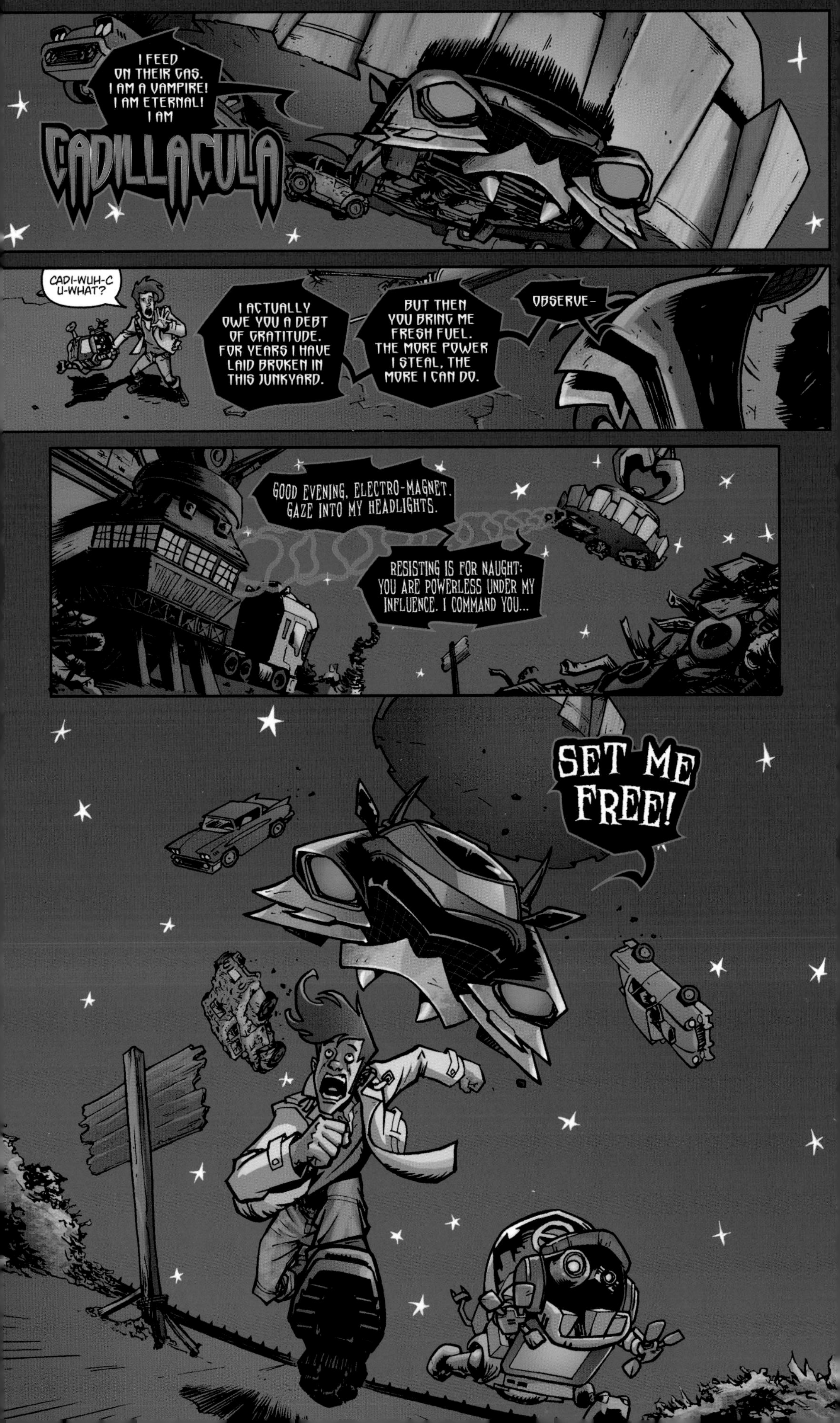

I FEED ON THEIR GAS. I AM A VAMPIRE! I AM ETERNAL! I AM
CADILLACULA
CADI-WUH-C U-WHAT?
I ACTUALLY OWE YOU A DEBT OF GRATITUDE. FOR YEARS I HAVE LAID BROKEN IN THIS JUNKYARD.
BUT THEN YOU BRING ME FRESH FUEL. THE MORE POWER I STEAL, THE MORE I CAN DO.
OBSERVE-
GOOD EVENING, ELECTRO-MAGNET. GAZE INTO MY HEADLIGHTS.
RESISTING IS FOR NAUGHT; YOU ARE POWERLESS UNDER MY INFLUENCE. I COMMAND YOU...
SET ME FREE!

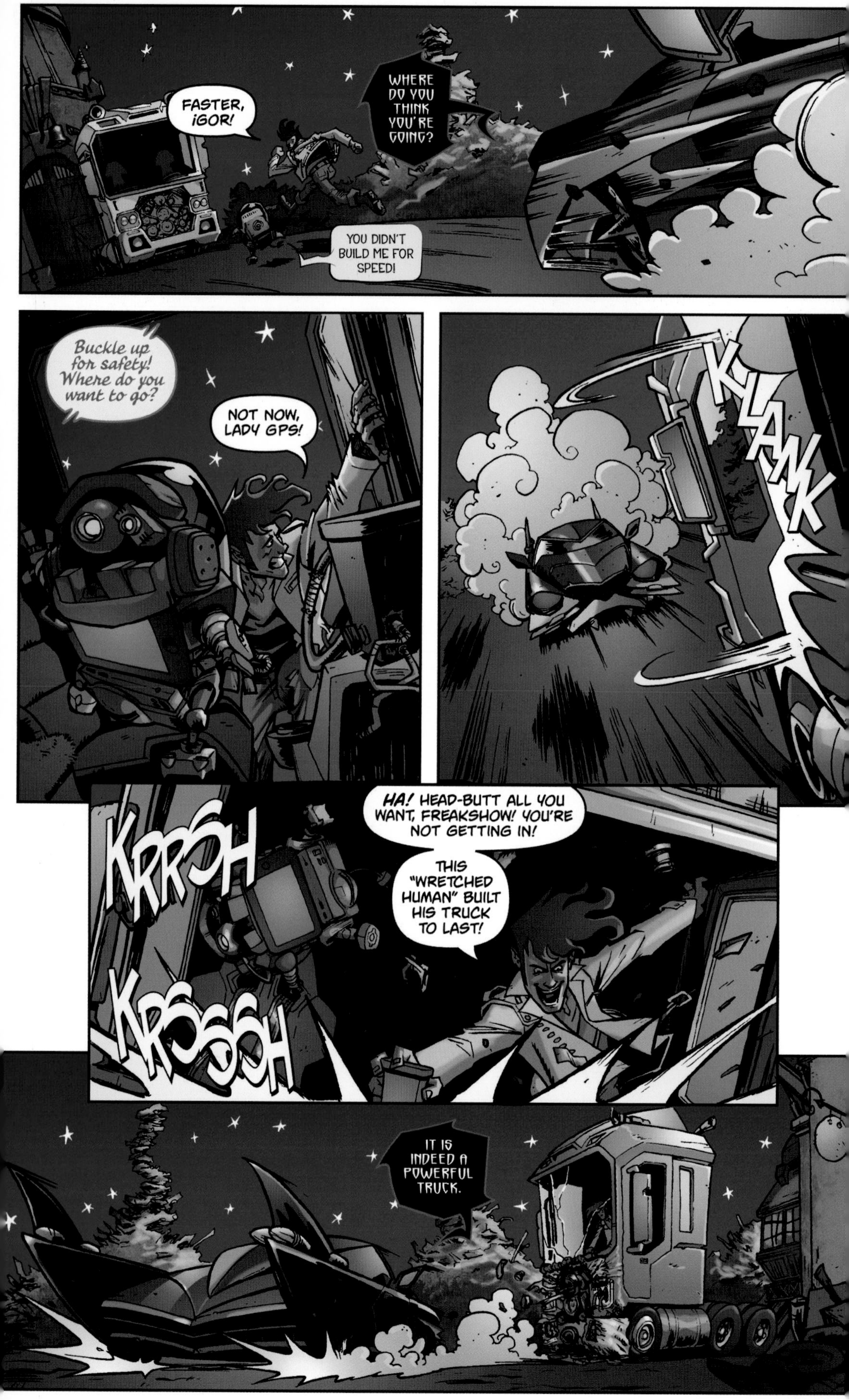
FASTER, ¡GOR!
WHERE DO YOU THINK YOU'RE GOING?
YOU DIDN'T BUILD ME FOR SPEED!
Buckle up for safety! Where do you want to go?
NOT NOW, LADY GPS!
KLANK
KRRSH
KRSSSH
HA! HEAD-BUTT ALL YOU WANT, FREAKSHOW! YOU'RE NOT GETTING IN!
THIS "WRETCHED HUMAN" BUILT HIS TRUCK TO LAST!
IT IS INDEED A POWERFUL TRUCK.

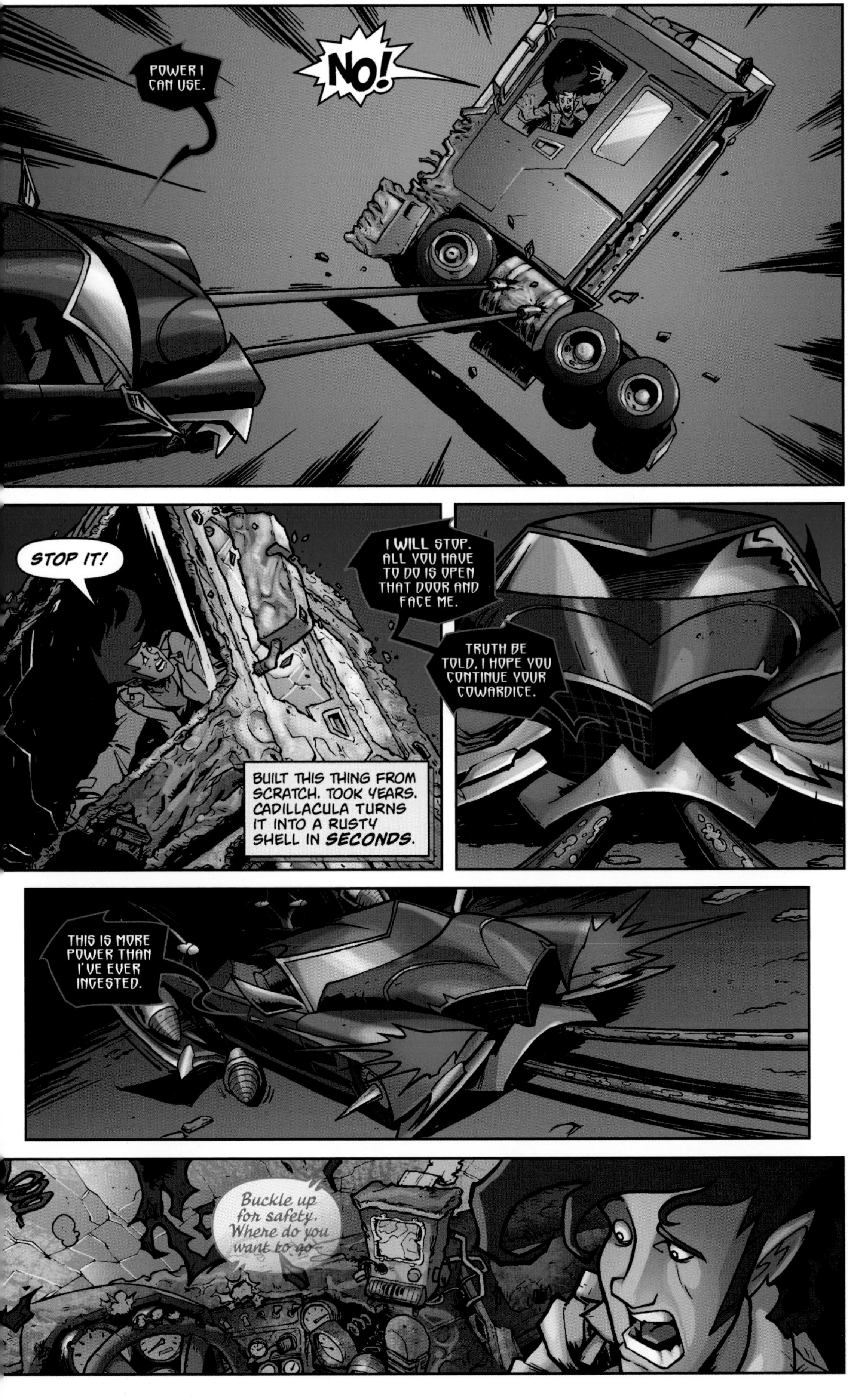
POWER I CAN USE.
NO!
STOP IT!
I WILL STOP. ALL YOU HAVE TO DO IS OPEN THAT DOOR AND FACE ME.
TRUTH BE TOLD, I HOPE YOU CONTINUE YOUR COWARDICE.
BUILT THIS THING FROM SCRATCH. TOOK YEARS. CADILLACULA TURNS IT INTO A RUSTY SHELL IN SECONDS.
THIS IS MORE POWER THAN I'VE EVER INGESTED.
Buckle up for safety. Where do you want to go

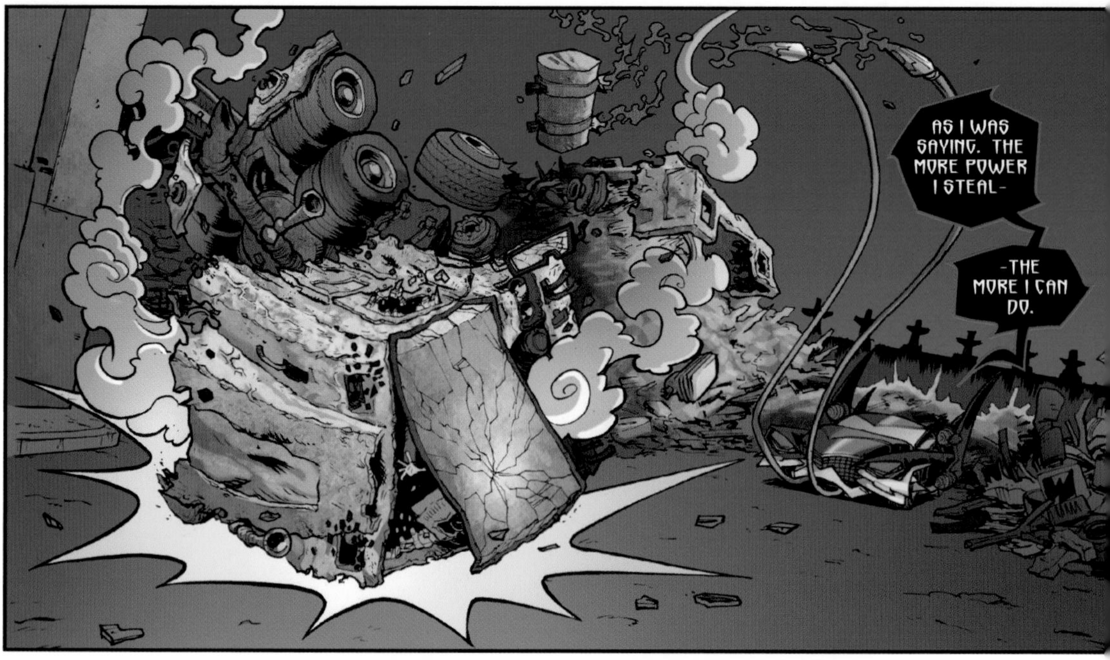
AS I WAS SAYING. THE MORE POWER I STEAL-
-THE MORE I CAN DO.

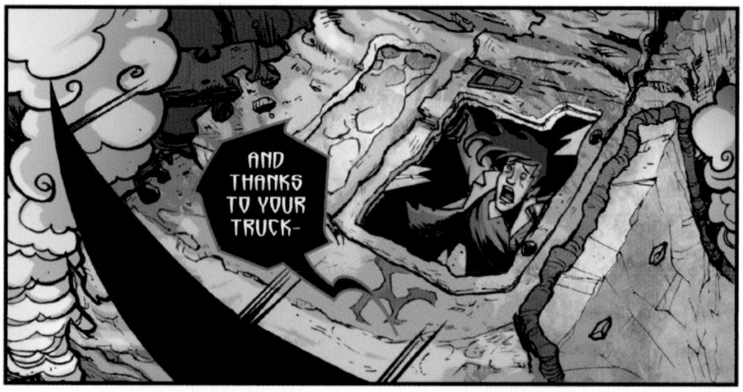
AND THANKS TO YOUR TRUCK-

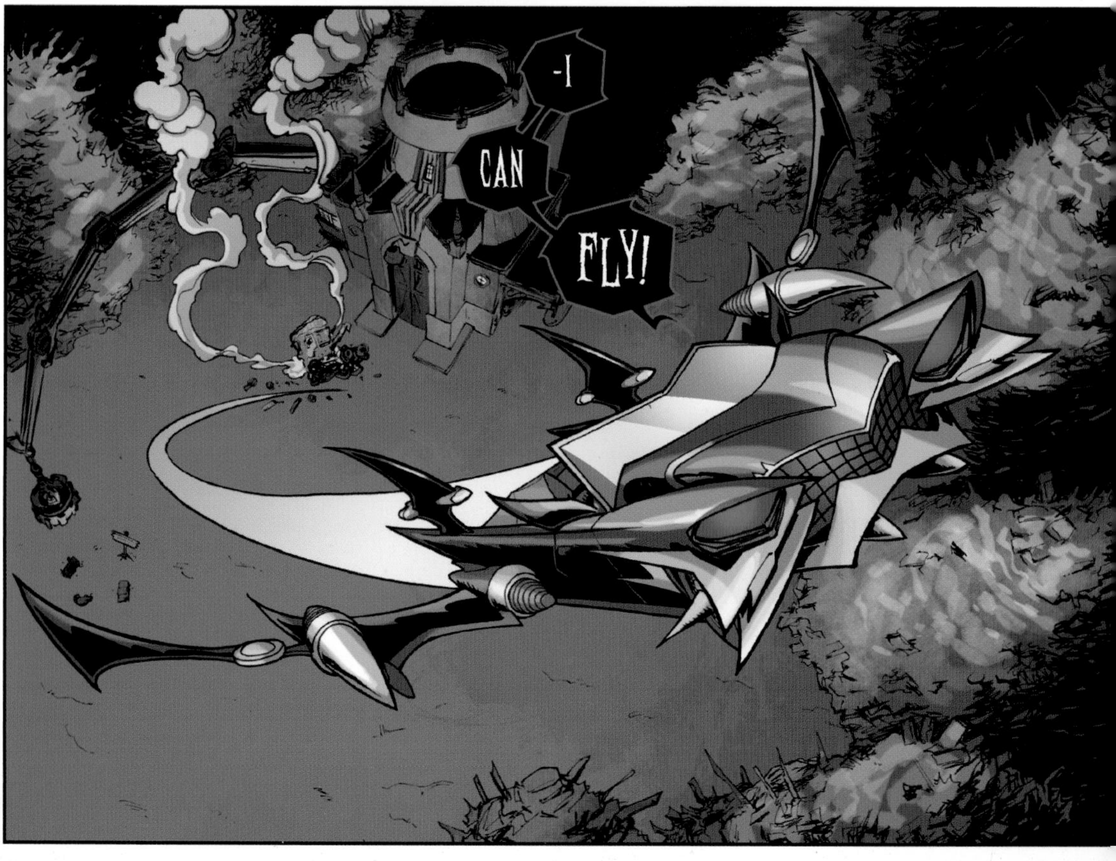
-I
CAN
FLY!

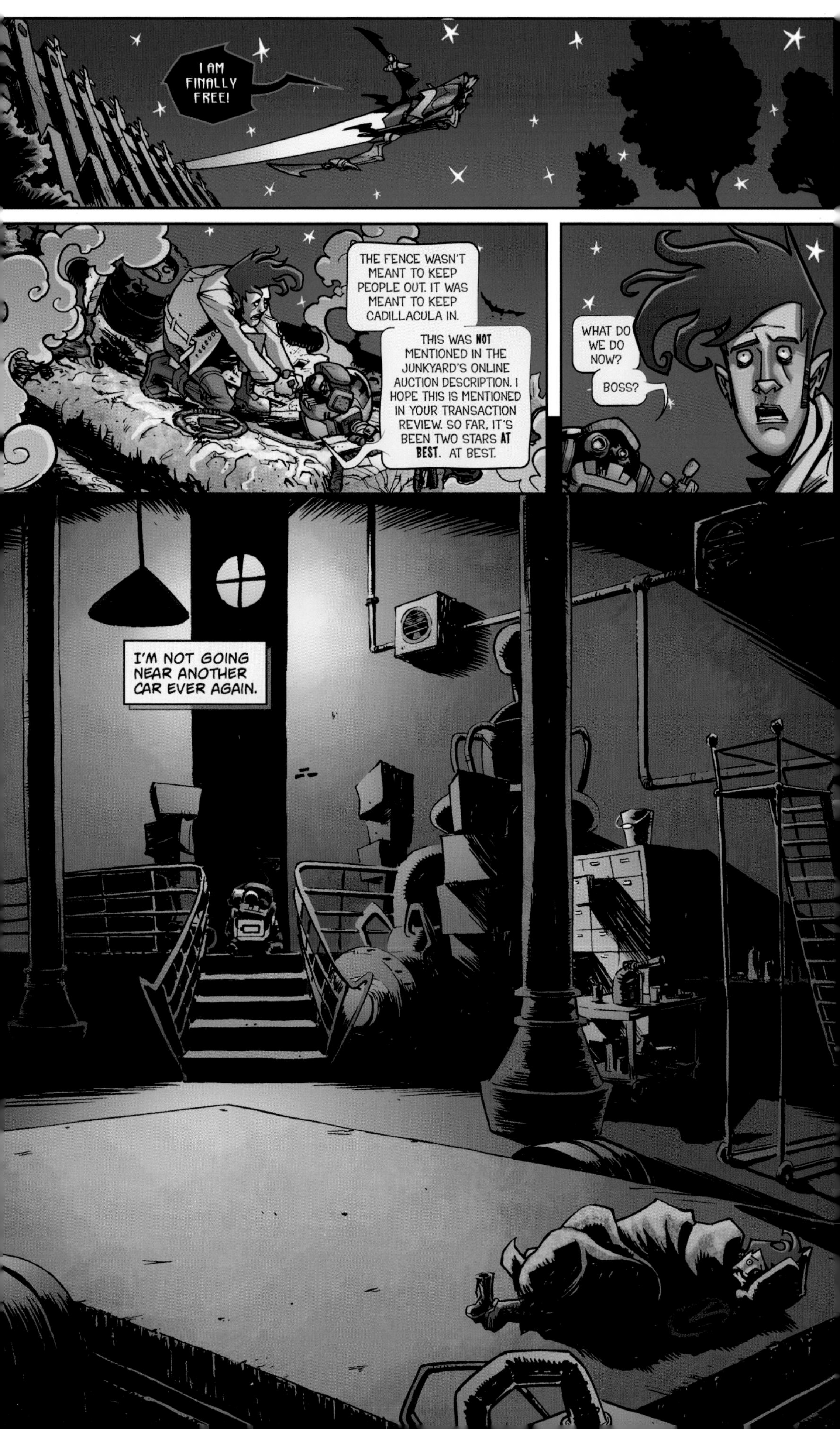
I AM FINALLY FREE!
THE FENCE WASN'T MEANT TO KEEP PEOPLE OUT. IT WAS MEANT TO KEEP CADILLACULA IN.
THIS WAS NOT MENTIONED IN THE JUNKYARD'S ONLINE AUCTION DESCRIPTION. I HOPE THIS IS MENTIONED IN YOUR TRANSACTION REVIEW. SO FAR, IT'S BEEN TWO STARS AT BEST. AT BEST.
WHAT DO WE DO NOW?
BOSS?
I'M NOT GOING NEAR ANOTHER CAR EVER AGAIN.

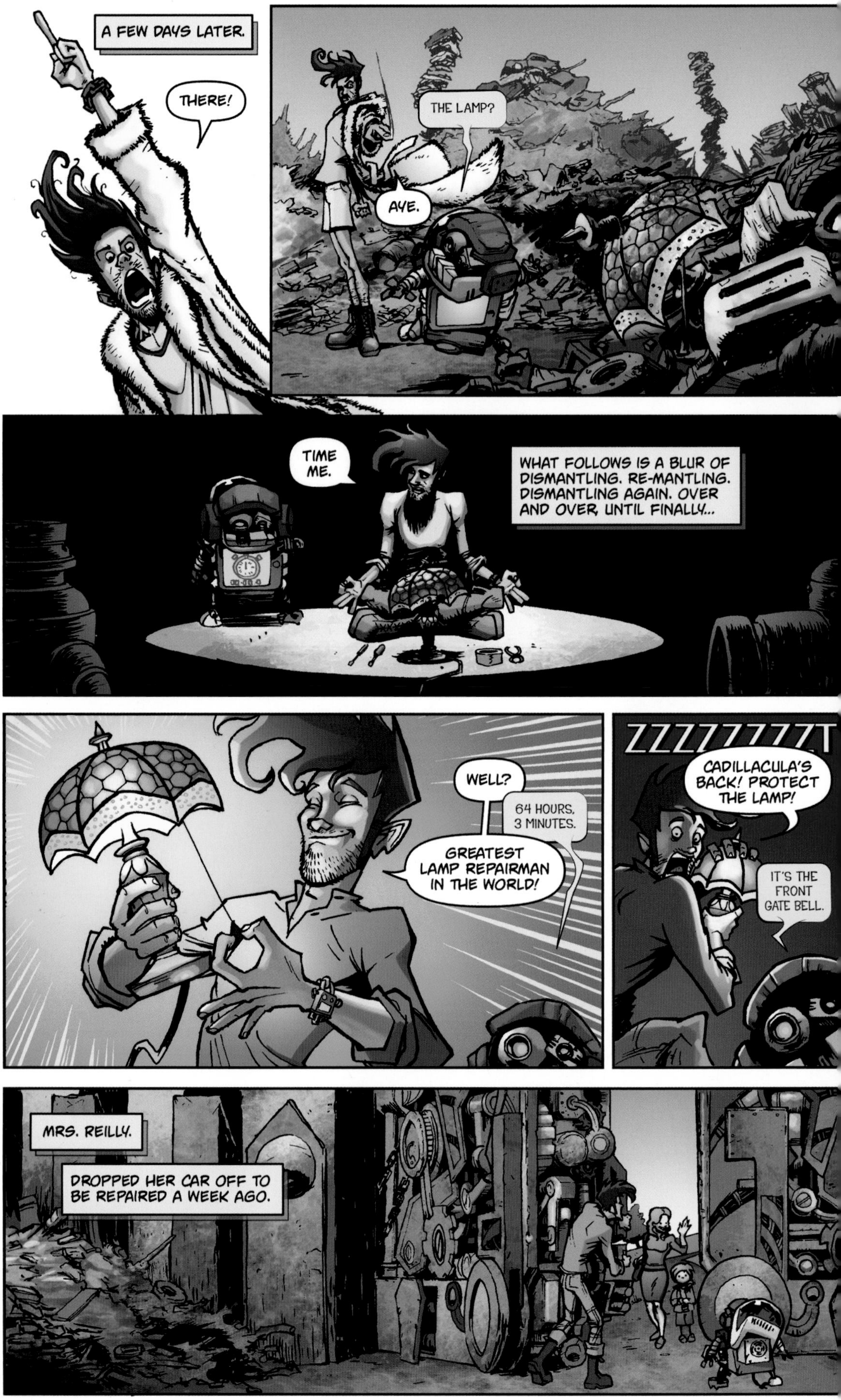
A FEW DAYS LATER.
THERE!
THE LAMP?
AYE.
TIME ME.
WHAT FOLLOWS IS A BLUR OF DISMANTLING. RE-MANTLING. DISMANTLING AGAIN. OVER AND OVER, UNTIL FINALLY...
WELL?
64 HOURS, 3 MINUTES.
GREATEST LAMP REPAIRMAN IN THE WORLD!
ZZZZZZZZT
CADILLACULA'S BACK! PROTECT THE LAMP!
IT'S THE FRONT GATE BELL.
MRS. REILLY.
DROPPED HER CAR OFF TO BE REPAIRED A WEEK AGO.

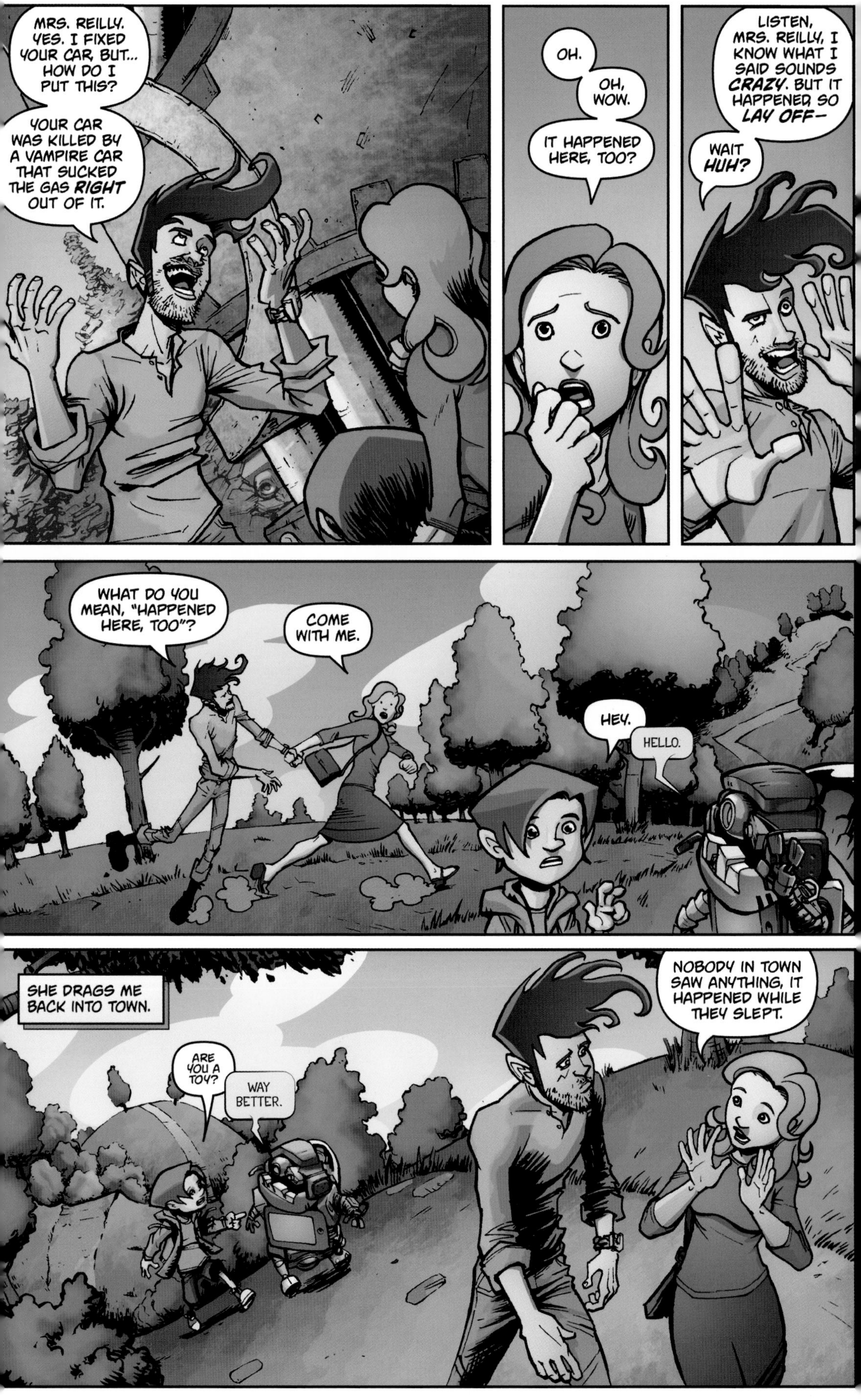

MRS. REILLY. YES. I FIXED YOUR CAR, BUT... HOW DO I PUT THIS?
YOUR CAR WAS KILLED BY A VAMPIRE CAR THAT SUCKED THE GAS RIGHT OUT OF IT.
OH.
OH, WOW.
IT HAPPENED HERE, TOO?
LISTEN, MRS. REILLY, I KNOW WHAT I SAID SOUNDS CRAZY. BUT IT HAPPENED, SO LAY OFF—
WAIT HUH?
WHAT DO YOU MEAN, "HAPPENED HERE, TOO"?
COME WITH ME.
HEY.
HELLO.
SHE DRAGS ME BACK INTO TOWN.
ARE YOU A TOY?
WAY BETTER.
NOBODY IN TOWN SAW ANYTHING, IT HAPPENED WHILE THEY SLEPT.

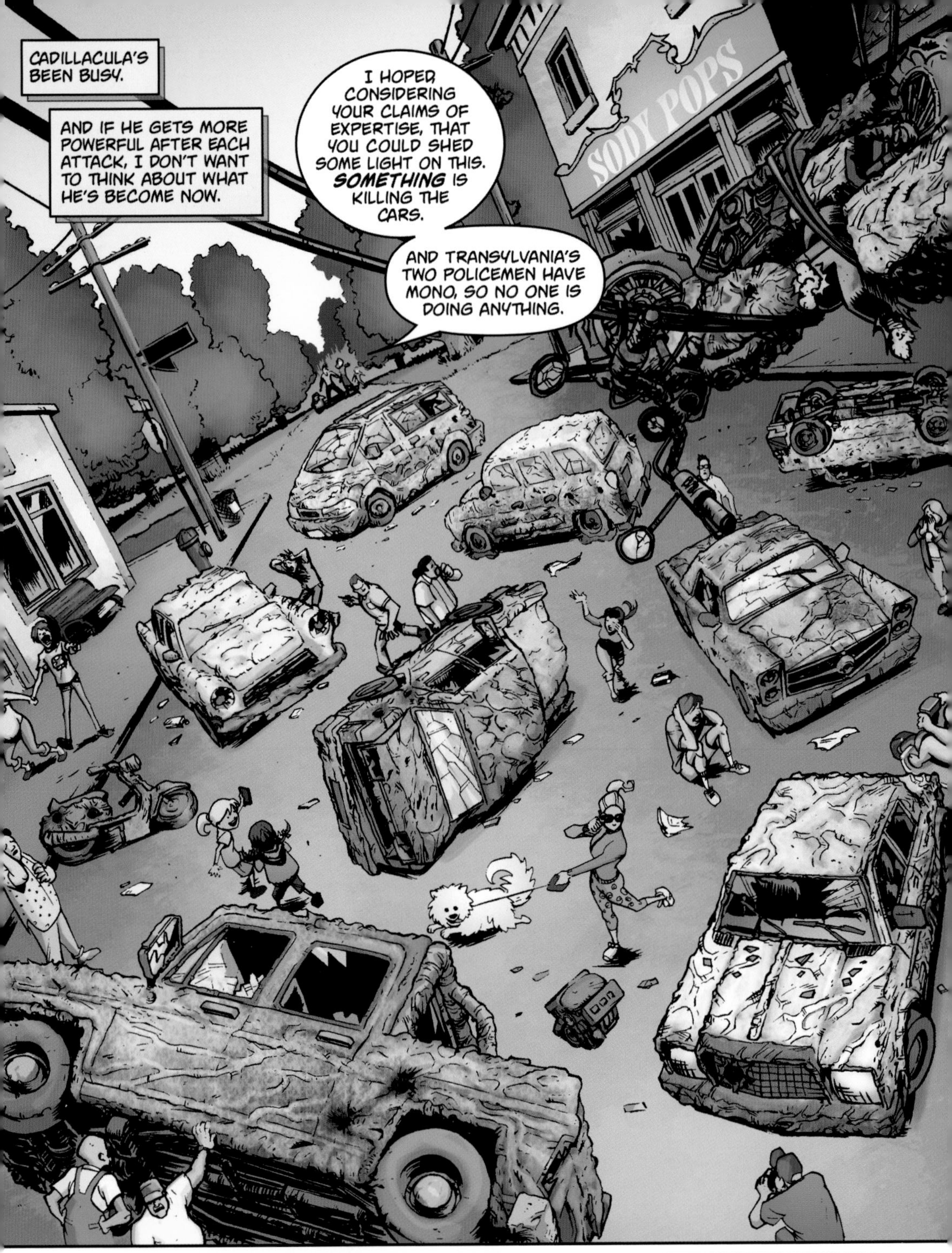
CADILLACULA'S BEEN BUSY.
AND IF HE GETS MORE POWERFUL AFTER EACH ATTACK, I DON'T WANT TO THINK ABOUT WHAT HE'S BECOME NOW.
I HOPED, CONSIDERING YOUR CLAIMS OF EXPERTISE, THAT YOU COULD SHED SOME LIGHT ON THIS. SOMETHING IS KILLING THE CARS.
AND TRANSYLVANIA'S TWO POLICEMEN HAVE MONO, SO NO ONE IS DOING ANYTHING.
SODY POPS

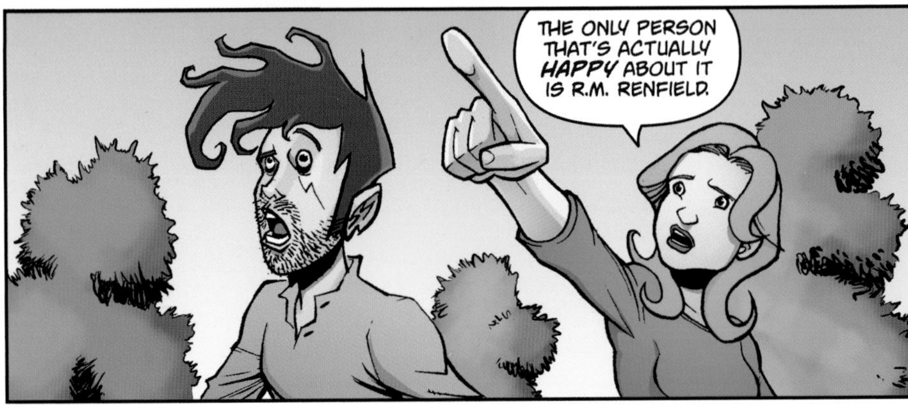
THE ONLY PERSON THAT'S ACTUALLY HAPPY ABOUT IT IS R.M. RENFIELD.

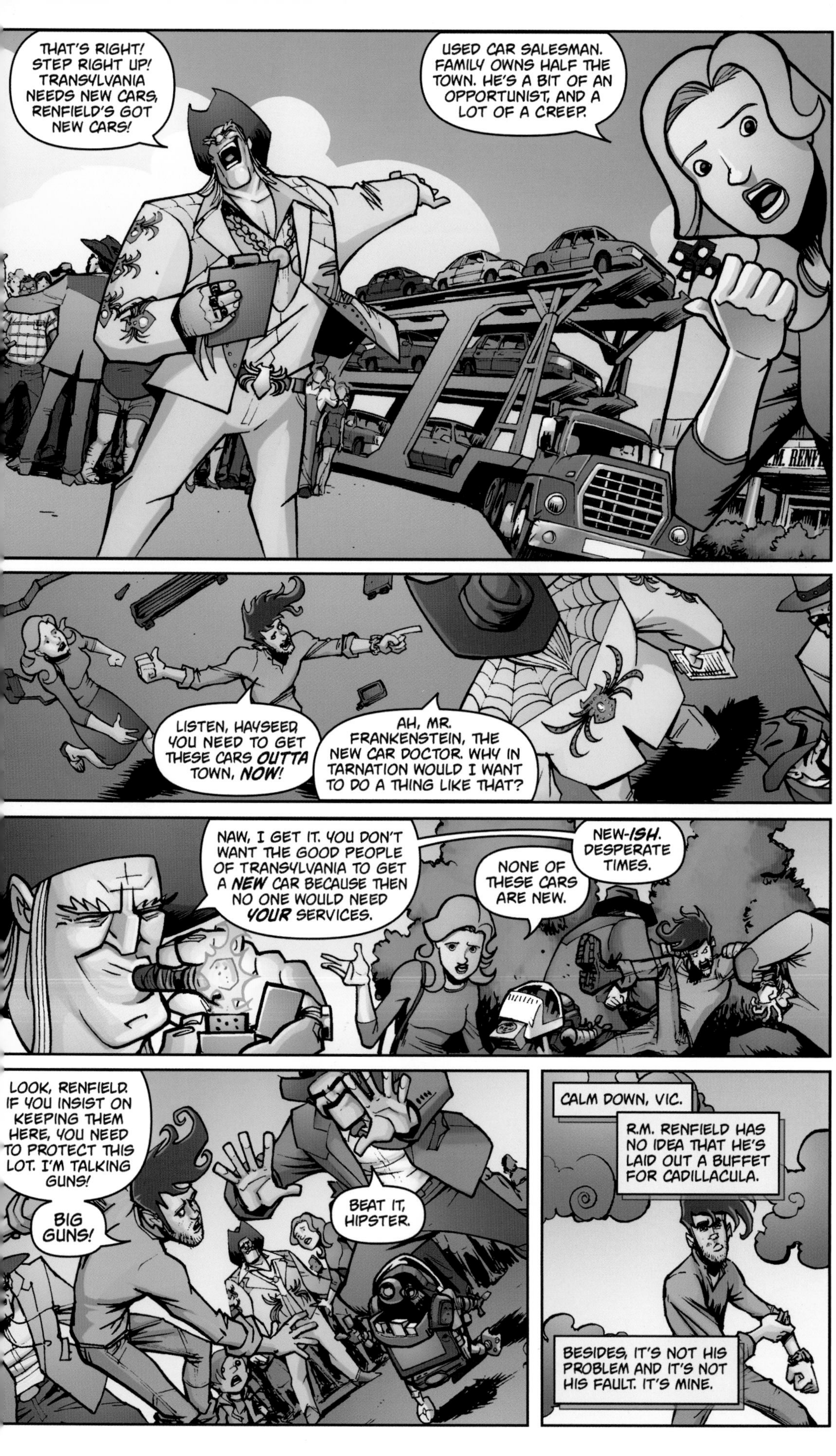
THAT'S RIGHT! STEP RIGHT UP! TRANSYLVANIA NEEDS NEW CARS, RENFIELD'S GOT NEW CARS!
USED CAR SALESMAN. FAMILY OWNS HALF THE TOWN. HE'S A BIT OF AN OPPORTUNIST, AND A LOT OF A CREEP.
LISTEN, HAYSEED, YOU NEED TO GET THESE CARS OUTTA TOWN, NOW!
AH, MR. FRANKENSTEIN, THE NEW CAR DOCTOR. WHY IN TARNATION WOULD I WANT TO DO A THING LIKE THAT?
NAW, I GET IT. YOU DON'T WANT THE GOOD PEOPLE OF TRANSYLVANIA TO GET A NEW CAR BECAUSE THEN NO ONE WOULD NEED YOUR SERVICES.
NONE OF THESE CARS ARE NEW.
NEW-ISH. DESPERATE TIMES.
LOOK, RENFIELD. IF YOU INSIST ON KEEPING THEM HERE, YOU NEED TO PROTECT THIS LOT. I'M TALKING GUNS!
BIG GUNS!
BEAT IT, HIPSTER.
CALM DOWN, VIC.
R.M. RENFIELD HAS NO IDEA THAT HE'S LAID OUT A BUFFET FOR CADILLACULA.
BESIDES, IT'S NOT HIS PROBLEM AND IT'S NOT HIS FAULT. IT'S MINE.

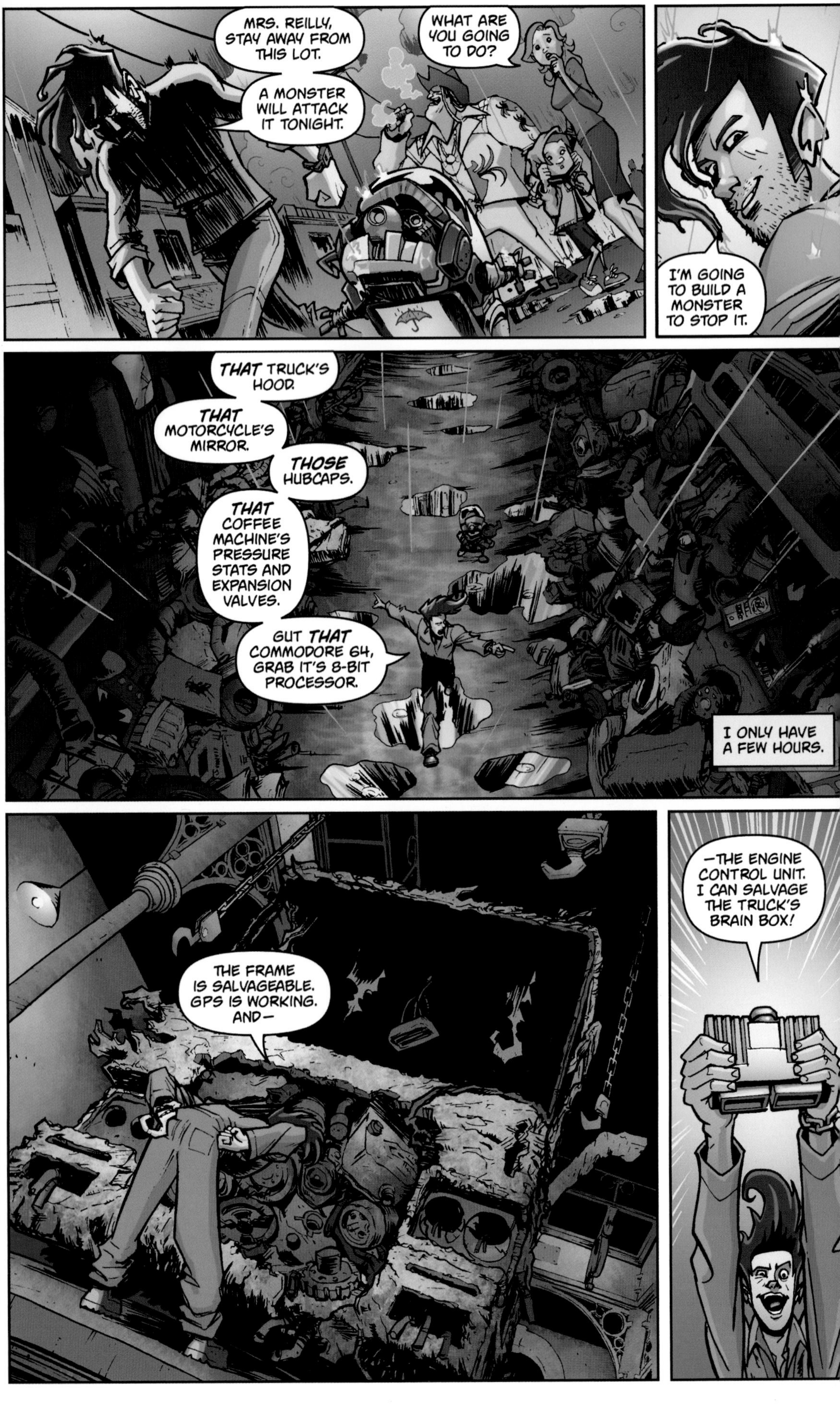
MRS. REILLY, STAY AWAY FROM THIS LOT.
A MONSTER WILL ATTACK IT TONIGHT.
WHAT ARE YOU GOING TO DO?
I'M GOING TO BUILD A MONSTER TO STOP IT.
THAT TRUCK'S HOOD.
THAT MOTORCYCLE'S MIRROR.
THOSE HUBCAPS.
THAT COFFEE MACHINE'S PRESSURE STATS AND EXPANSION VALVES.
GUT *THAT* COMMODORE 64, GRAB IT'S 8-BIT PROCESSOR.
I ONLY HAVE A FEW HOURS.
THE FRAME IS SALVAGEABLE. GPS IS WORKING. AND—
—THE ENGINE CONTROL UNIT. I CAN SALVAGE THE TRUCK'S BRAIN BOX!

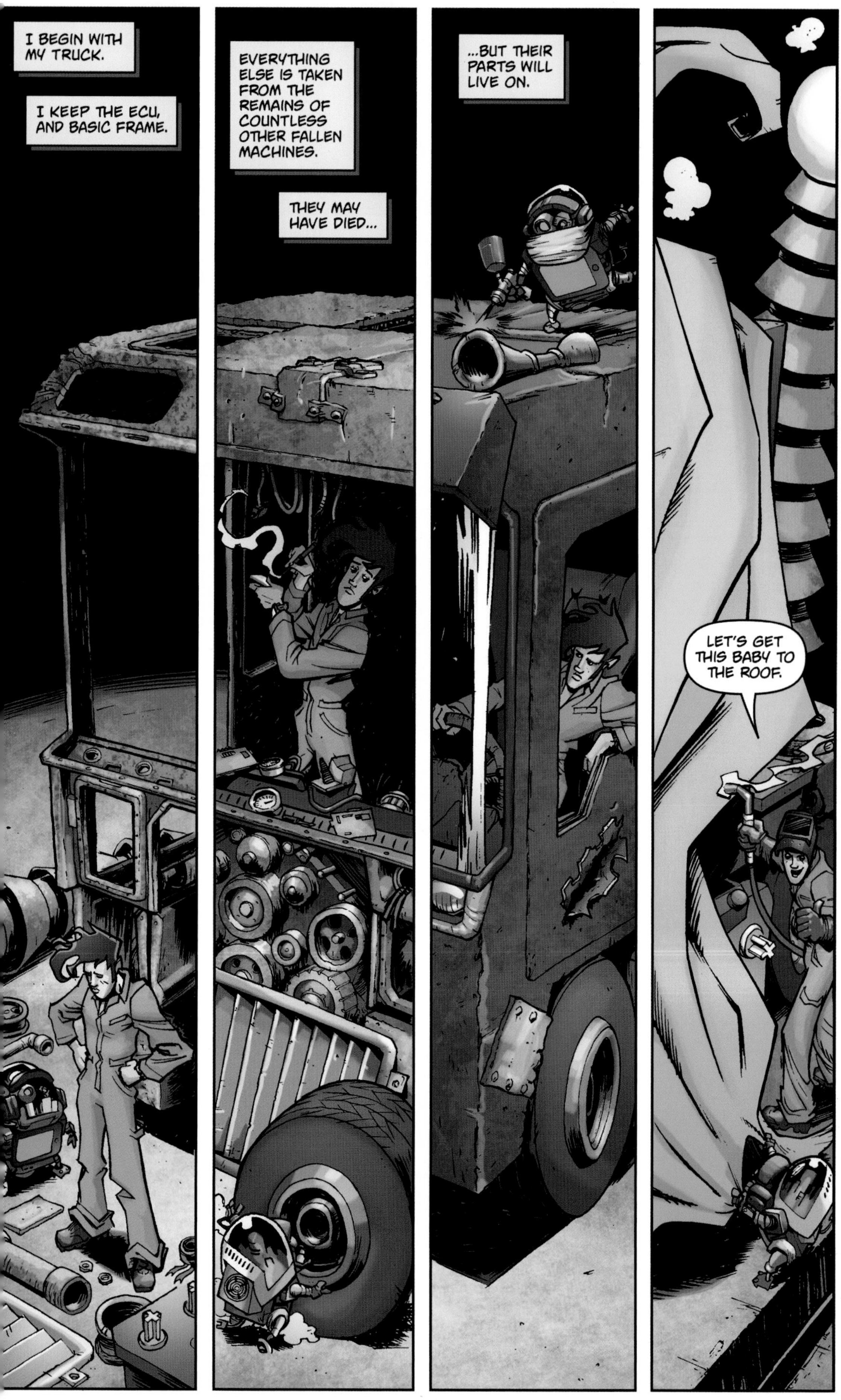
I BEGIN WITH MY TRUCK.
I KEEP THE ECU, AND BASIC FRAME.
EVERYTHING ELSE IS TAKEN FROM THE REMAINS OF COUNTLESS OTHER FALLEN MACHINES.
THEY MAY HAVE DIED...
...BUT THEIR PARTS WILL LIVE ON.
LET'S GET THIS BABY TO THE ROOF.

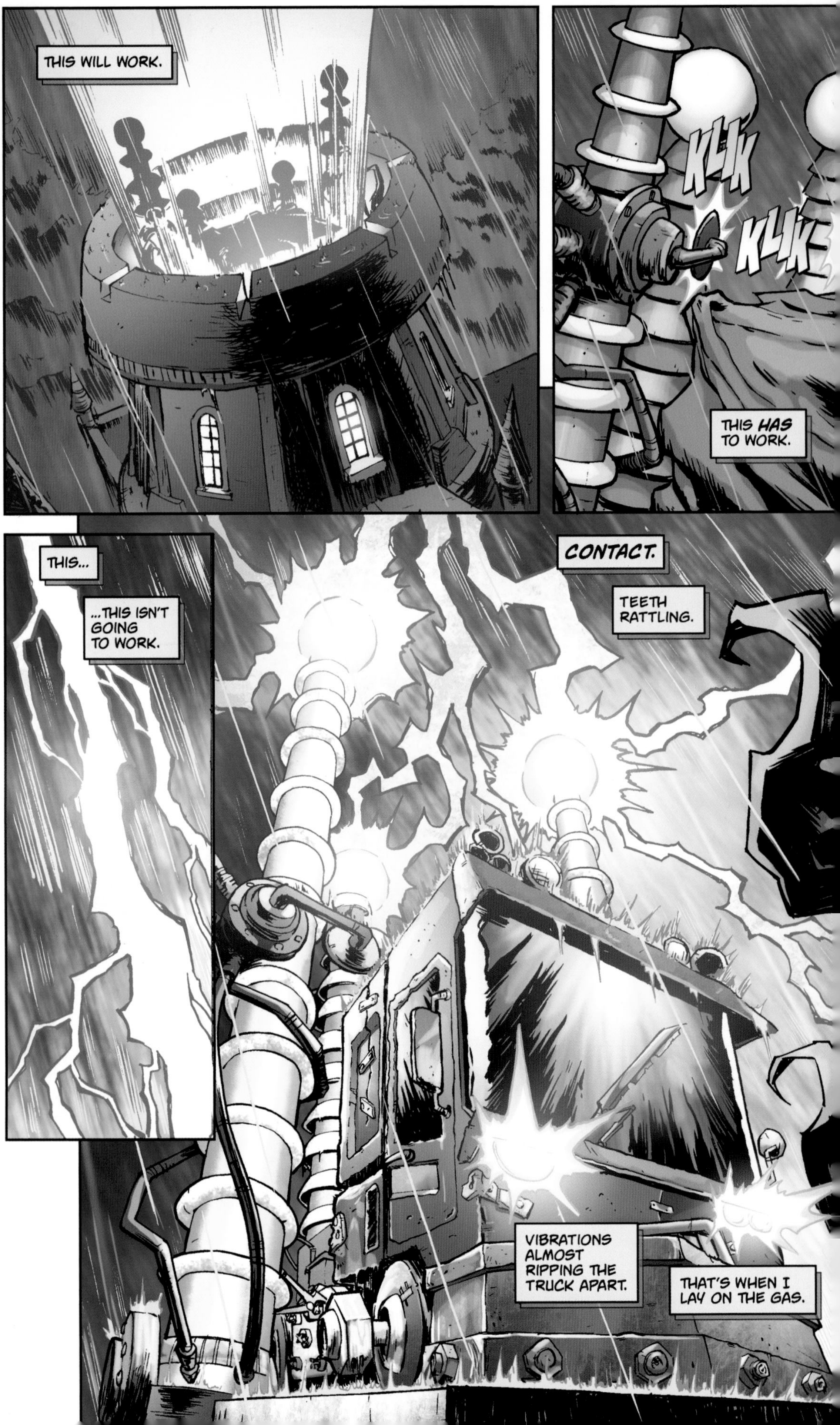
THIS WILL WORK.
KLIK
KLIK
THIS HAS TO WORK.
THIS...
...THIS ISN'T GOING TO WORK.
CONTACT.
TEETH RATTLING.
VIBRATIONS ALMOST RIPPING THE TRUCK APART.
THAT'S WHEN I LAY ON THE GAS.

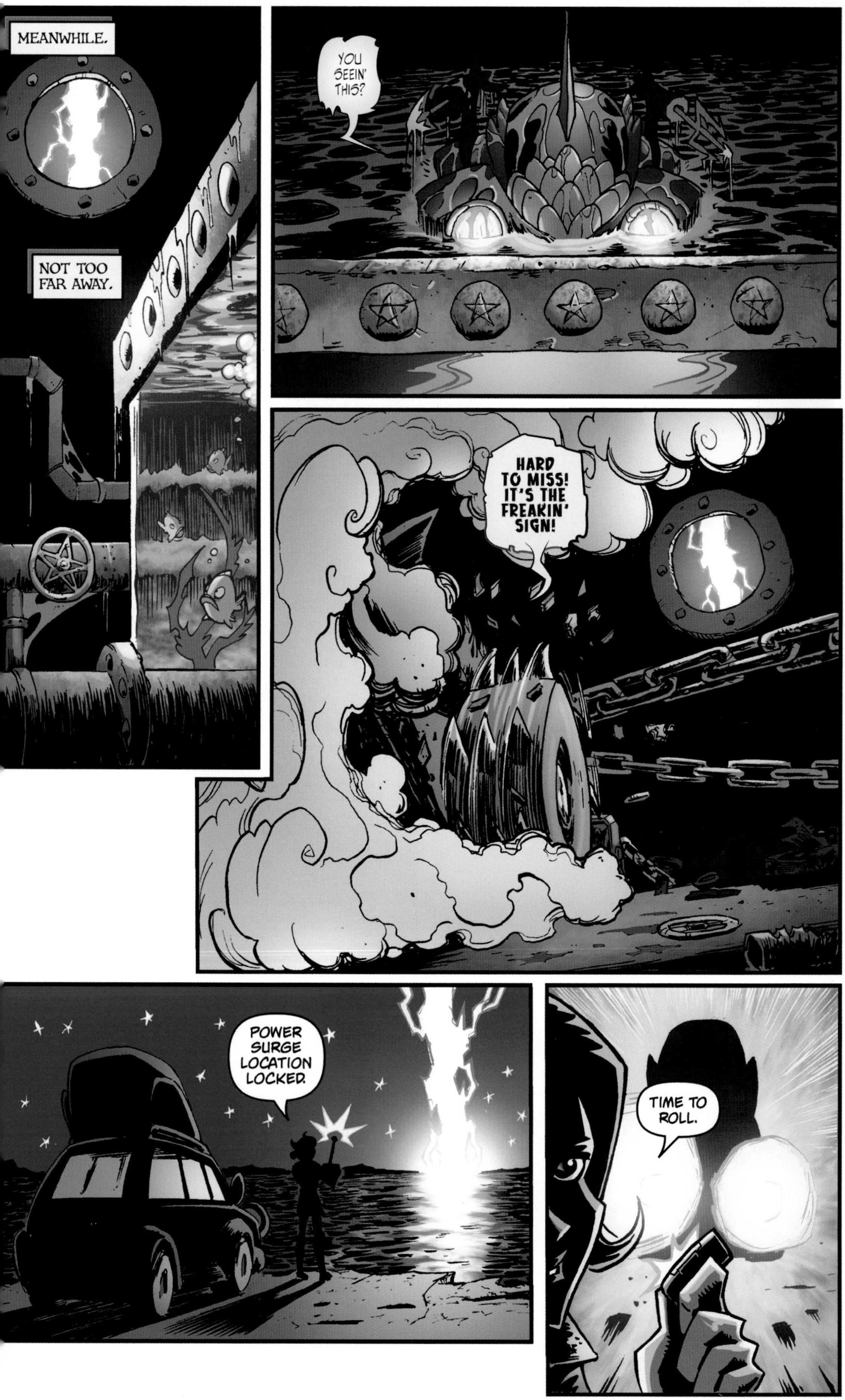
MEANWHILE.
NOT TOO FAR AWAY.
YOU SEEIN' THIS?
HARD TO MISS! IT'S THE FREAKIN' SIGN!
POWER SURGE LOCATION LOCKED.
TIME TO ROLL.

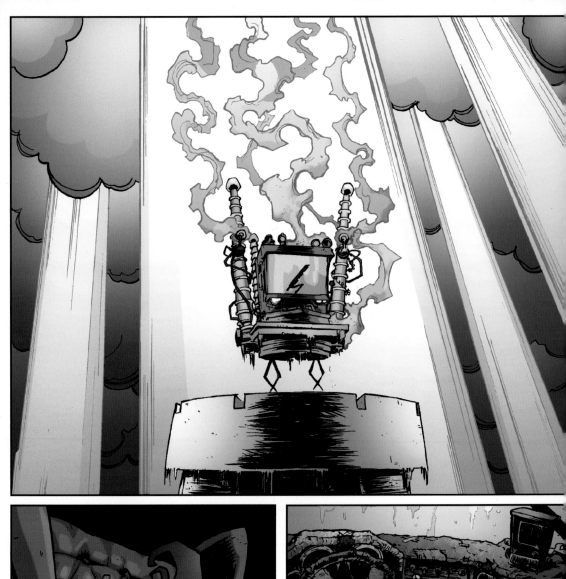

BU BU BU

BUCKLE UP FOR SAFETY. WHERE DO YOU WANT TO GO?

WHOA.

NEW VOICE.

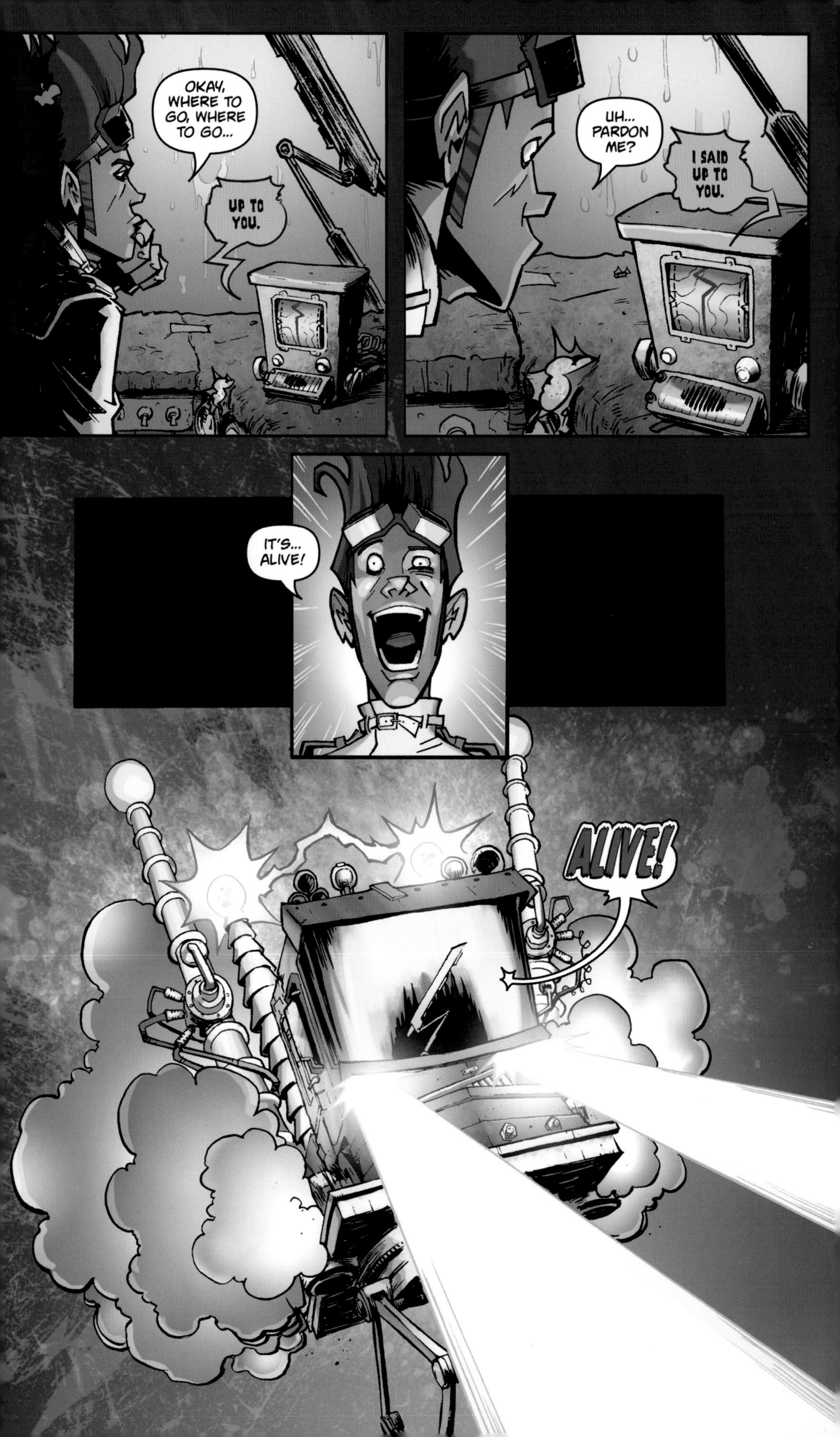
OKAY, WHERE TO GO, WHERE TO GO...
UP TO YOU.
UH... PARDON ME?
I SAID UP TO YOU.
IT'S... ALIVE!
ALIVE!

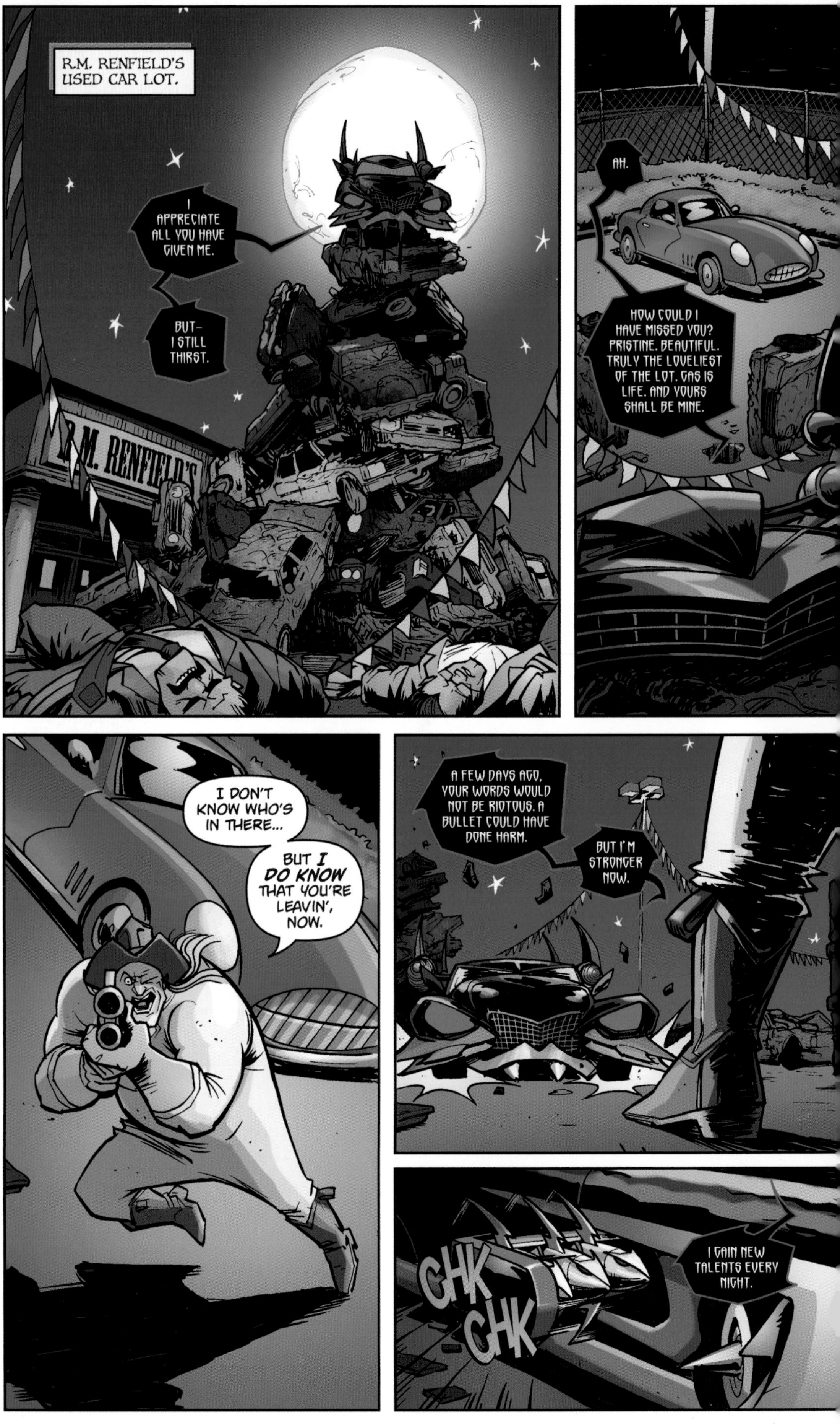
R.M. RENFIELD'S USED CAR LOT.
I APPRECIATE ALL YOU HAVE GIVEN ME.
BUT– I STILL THIRST.
R.M. RENFIELD'S
AH.
HOW COULD I HAVE MISSED YOU? PRISTINE. BEAUTIFUL. TRULY THE LOVELIEST OF THE LOT. GAS IS LIFE. AND YOURS SHALL BE MINE.
I DON'T KNOW WHO'S IN THERE...
BUT *I* ***DO KNOW*** THAT YOU'RE LEAVIN', NOW.
A FEW DAYS AGO, YOUR WORDS WOULD NOT BE RIOTOUS. A BULLET COULD HAVE DONE HARM.
BUT I'M STRONGER NOW.
CHK CHK
I GAIN NEW TALENTS EVERY NIGHT.

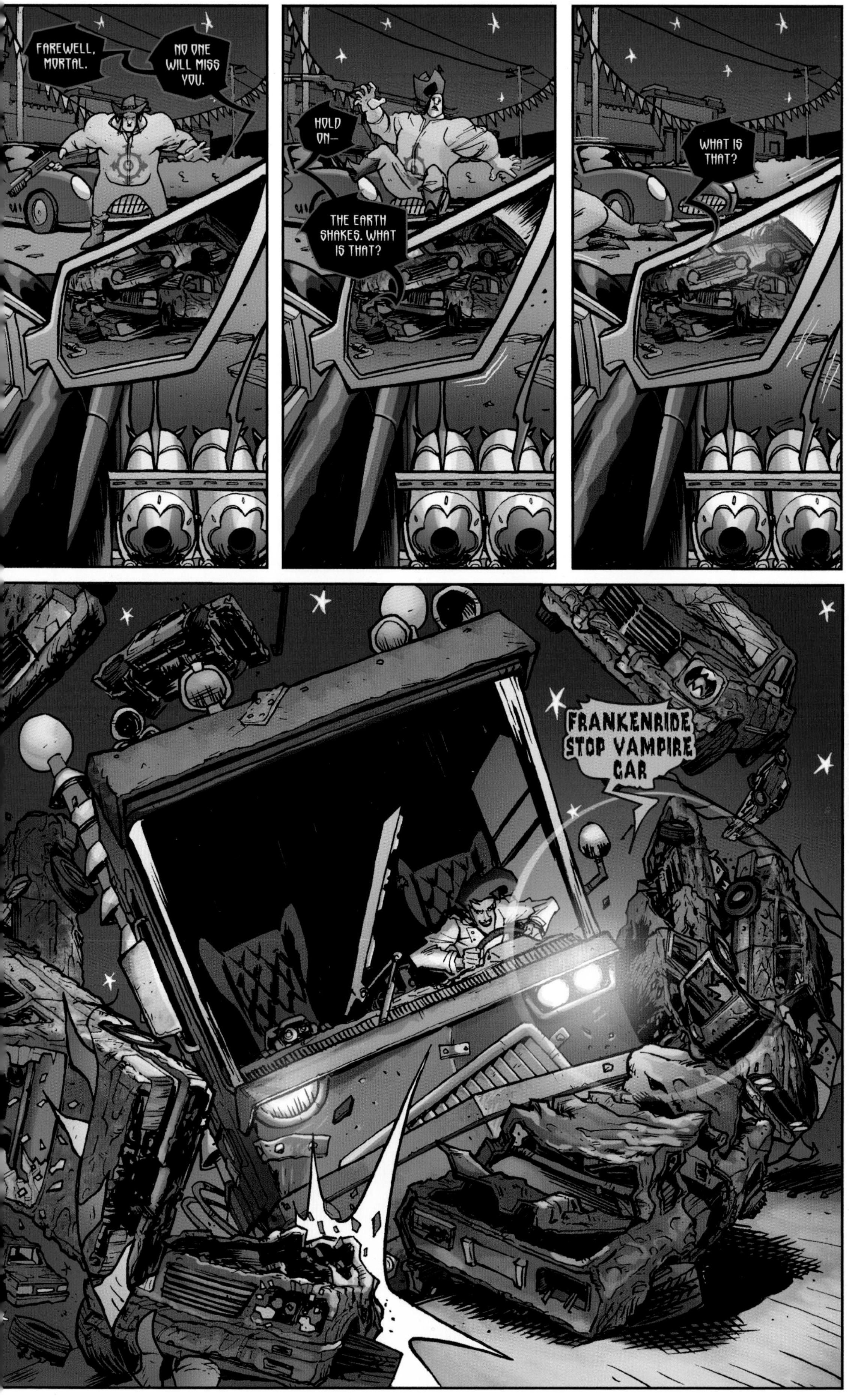
FAREWELL, MORTAL.
NO ONE WILL MISS YOU.
HOLD ON—
THE EARTH SHAKES. WHAT IS THAT?
WHAT IS THAT?
FRANKENRIDE STOP VAMPIRE CAR

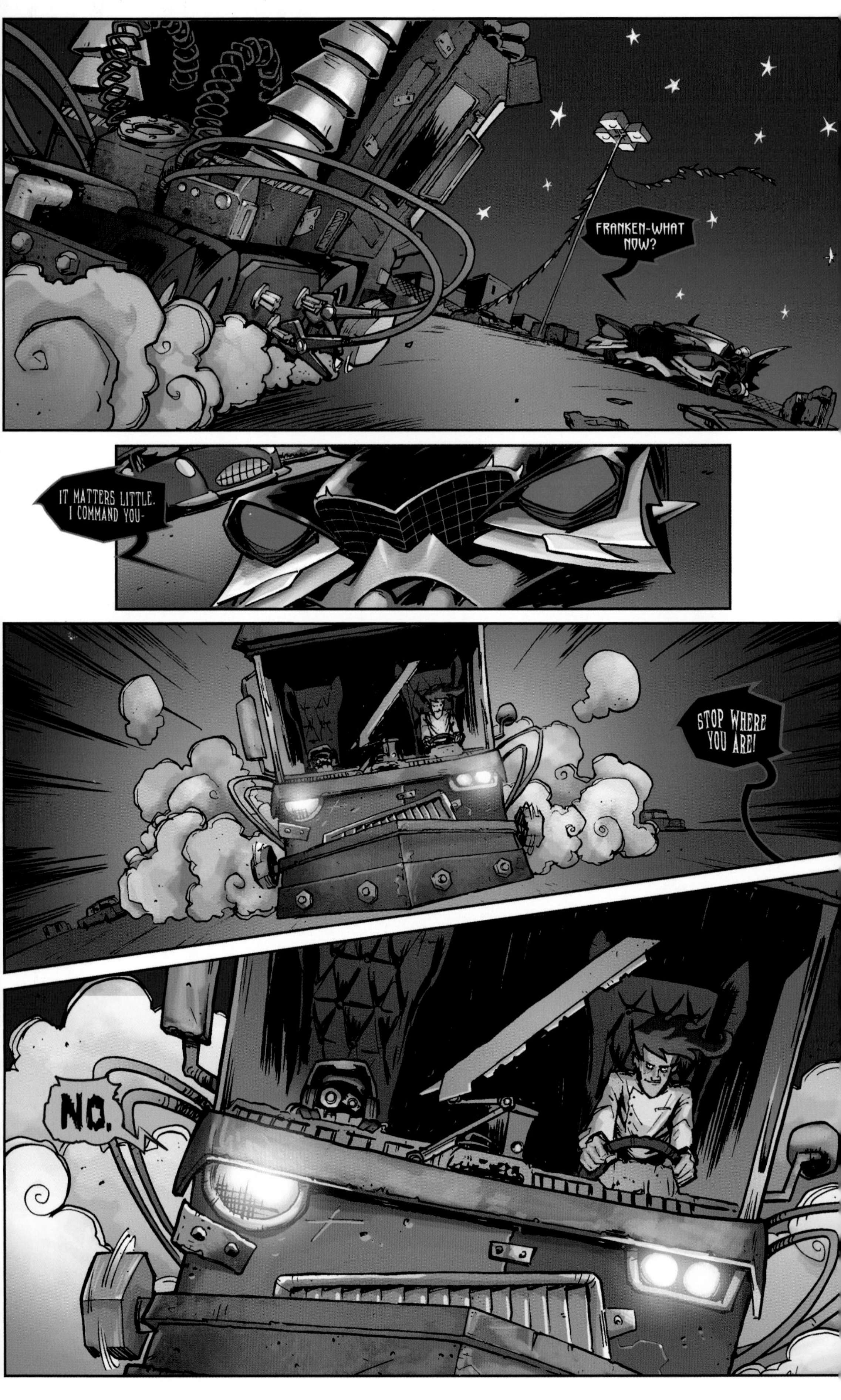
FRANKEN-WHAT NOW?
IT MATTERS LITTLE. I COMMAND YOU-
STOP WHERE YOU ARE!
NO.

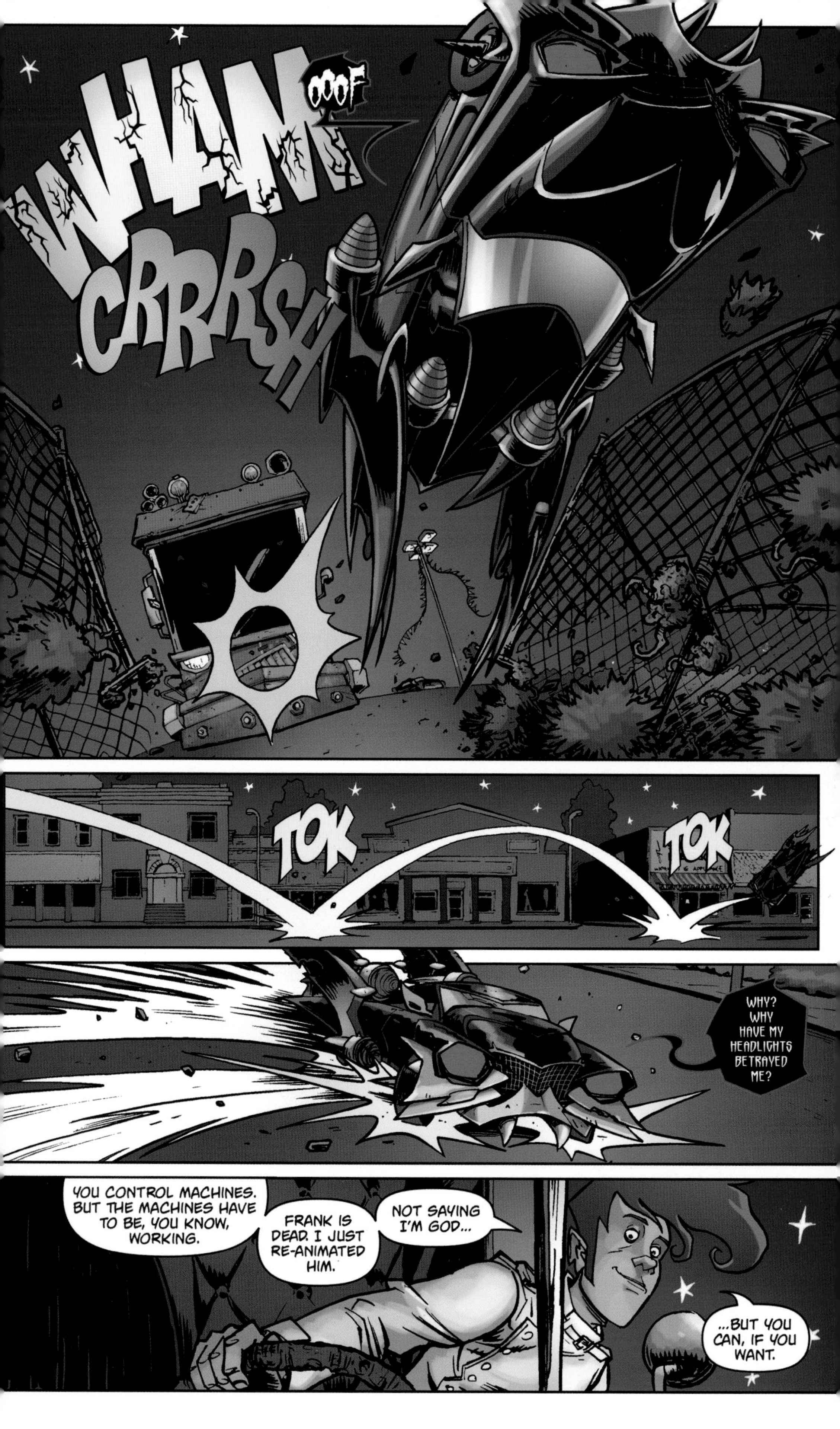
WHAM
OOOF
CRRRSH
TOK
TOK
WHY? WHY HAVE MY HEADLIGHTS BETRAYED ME?
YOU CONTROL MACHINES. BUT THE MACHINES HAVE TO BE, YOU KNOW, WORKING.
FRANK IS DEAD. I JUST RE-ANIMATED HIM.
NOT SAYING I'M GOD...
...BUT YOU CAN, IF YOU WANT.

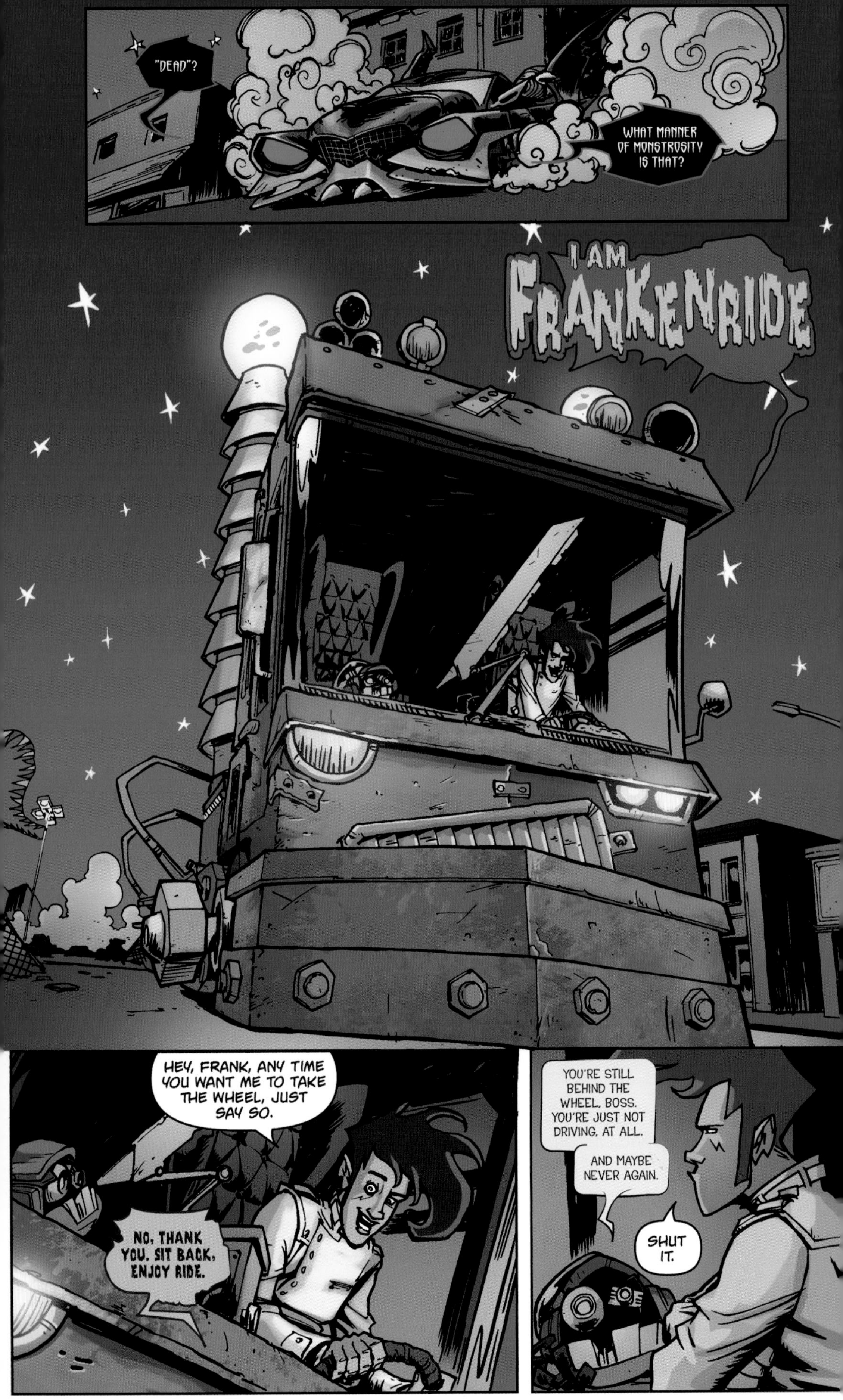
"DEAD"?
WHAT MANNER OF MONSTROSITY IS THAT?
I AM FRANKENRIDE
HEY, FRANK, ANY TIME YOU WANT ME TO TAKE THE WHEEL, JUST SAY SO.
NO, THANK YOU. SIT BACK, ENJOY RIDE.
YOU'RE STILL BEHIND THE WHEEL, BOSS. YOU'RE JUST NOT DRIVING, AT ALL.
AND MAYBE NEVER AGAIN.
SHUT IT.

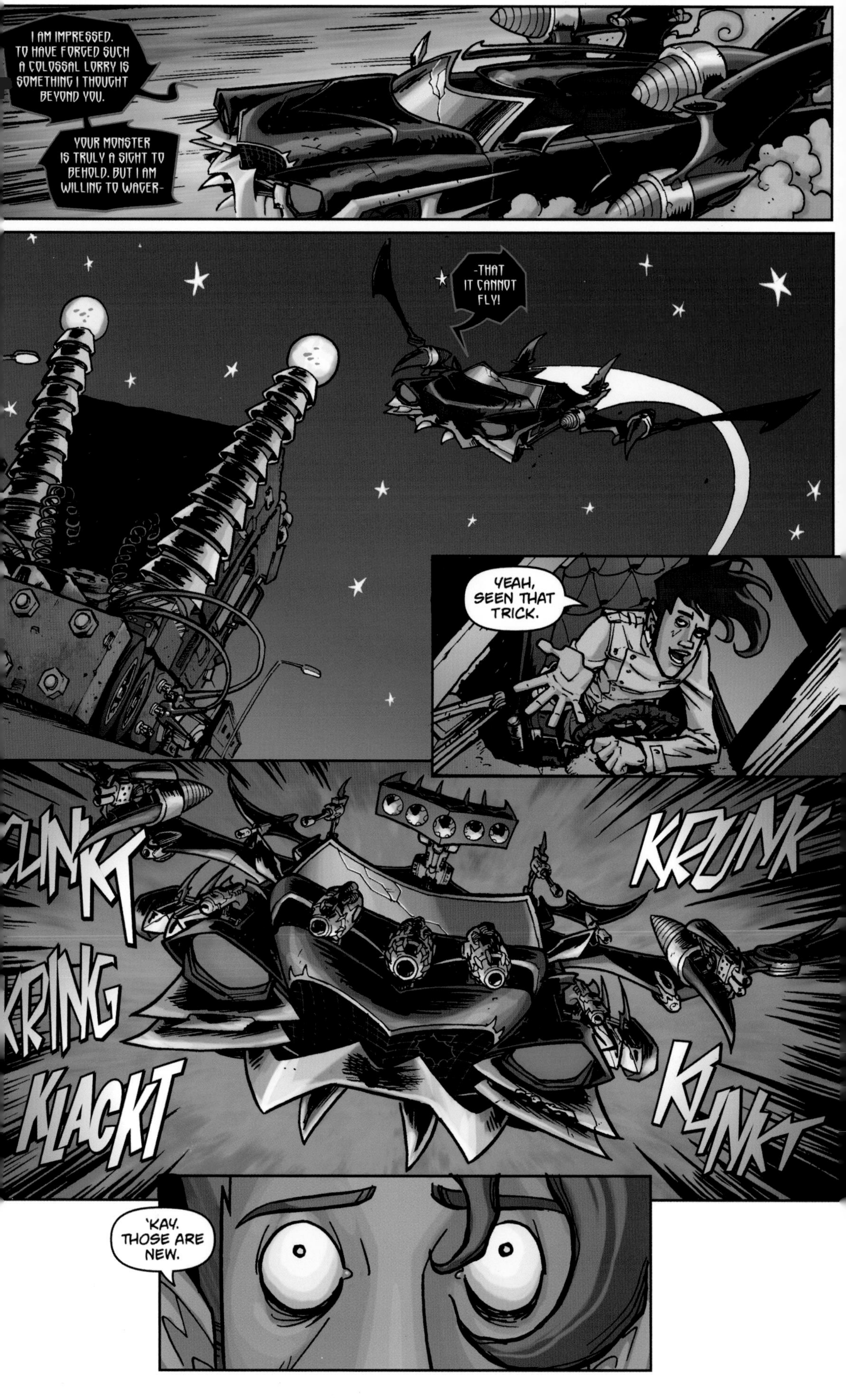
I AM IMPRESSED. TO HAVE FORGED SUCH A COLOSSAL LORRY IS SOMETHING I THOUGHT BEYOND YOU.
YOUR MONSTER IS TRULY A SIGHT TO BEHOLD. BUT I AM WILLING TO WAGER-
-THAT IT CANNOT FLY!
YEAH, SEEN THAT TRICK.
KRUNK
KRING
KLACKT
KLINKT
'KAY. THOSE ARE NEW.

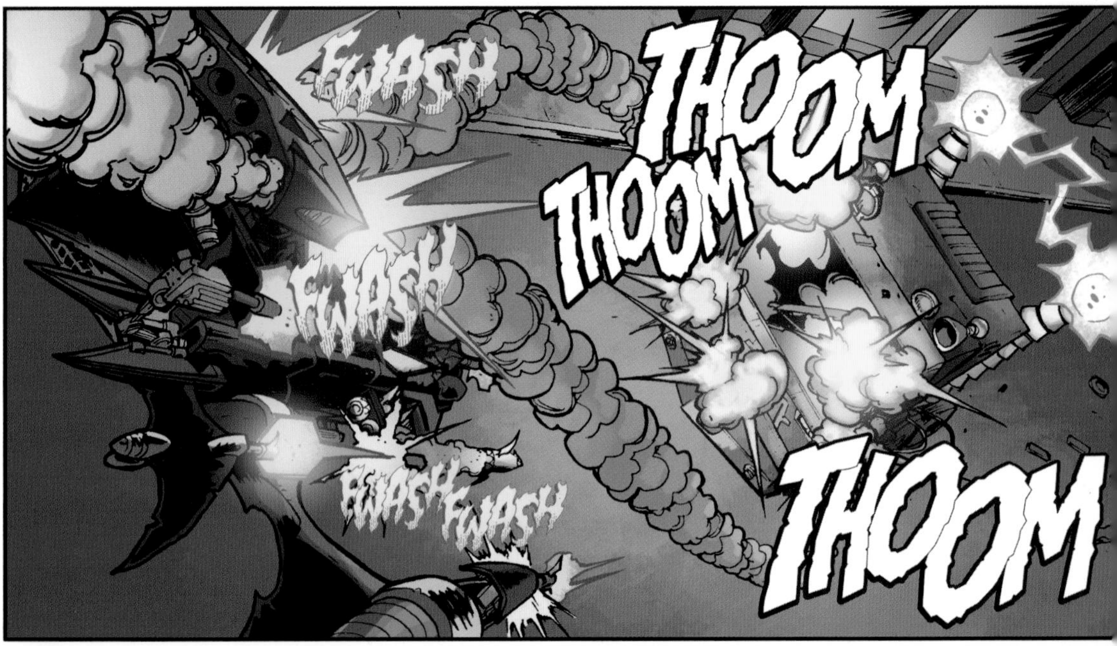
FWASH
THOOM
THOOM
FWASH
FWASH
FWASH
THOOM

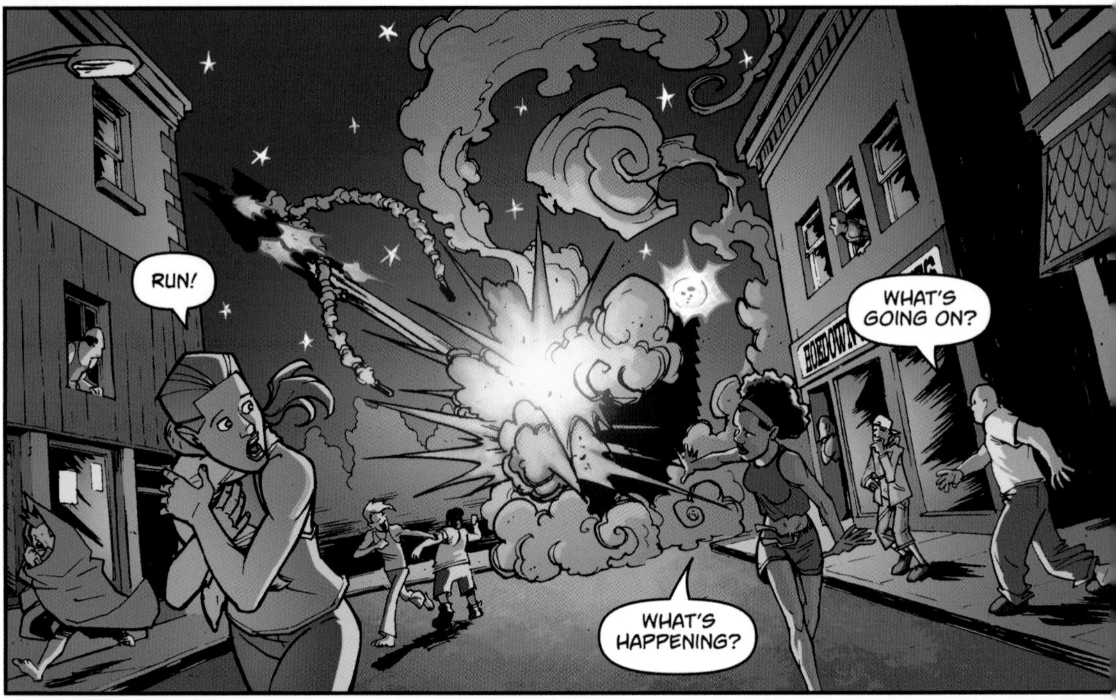
RUN!
WHAT'S GOING ON?
WHAT'S HAPPENING?

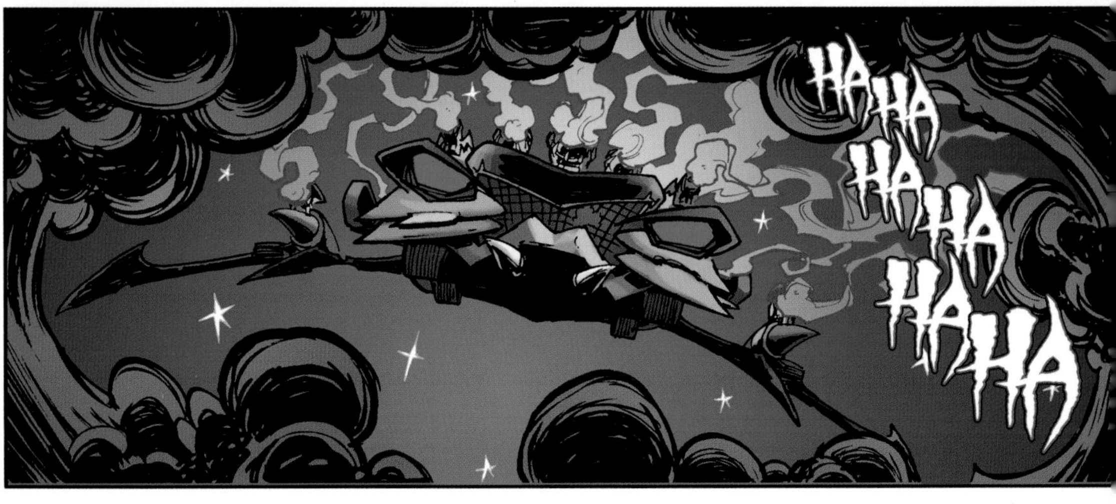
HA HA HA HA HA HA HA HA HA

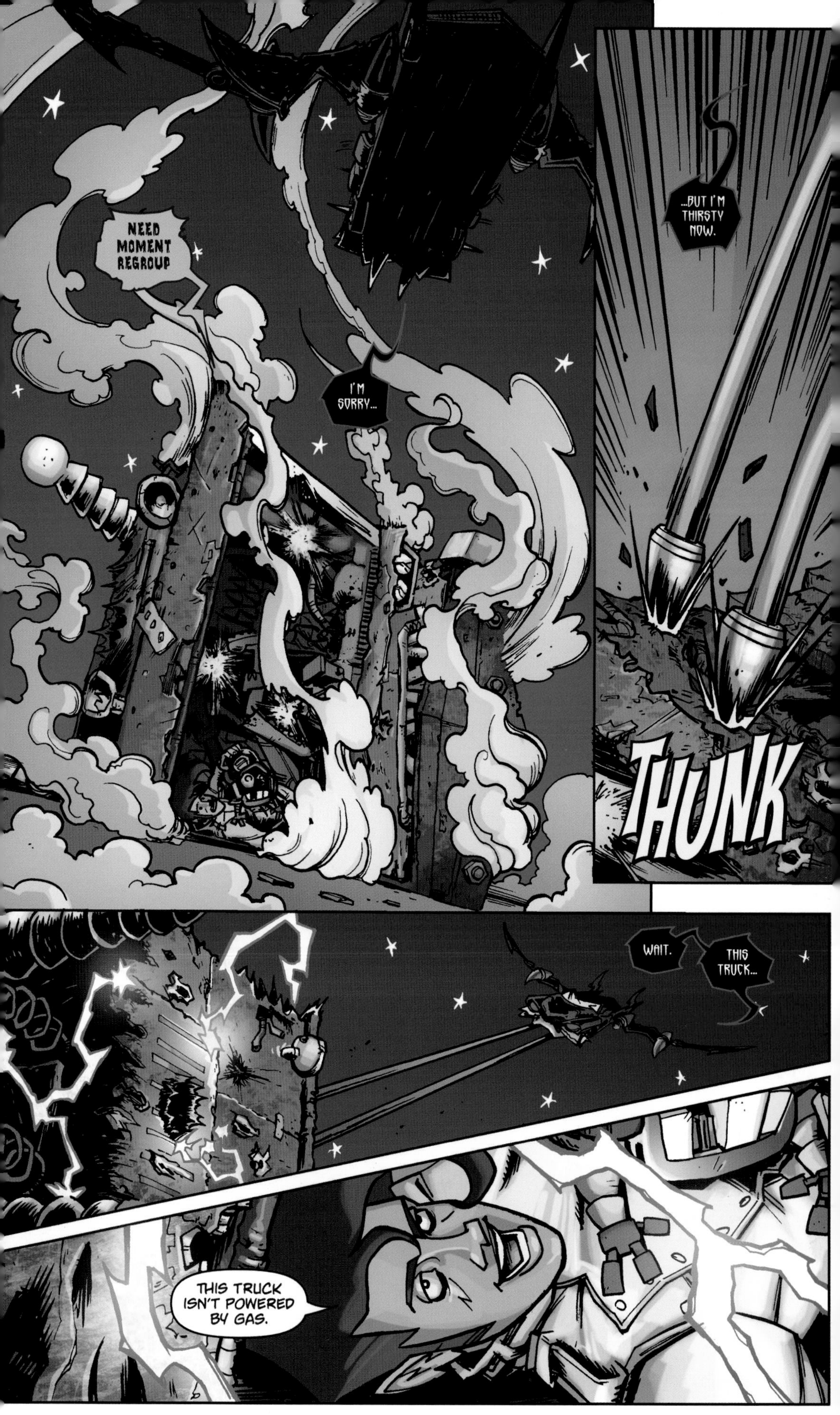
NEED MOMENT REGROUP
I'M SORRY...
...BUT I'M THIRSTY NOW.
THUNK
WAIT.
THIS TRUCK...
THIS TRUCK ISN'T POWERED BY GAS.

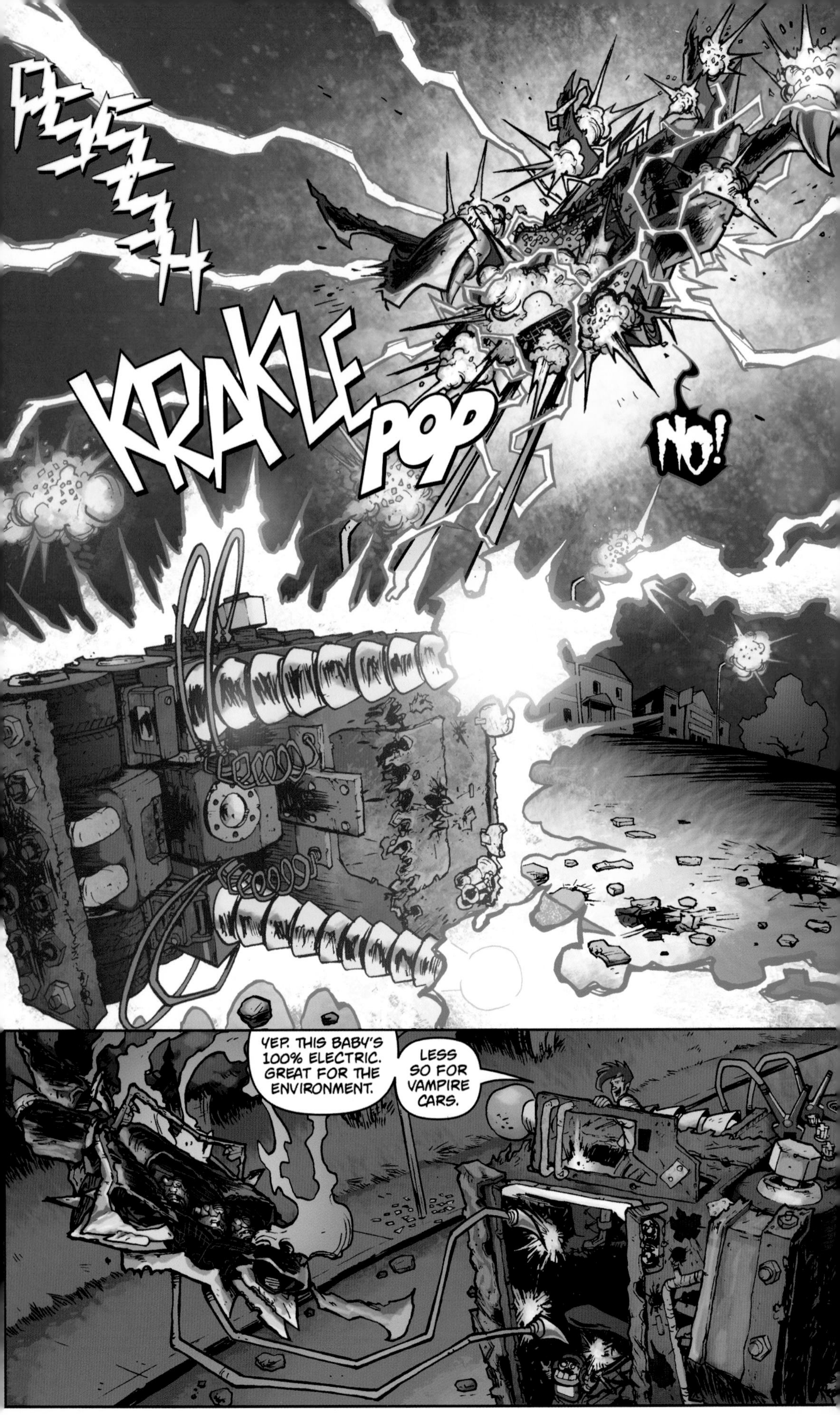
BZZZZZZT
KRAKLE POP
NO!
YEP. THIS BABY'S 100% ELECTRIC. GREAT FOR THE ENVIRONMENT.
LESS SO FOR VAMPIRE CARS.

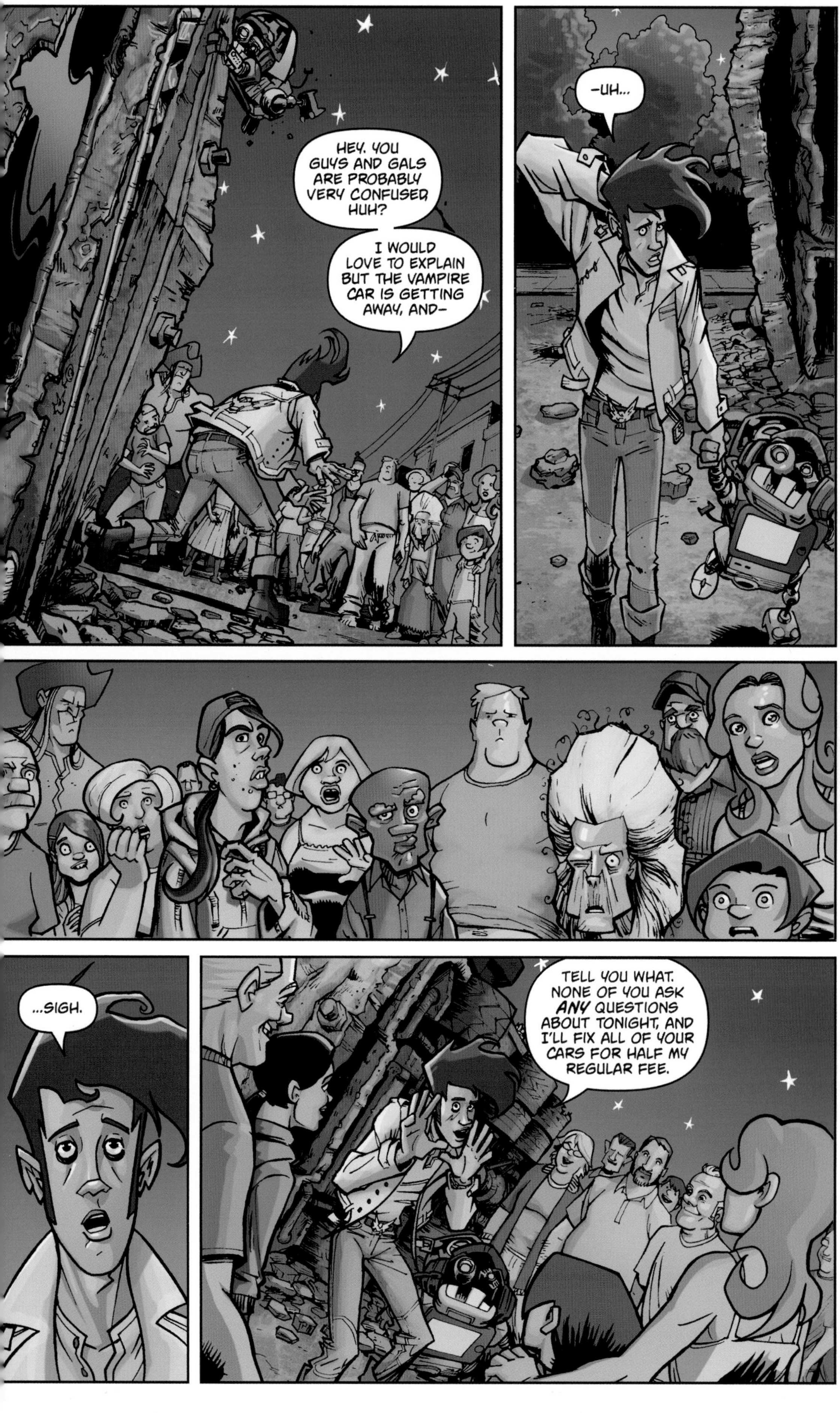
HEY. YOU GUYS AND GALS ARE PROBABLY VERY CONFUSED, HUH?
I WOULD LOVE TO EXPLAIN BUT THE VAMPIRE CAR IS GETTING AWAY, AND–
–UH...
...SIGH.
TELL YOU WHAT. NONE OF YOU ASK ANY QUESTIONS ABOUT TONIGHT, AND I'LL FIX ALL OF YOUR CARS FOR HALF MY REGULAR FEE.

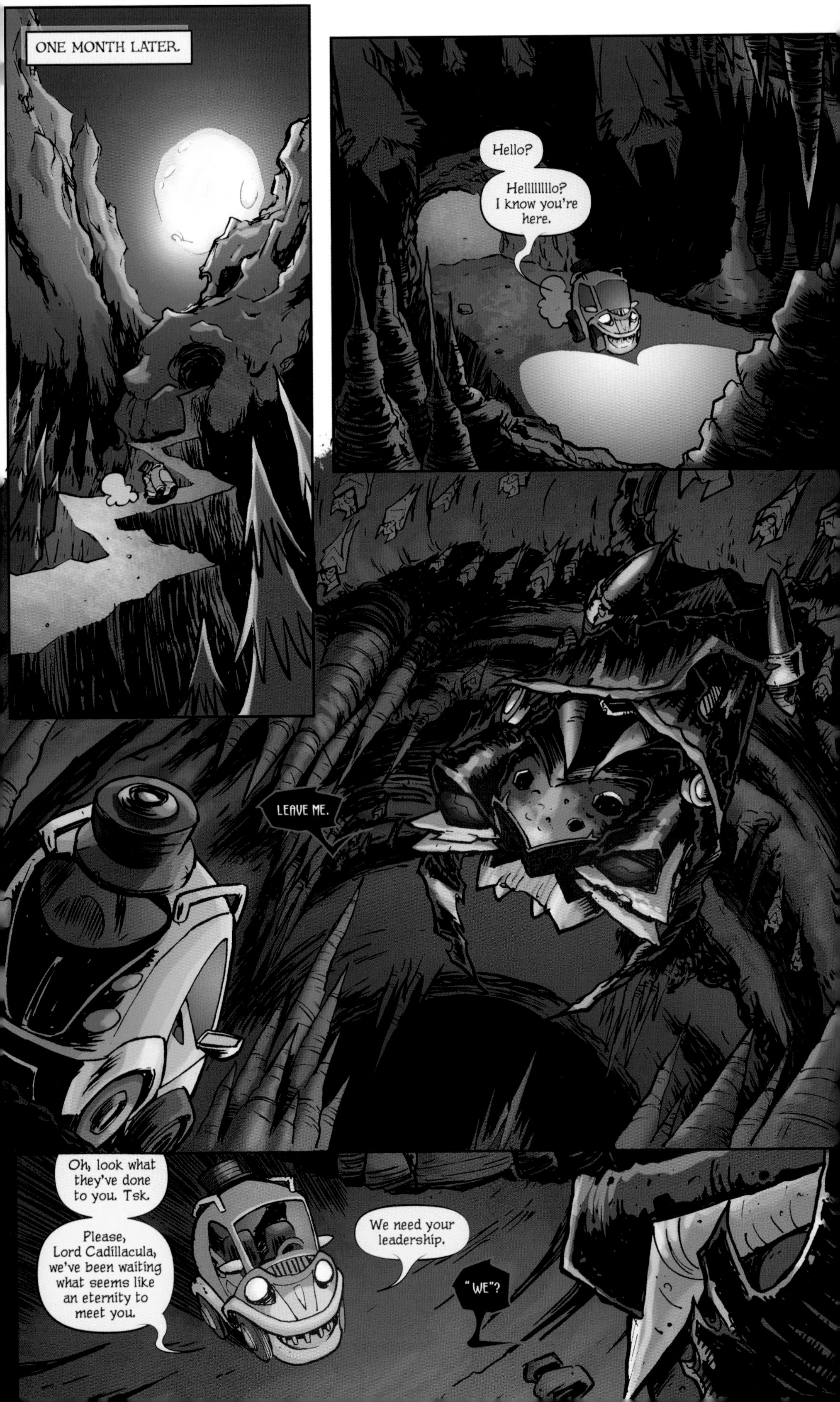
ONE MONTH LATER.
Hello?
Hellllllllo? I know you're here.
LEAVE ME.
Oh, look what they've done to you. Tsk.
Please, Lord Cadillacula, we've been waiting what seems like an eternity to meet you.
We need your leadership.
"WE"?

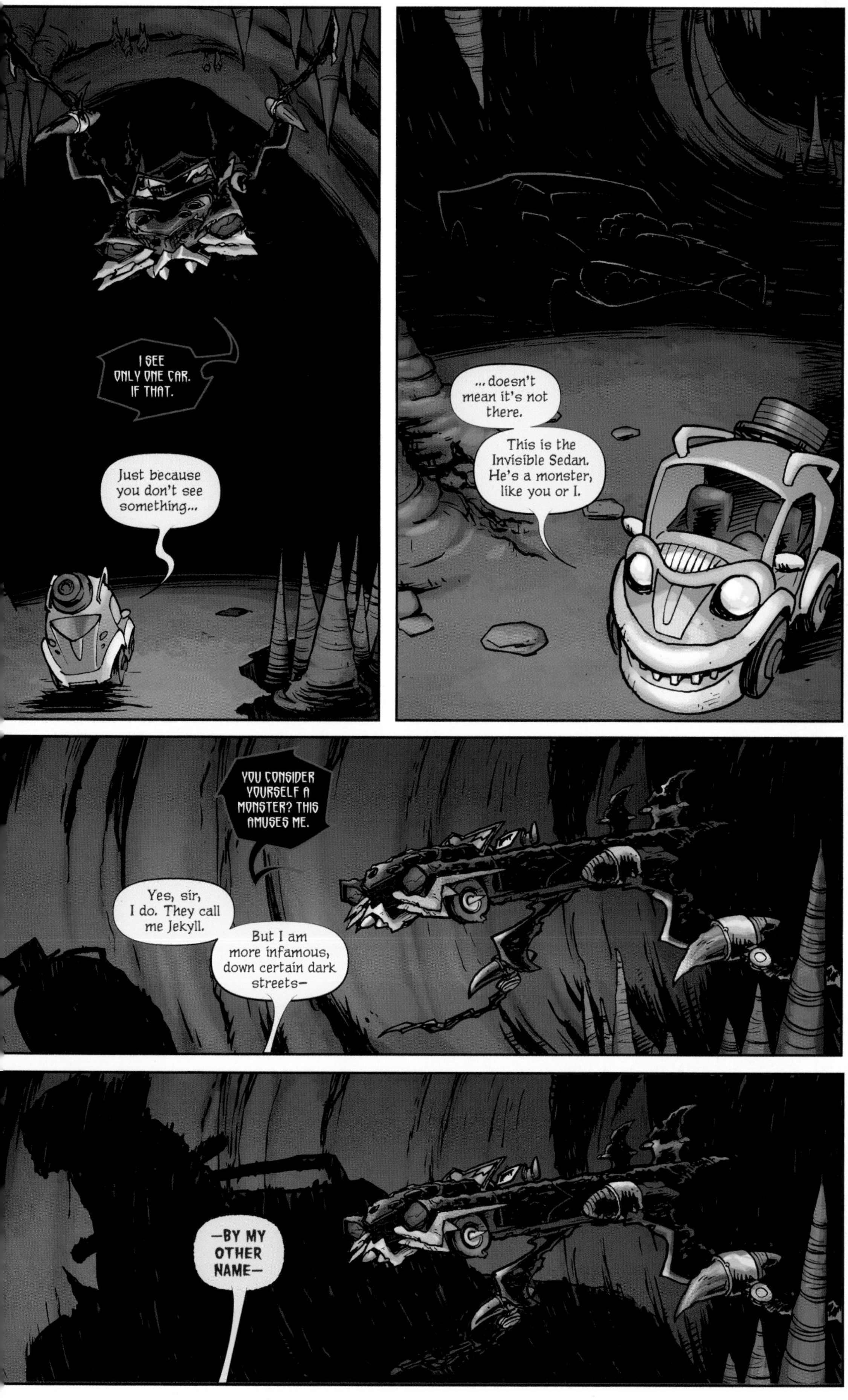
I SEE ONLY ONE CAR. IF THAT.
Just because you don't see something...
...doesn't mean it's not there.
This is the Invisible Sedan. He's a monster, like you or I.
YOU CONSIDER YOURSELF A MONSTER? THIS AMUSES ME.
Yes, sir, I do. They call me Jekyll.
But I am more infamous, down certain dark streets—
—BY MY OTHER NAME—

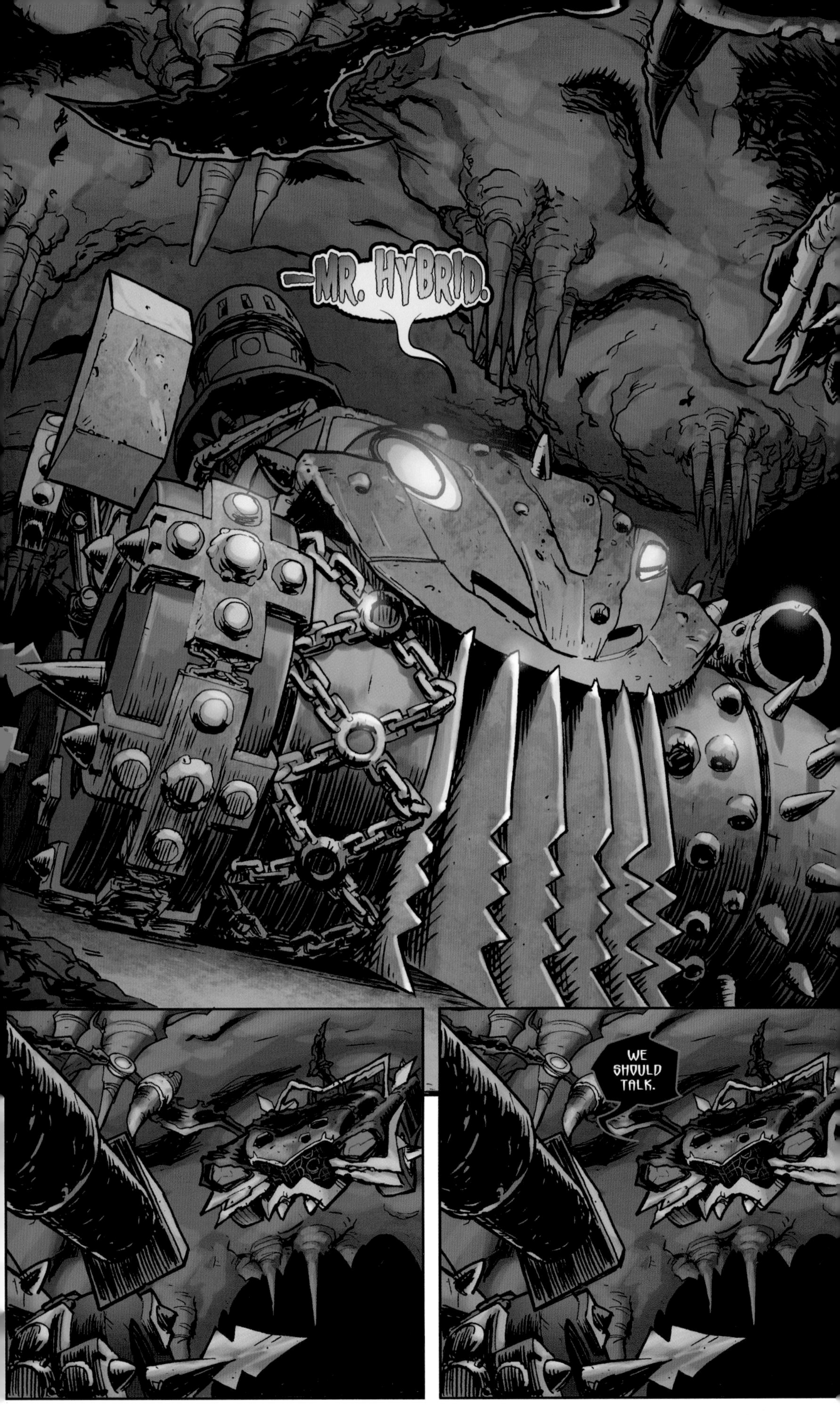
—MR. HYBRID.
WE SHOULD TALK.

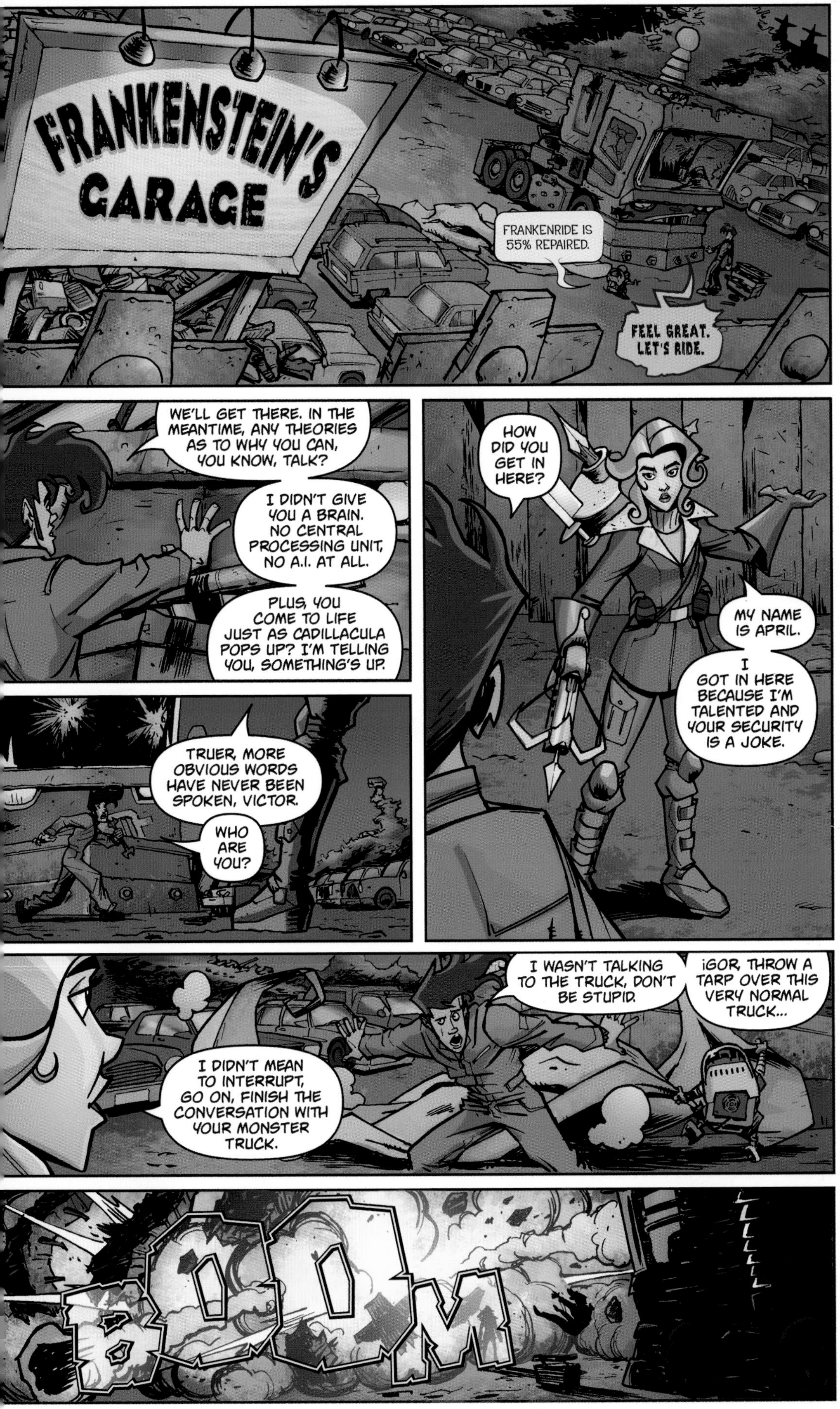
FRANKENSTEIN'S GARAGE
FRANKENRIDE IS 55% REPAIRED.
FEEL GREAT. LET'S RIDE.
WE'LL GET THERE. IN THE MEANTIME, ANY THEORIES AS TO WHY YOU CAN, YOU KNOW, TALK?
I DIDN'T GIVE YOU A BRAIN. NO CENTRAL PROCESSING UNIT, NO A.I. AT ALL.
PLUS, YOU COME TO LIFE JUST AS CADILLACULA POPS UP? I'M TELLING YOU, SOMETHING'S UP.
TRUER, MORE OBVIOUS WORDS HAVE NEVER BEEN SPOKEN, VICTOR.
WHO ARE YOU?
HOW DID YOU GET IN HERE?
MY NAME IS APRIL.
I GOT IN HERE BECAUSE I'M TALENTED AND YOUR SECURITY IS A JOKE.
I WASN'T TALKING TO THE TRUCK, DON'T BE STUPID.
iGOR, THROW A TARP OVER THIS VERY NORMAL TRUCK...
I DIDN'T MEAN TO INTERRUPT, GO ON, FINISH THE CONVERSATION WITH YOUR MONSTER TRUCK.
BOOM

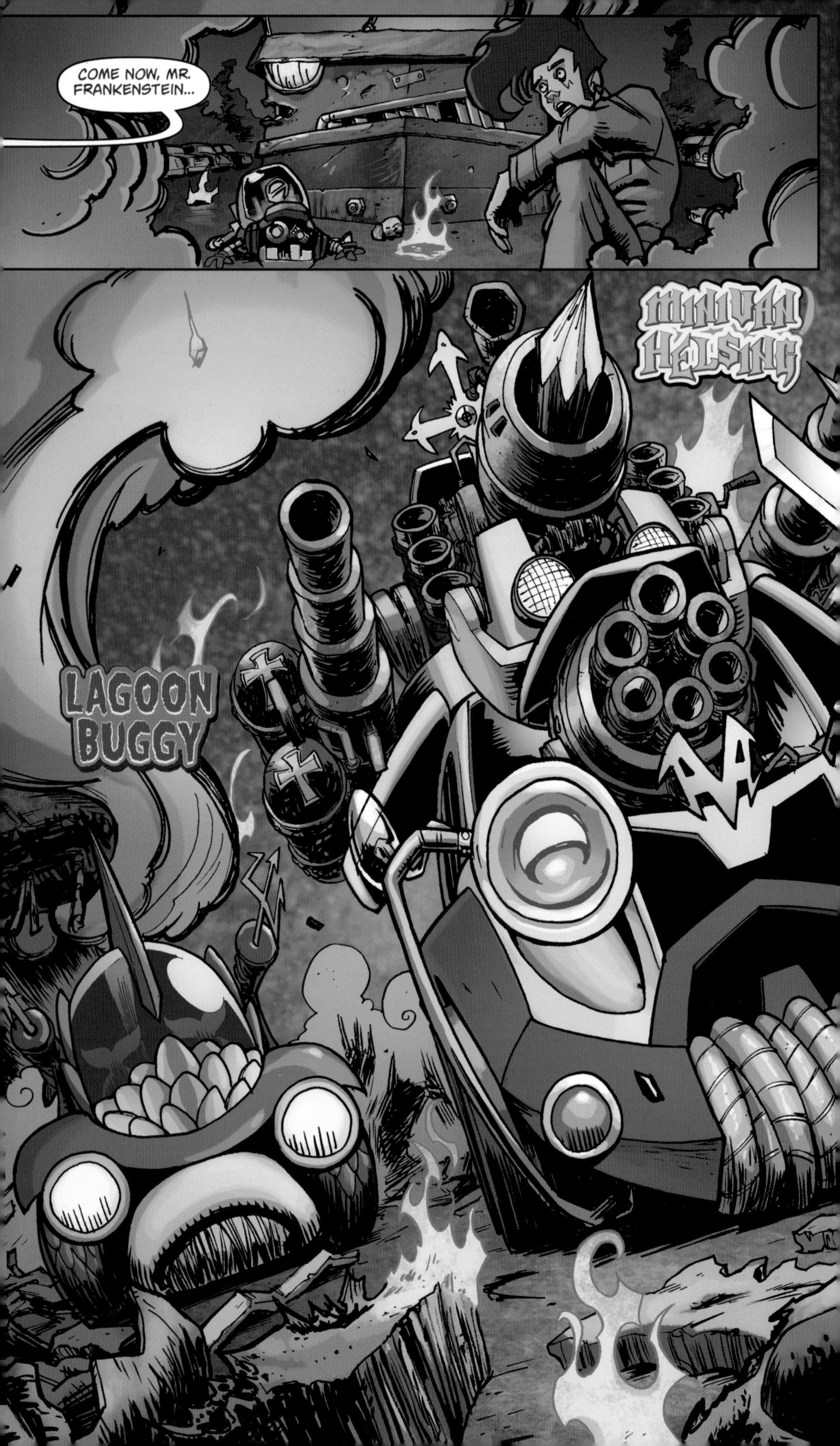
COME NOW, MR. FRANKENSTEIN...
MINIVAN HELSING
LAGOON BUGGY

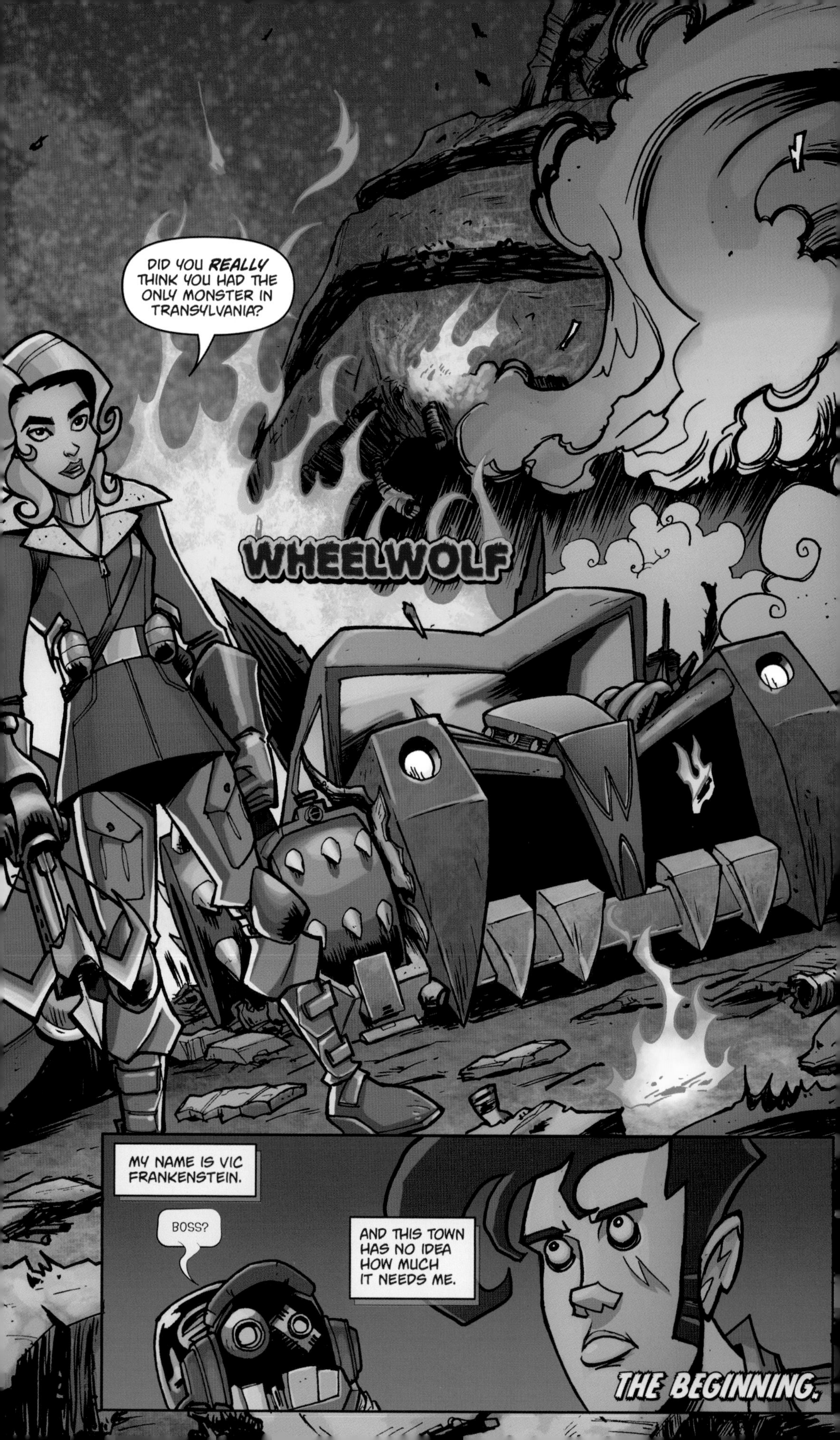
DID YOU REALLY THINK YOU HAD THE ONLY MONSTER IN TRANSYLVANIA?
WHEELWOLF
MY NAME IS VIC FRANKENSTEIN.
BOSS?
AND THIS TOWN HAS NO IDEA HOW MUCH IT NEEDS ME.
THE BEGINNING.

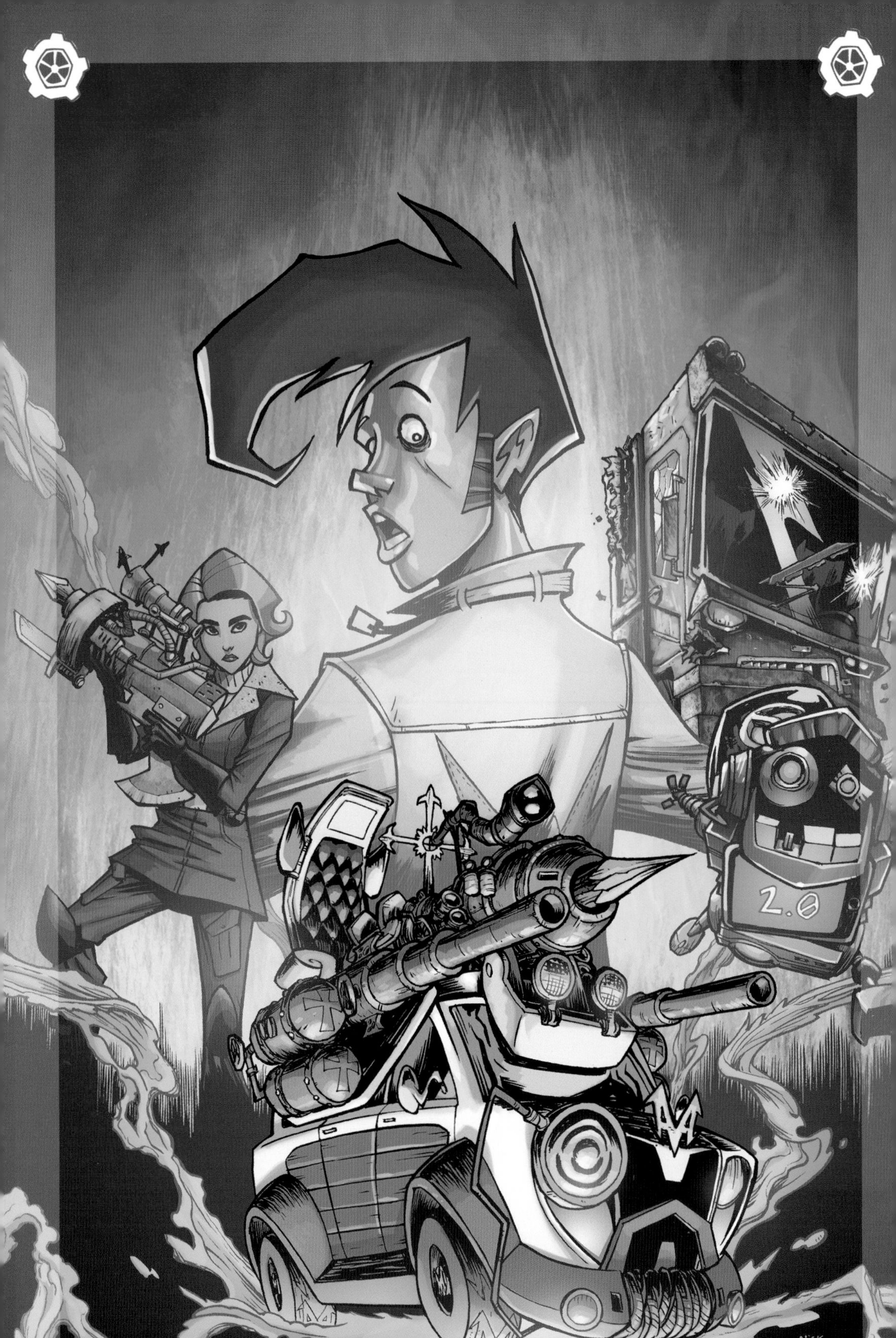
2.0
NICK ROCHE 2014

THE CURSE *of* MINIVAN HELSING, PART 1

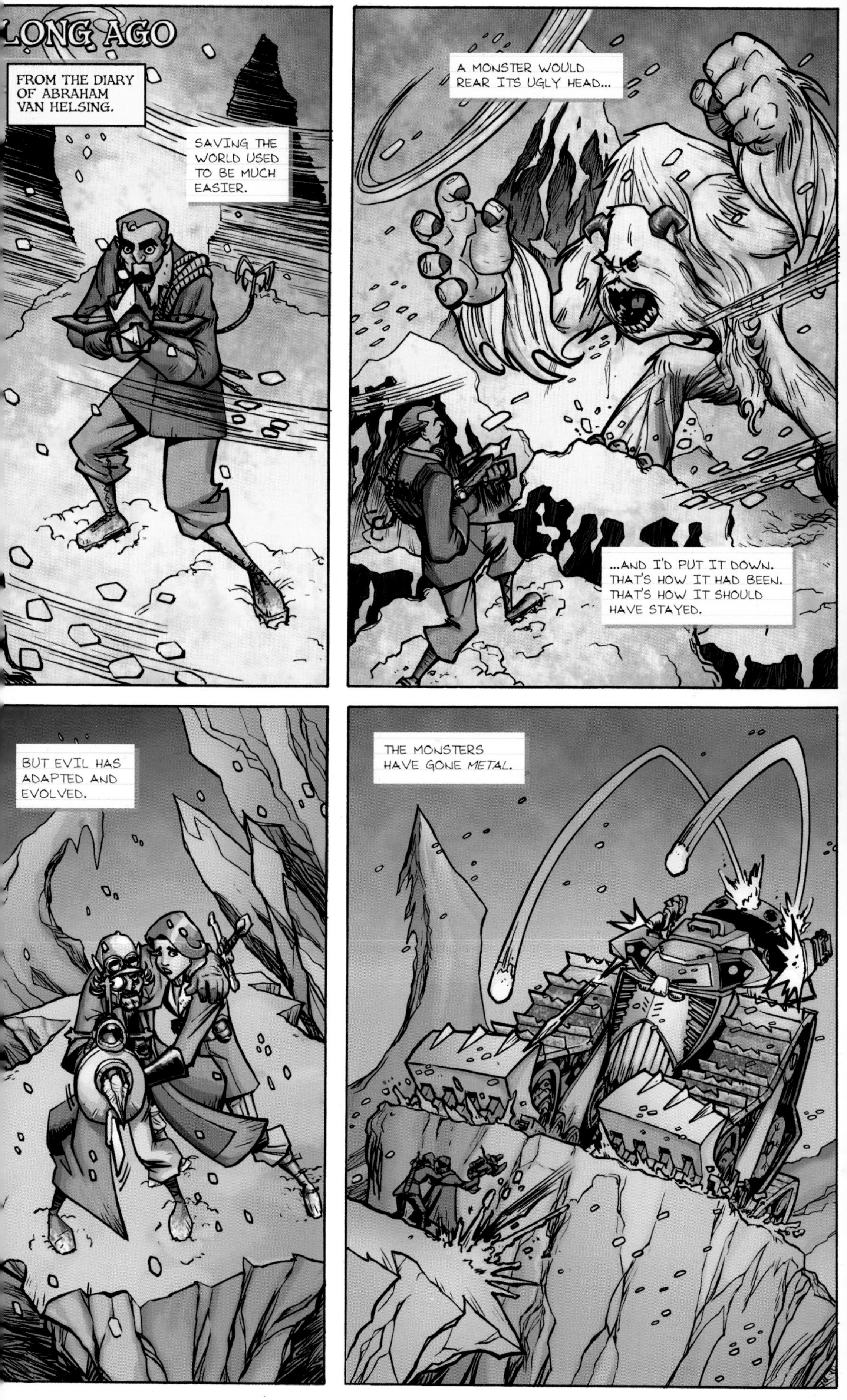
LONG AGO
FROM THE DIARY OF ABRAHAM VAN HELSING.
SAVING THE WORLD USED TO BE MUCH EASIER.
A MONSTER WOULD REAR ITS UGLY HEAD...
...AND I'D PUT IT DOWN. THAT'S HOW IT HAD BEEN. THAT'S HOW IT SHOULD HAVE STAYED.
BUT EVIL HAS ADAPTED AND EVOLVED.
THE MONSTERS HAVE GONE *METAL*.

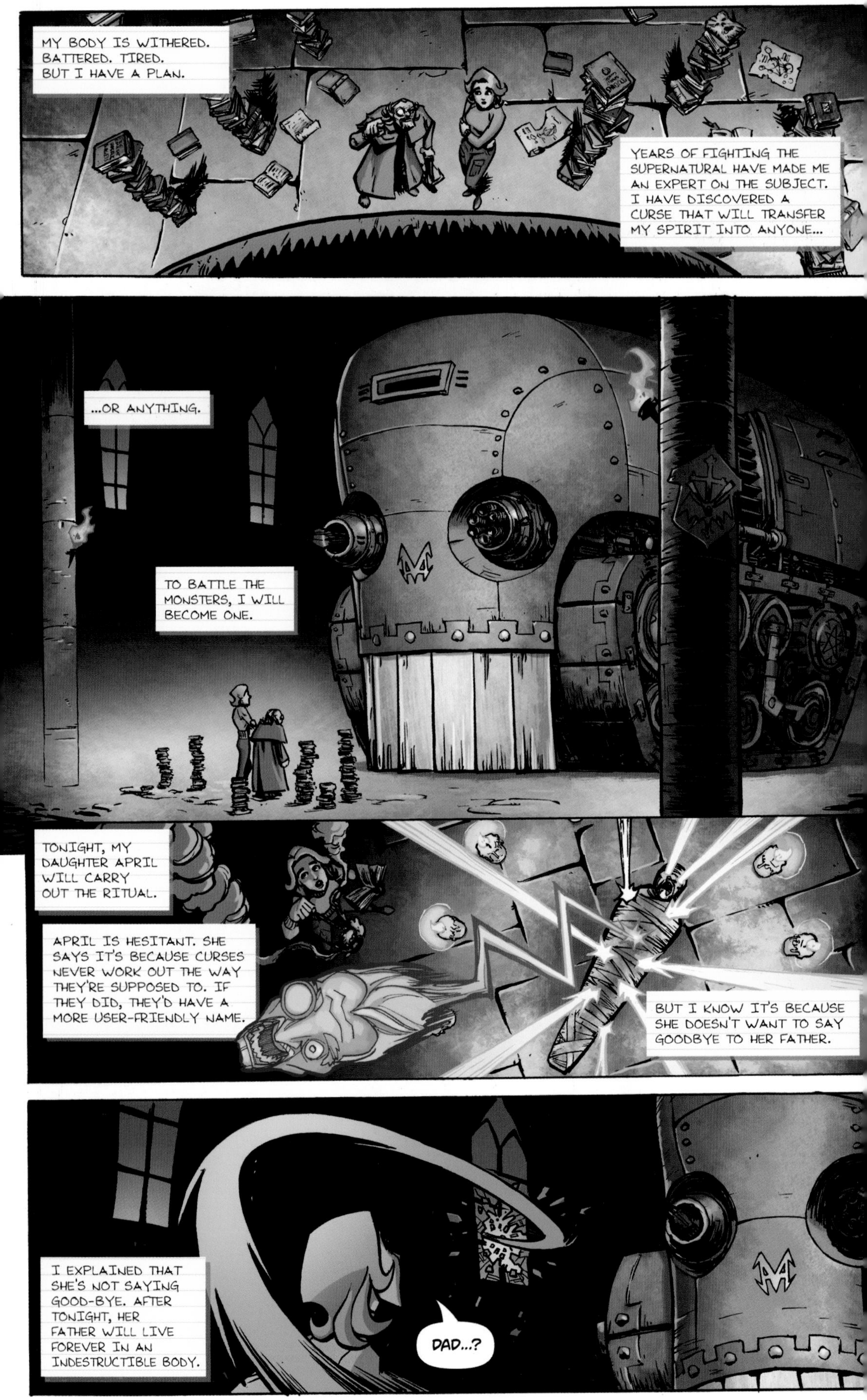
MY BODY IS WITHERED. BATTERED. TIRED. BUT I HAVE A PLAN.
YEARS OF FIGHTING THE SUPERNATURAL HAVE MADE ME AN EXPERT ON THE SUBJECT. I HAVE DISCOVERED A CURSE THAT WILL TRANSFER MY SPIRIT INTO ANYONE...
...OR ANYTHING.
TO BATTLE THE MONSTERS, I WILL BECOME ONE.
TONIGHT, MY DAUGHTER APRIL WILL CARRY OUT THE RITUAL.
APRIL IS HESITANT. SHE SAYS IT'S BECAUSE CURSES NEVER WORK OUT THE WAY THEY'RE SUPPOSED TO. IF THEY DID, THEY'D HAVE A MORE USER-FRIENDLY NAME.
BUT I KNOW IT'S BECAUSE SHE DOESN'T WANT TO SAY GOODBYE TO HER FATHER.
I EXPLAINED THAT SHE'S NOT SAYING GOOD-BYE. AFTER TONIGHT, HER FATHER WILL LIVE FOREVER IN AN INDESTRUCTIBLE BODY.
DAD...?

WHOOOOSH
WHAT HAPPENED? DID IT WORK?

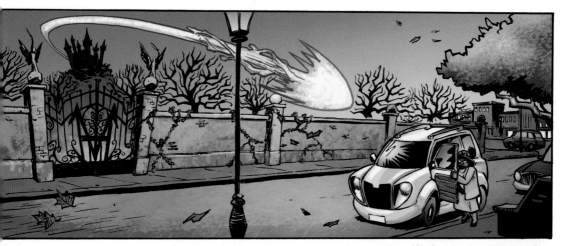

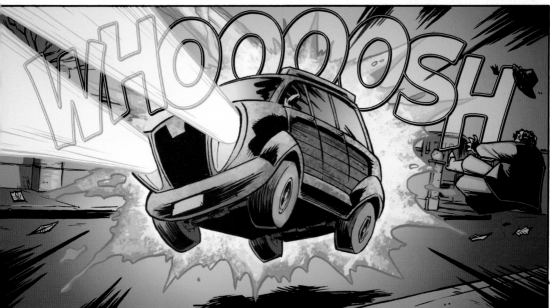

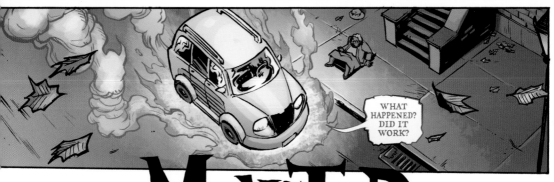

MONSTER MOTORS

THE CURSE OF MINIVAN HELSING

PART 1 OF 2

BY BRIAN LYNCH, NICK ROCHE, LEN O'GRADY AND TOM B. LONG

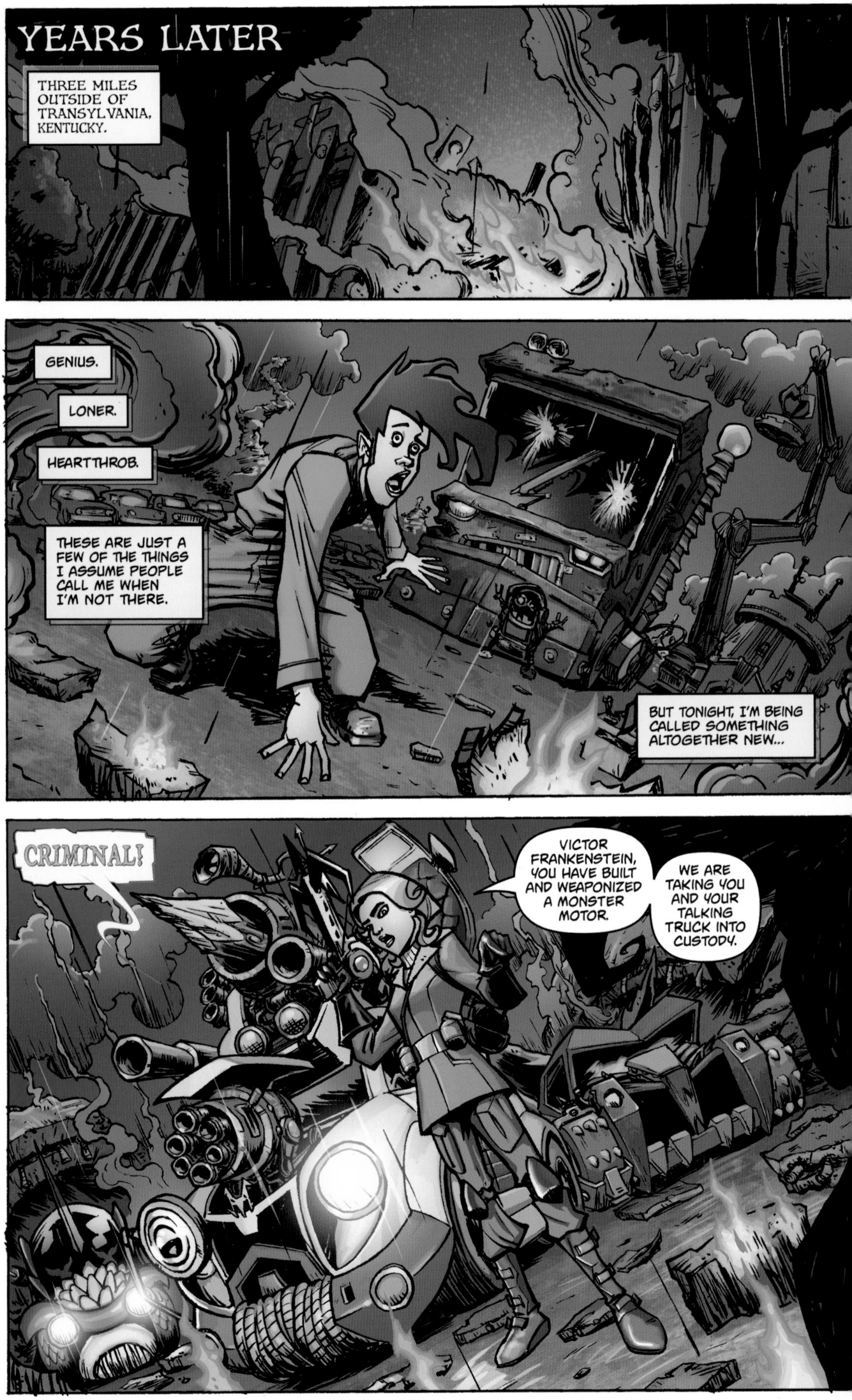
YEARS LATER
THREE MILES OUTSIDE OF TRANSYLVANIA, KENTUCKY.
GENIUS.
LONER.
HEARTTHROB.
THESE ARE JUST A FEW OF THE THINGS I ASSUME PEOPLE CALL ME WHEN I'M NOT THERE.
BUT TONIGHT, I'M BEING CALLED SOMETHING ALTOGETHER NEW...
CRIMINAL!
VICTOR FRANKENSTEIN, YOU HAVE BUILT AND WEAPONIZED A MONSTER MOTOR.
WE ARE TAKING YOU AND YOUR TALKING TRUCK INTO CUSTODY.

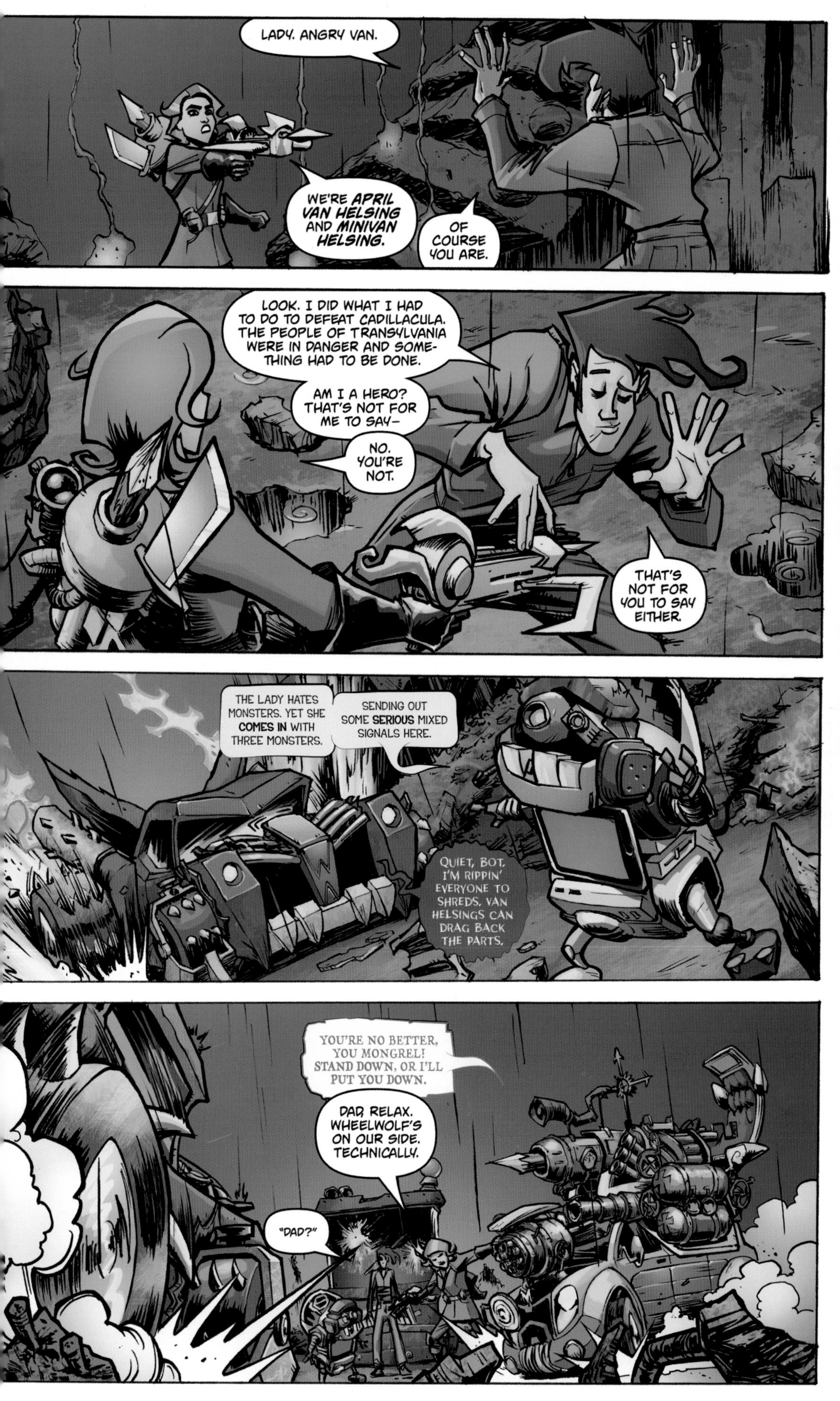
LADY. ANGRY VAN.
WE'RE APRIL VAN HELSING AND MINIVAN HELSING.
OF COURSE YOU ARE.
LOOK. I DID WHAT I HAD TO DO TO DEFEAT CADILLACULA. THE PEOPLE OF TRANSYLVANIA WERE IN DANGER AND SOMETHING HAD TO BE DONE.
AM I A HERO? THAT'S NOT FOR ME TO SAY–
NO. YOU'RE NOT.
THAT'S NOT FOR YOU TO SAY EITHER.
THE LADY HATES MONSTERS. YET SHE COMES IN WITH THREE MONSTERS.
SENDING OUT SOME SERIOUS MIXED SIGNALS HERE.
QUIET, BOT. I'M RIPPIN' EVERYONE TO SHREDS. VAN HELSINGS CAN DRAG BACK THE PARTS.
YOU'RE NO BETTER, YOU MONGREL! STAND DOWN, OR I'LL PUT YOU DOWN.
DAD, RELAX. WHEELWOLF'S ON OUR SIDE. TECHNICALLY.
"DAD?"

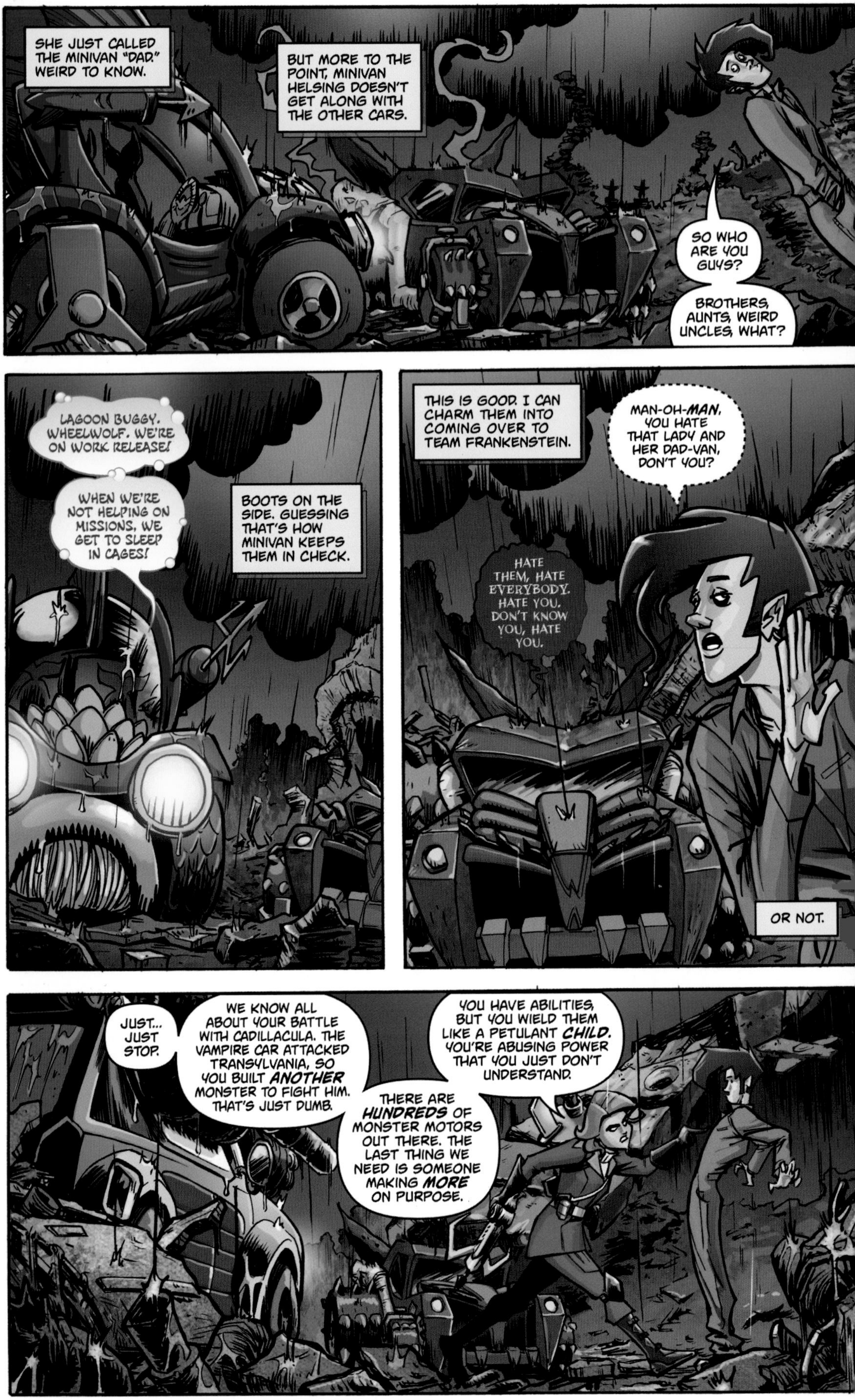

SHE JUST CALLED THE MINIVAN "DAD." WEIRD TO KNOW.
BUT MORE TO THE POINT, MINIVAN HELSING DOESN'T GET ALONG WITH THE OTHER CARS.
SO WHO ARE YOU GUYS?
BROTHERS, AUNTS, WEIRD UNCLES, WHAT?
LAGOON BUGGY. WHEELWOLF. WE'RE ON WORK RELEASE!
WHEN WE'RE NOT HELPING ON MISSIONS, WE GET TO SLEEP IN CAGES!
BOOTS ON THE SIDE. GUESSING THAT'S HOW MINIVAN KEEPS THEM IN CHECK.
THIS IS GOOD. I CAN CHARM THEM INTO COMING OVER TO TEAM FRANKENSTEIN.
MAN-OH-MAN, YOU HATE THAT LADY AND HER DAD-VAN, DON'T YOU?
HATE THEM, HATE EVERYBODY. HATE YOU. DON'T KNOW YOU, HATE YOU.
OR NOT.
JUST... JUST STOP.
WE KNOW ALL ABOUT YOUR BATTLE WITH CADILLACULA. THE VAMPIRE CAR ATTACKED TRANSYLVANIA, SO YOU BUILT ANOTHER MONSTER TO FIGHT HIM. THAT'S JUST DUMB.
YOU HAVE ABILITIES, BUT YOU WIELD THEM LIKE A PETULANT CHILD. YOU'RE ABUSING POWER THAT YOU JUST DON'T UNDERSTAND.
THERE ARE HUNDREDS OF MONSTER MOTORS OUT THERE. THE LAST THING WE NEED IS SOMEONE MAKING MORE ON PURPOSE.

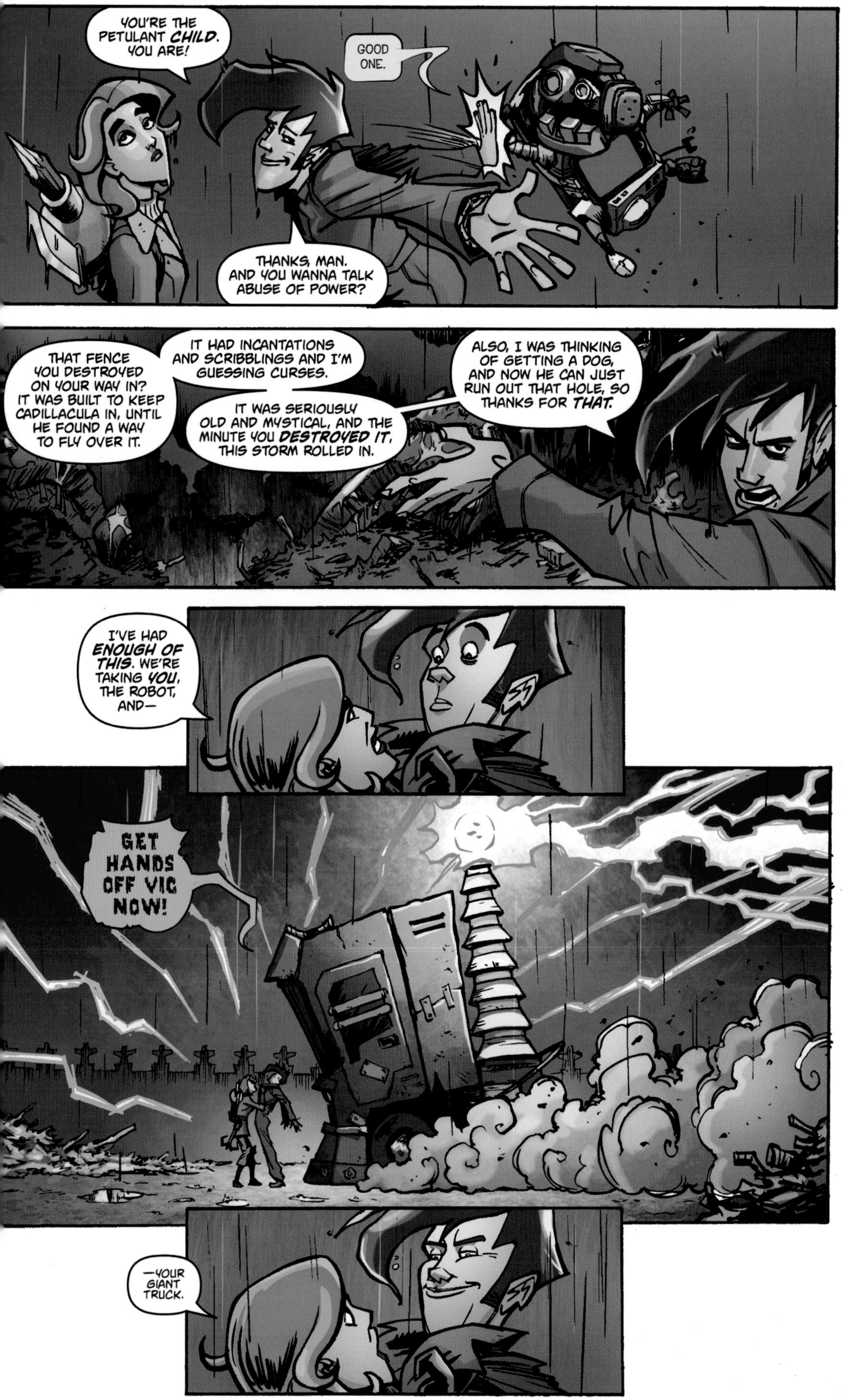
YOU'RE THE PETULANT CHILD. YOU ARE!
GOOD ONE.
THANKS, MAN. AND YOU WANNA TALK ABUSE OF POWER?
THAT FENCE YOU DESTROYED ON YOUR WAY IN? IT WAS BUILT TO KEEP CADILLACULA IN, UNTIL HE FOUND A WAY TO FLY OVER IT.
IT HAD INCANTATIONS AND SCRIBBLINGS AND I'M GUESSING CURSES.
IT WAS SERIOUSLY OLD AND MYSTICAL, AND THE MINUTE YOU DESTROYED IT, THIS STORM ROLLED IN.
ALSO, I WAS THINKING OF GETTING A DOG, AND NOW HE CAN JUST RUN OUT THAT HOLE, SO THANKS FOR THAT.
I'VE HAD ENOUGH OF THIS. WE'RE TAKING YOU, THE ROBOT, AND—
GET HANDS OFF VIC NOW!
—YOUR GIANT TRUCK.

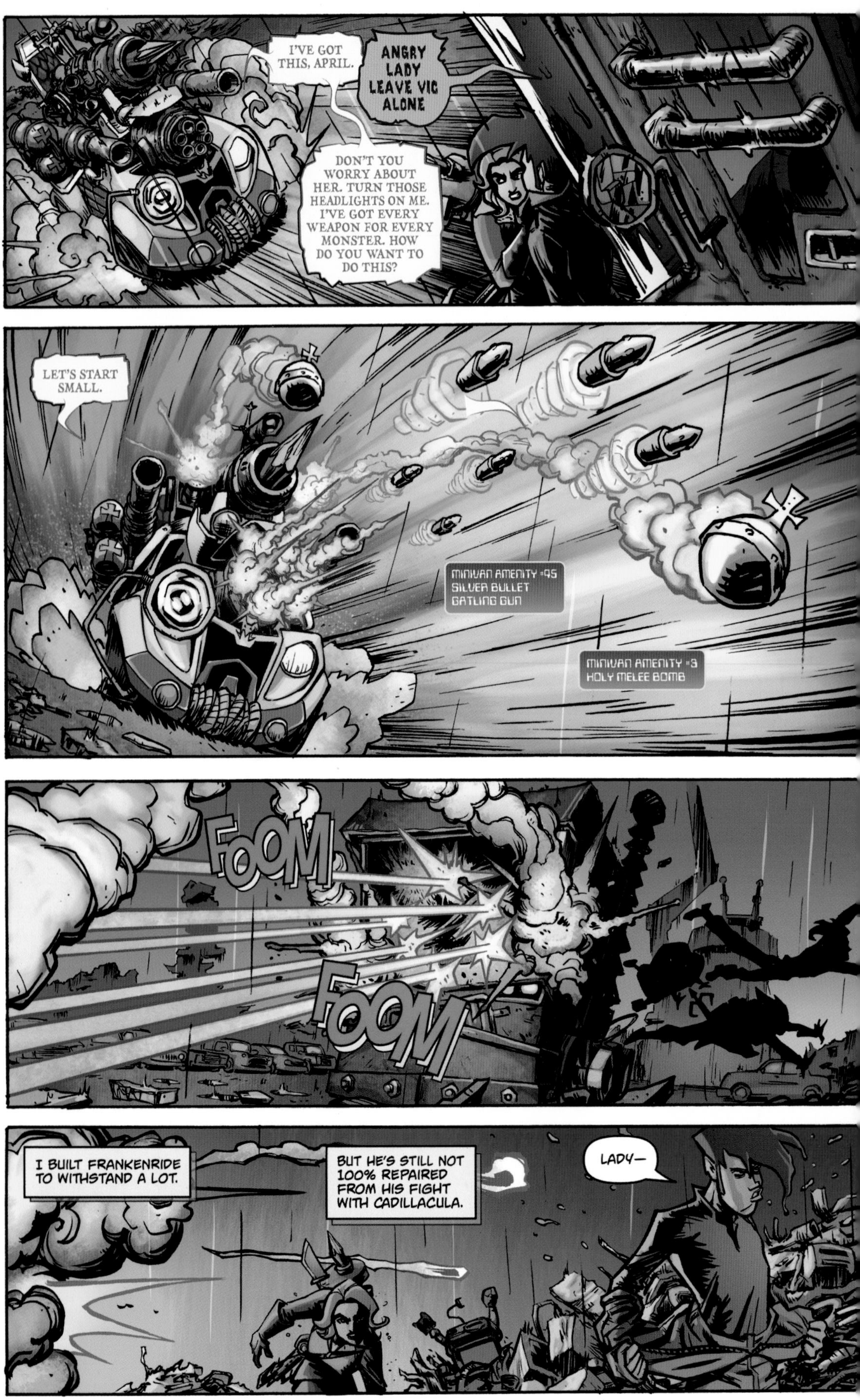
I'VE GOT THIS, APRIL.
ANGRY LADY LEAVE VIC ALONE
DON'T YOU WORRY ABOUT HER. TURN THOSE HEADLIGHTS ON ME. I'VE GOT EVERY WEAPON FOR EVERY MONSTER. HOW DO YOU WANT TO DO THIS?
LET'S START SMALL.
MINIVAN AMENITY #45 SILVER BULLET GATLING GUN
MINIVAN AMENITY #3 HOLY MELEE BOMB
FOOM
FOOM
I BUILT FRANKENRIDE TO WITHSTAND A LOT.
BUT HE'S STILL NOT 100% REPAIRED FROM HIS FIGHT WITH CADILLACULA.
LADY—

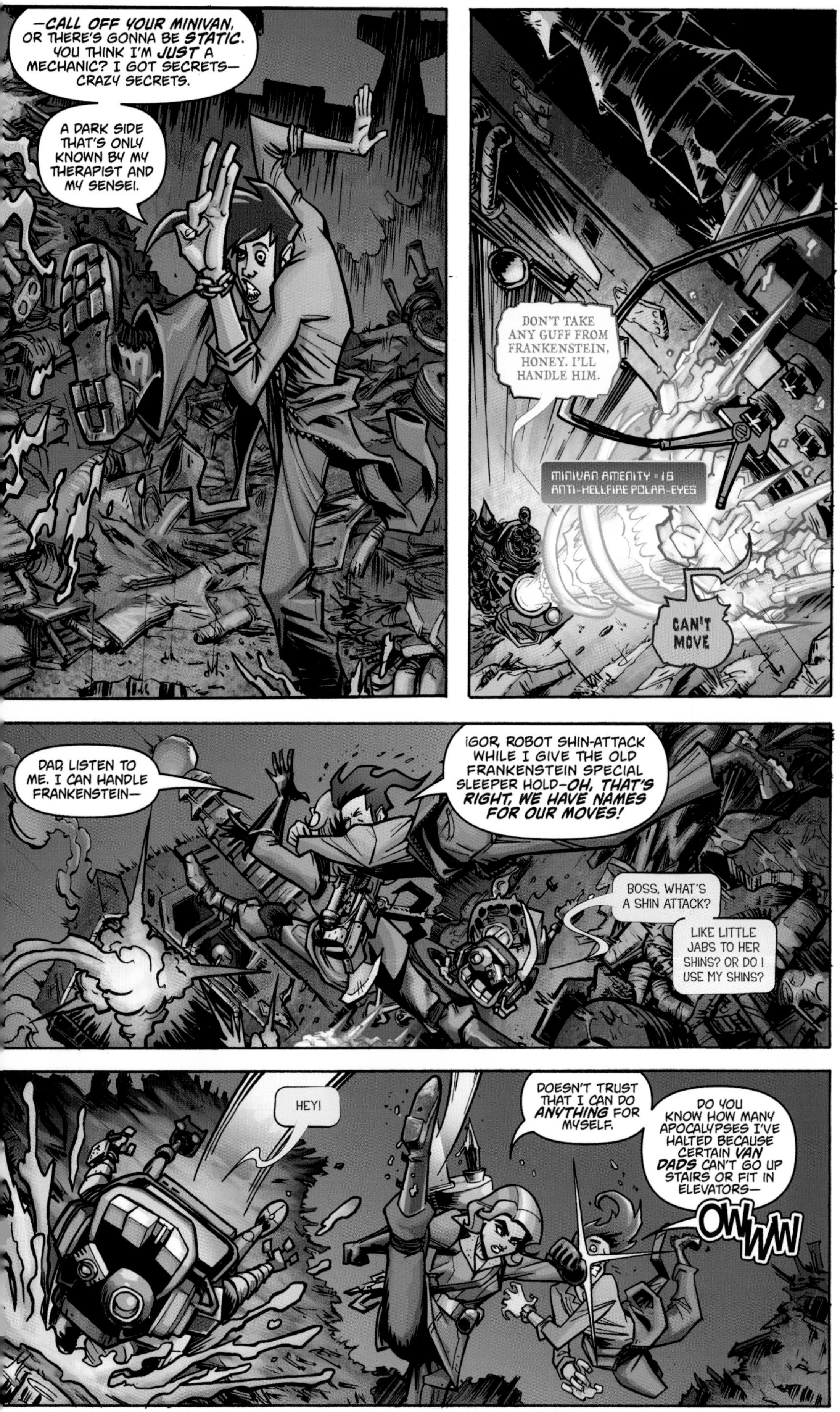
—CALL OFF YOUR MINIVAN, OR THERE'S GONNA BE STATIC. YOU THINK I'M JUST A MECHANIC? I GOT SECRETS— CRAZY SECRETS.
A DARK SIDE THAT'S ONLY KNOWN BY MY THERAPIST AND MY SENSEI.
DON'T TAKE ANY GUFF FROM FRANKENSTEIN, HONEY. I'LL HANDLE HIM.
MINIVAN AMENITY #16 ANTI-HELLFIRE POLAR-EYES
CAN'T MOVE
DAD, LISTEN TO ME. I CAN HANDLE FRANKENSTEIN—
¡GOR, ROBOT SHIN-ATTACK WHILE I GIVE THE OLD FRANKENSTEIN SPECIAL SLEEPER HOLD—OH, THAT'S RIGHT, WE HAVE NAMES FOR OUR MOVES!
BOSS, WHAT'S A SHIN ATTACK?
LIKE LITTLE JABS TO HER SHINS? OR DO I USE MY SHINS?
HEY!
DOESN'T TRUST THAT I CAN DO ANYTHING FOR MYSELF.
DO YOU KNOW HOW MANY APOCALYPSES I'VE HALTED BECAUSE CERTAIN VAN DADS CAN'T GO UP STAIRS OR FIT IN ELEVATORS—
OWWW

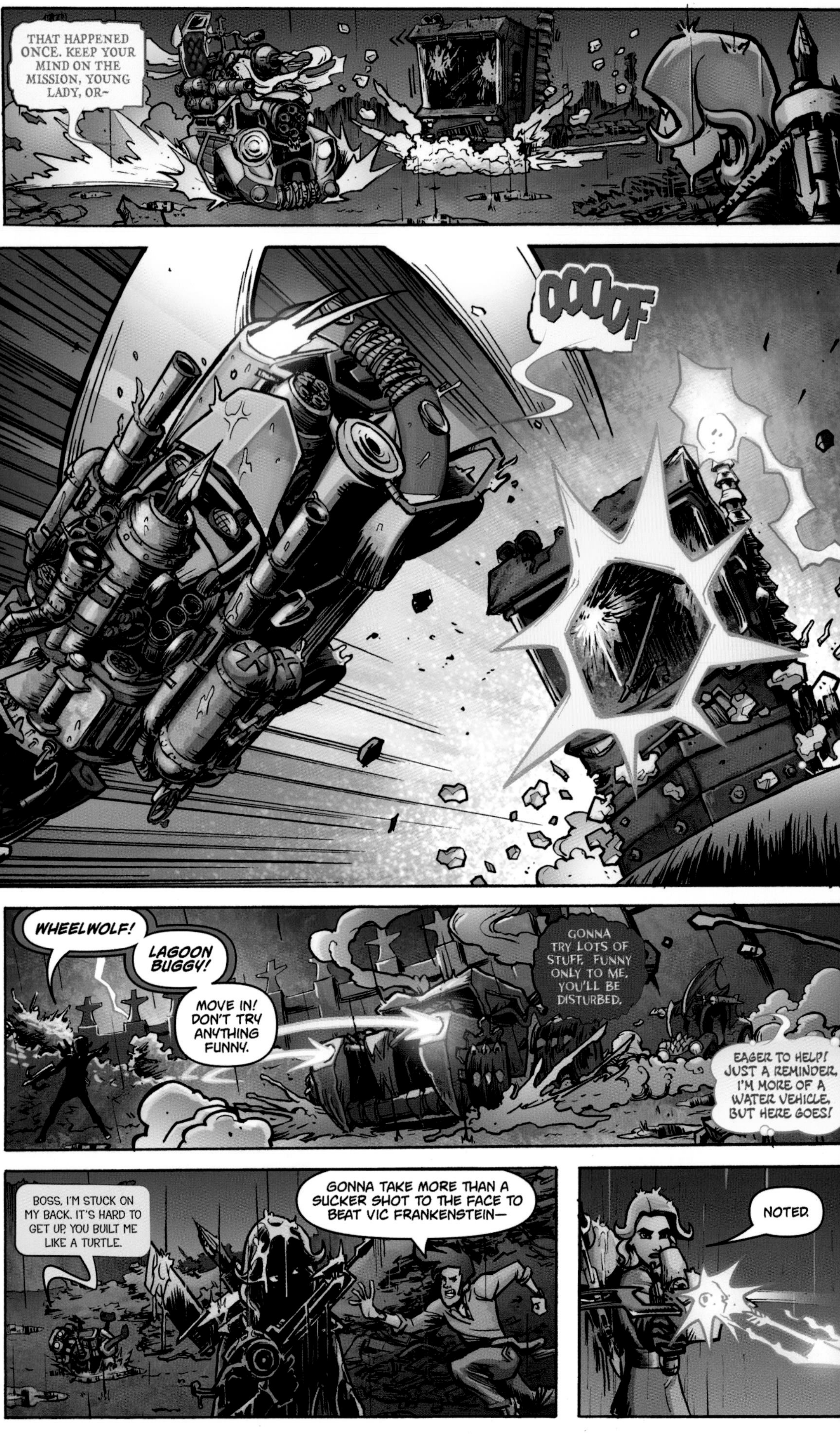
THAT HAPPENED ONCE. KEEP YOUR MIND ON THE MISSION, YOUNG LADY, OR~
OOOOF
WHEELWOLF!
LAGOON BUGGY!
MOVE IN! DON'T TRY ANYTHING FUNNY.
GONNA TRY LOTS OF STUFF, FUNNY ONLY TO ME, YOU'LL BE DISTURBED.
EAGER TO HELP! JUST A REMINDER, I'M MORE OF A WATER VEHICLE, BUT HERE GOES!
BOSS, I'M STUCK ON MY BACK. IT'S HARD TO GET UP, YOU BUILT ME LIKE A TURTLE.
GONNA TAKE MORE THAN A SUCKER SHOT TO THE FACE TO BEAT VIC FRANKENSTEIN—
NOTED.

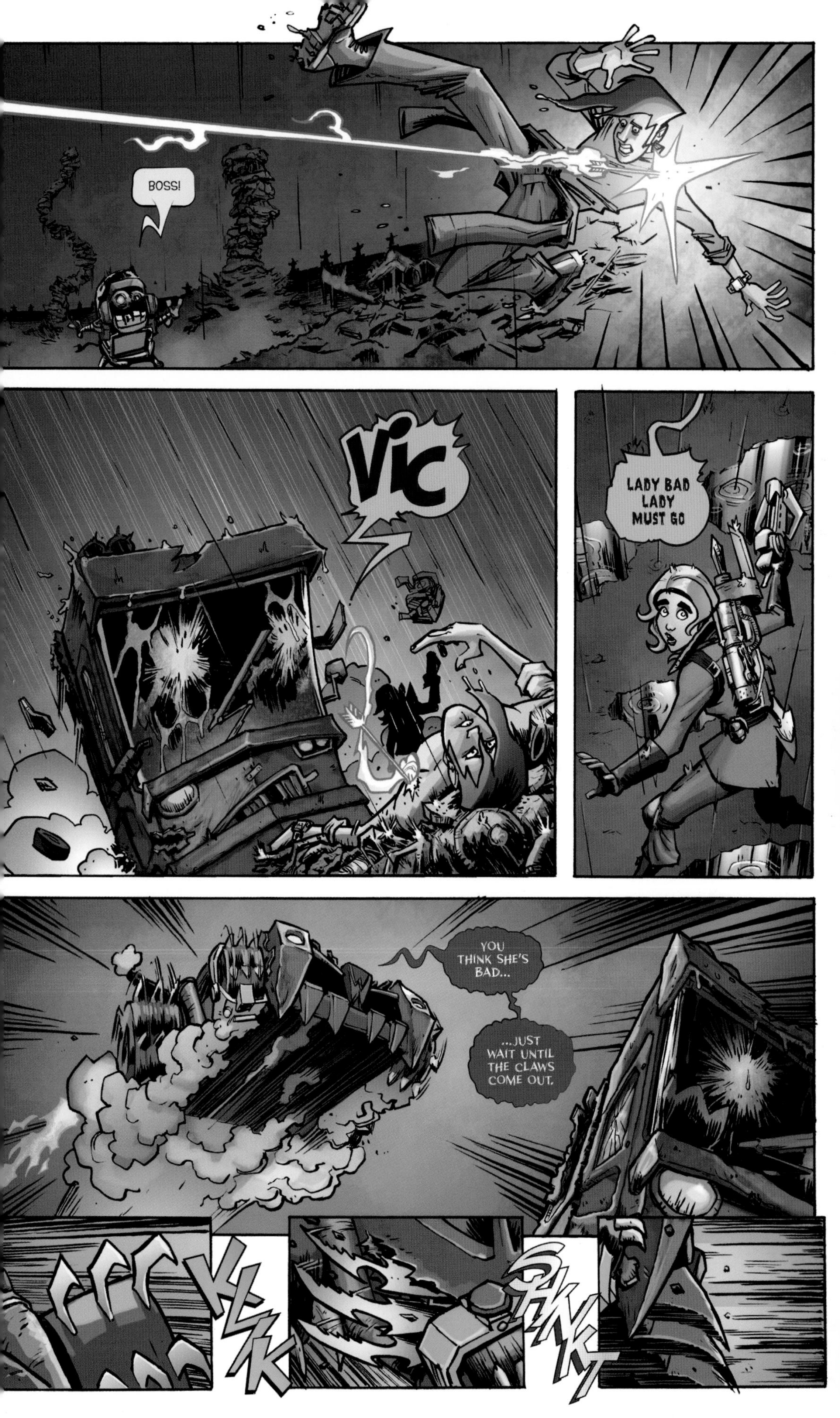
BOSS!
VIC
LADY BAD LADY MUST GO
YOU THINK SHE'S BAD...
...JUST WAIT UNTIL THE CLAWS COME OUT.
KLIK
SHKKT

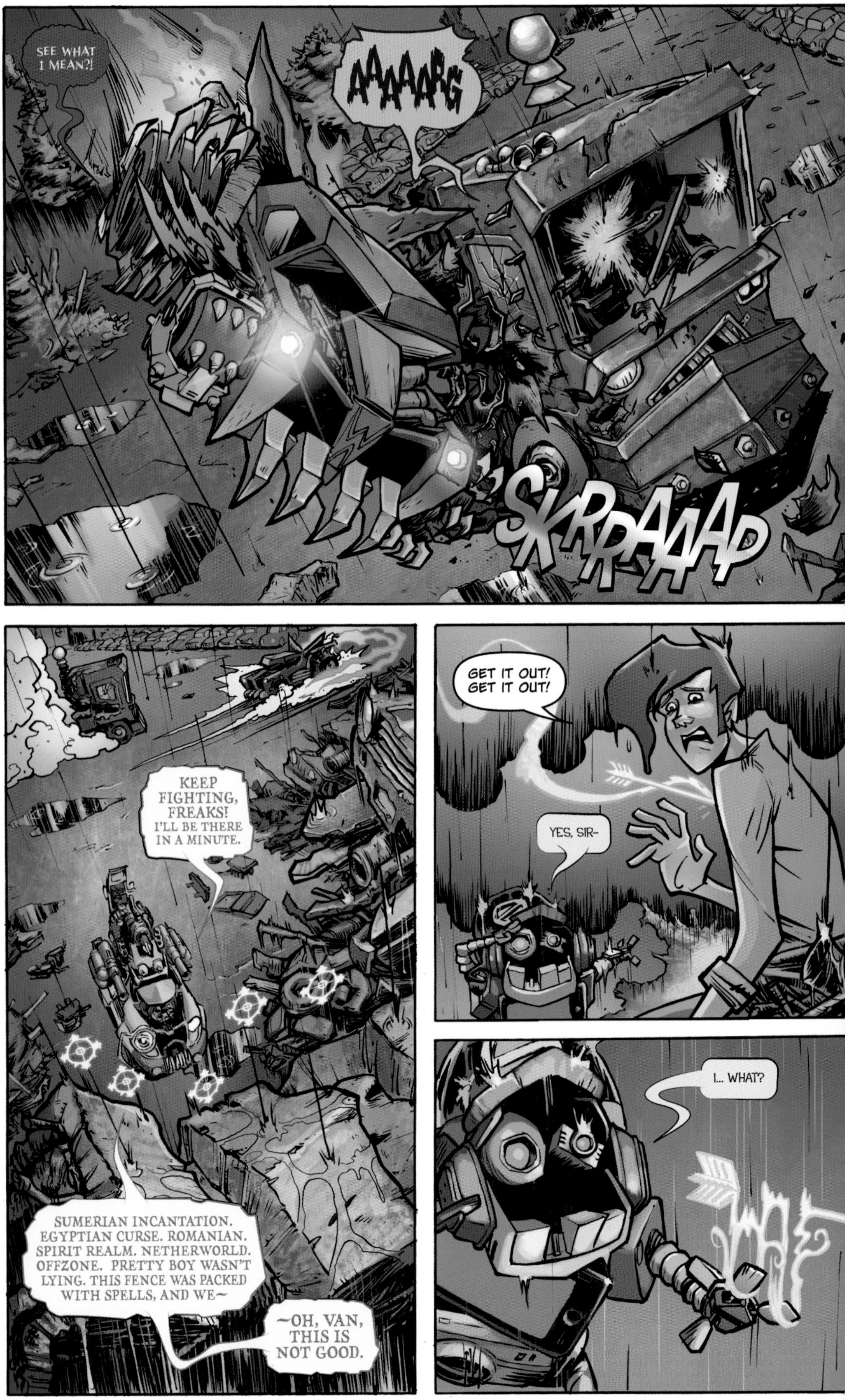
SEE WHAT I MEAN?!
AAAAARG
SKRRAAAAP
KEEP FIGHTING, FREAKS! I'LL BE THERE IN A MINUTE.
SUMERIAN INCANTATION. EGYPTIAN CURSE. ROMANIAN. SPIRIT REALM. NETHERWORLD. OFFZONE. PRETTY BOY WASN'T LYING. THIS FENCE WAS PACKED WITH SPELLS, AND WE~
~OH, VAN, THIS IS NOT GOOD.
GET IT OUT! GET IT OUT!
YES, SIR-
I... WHAT?

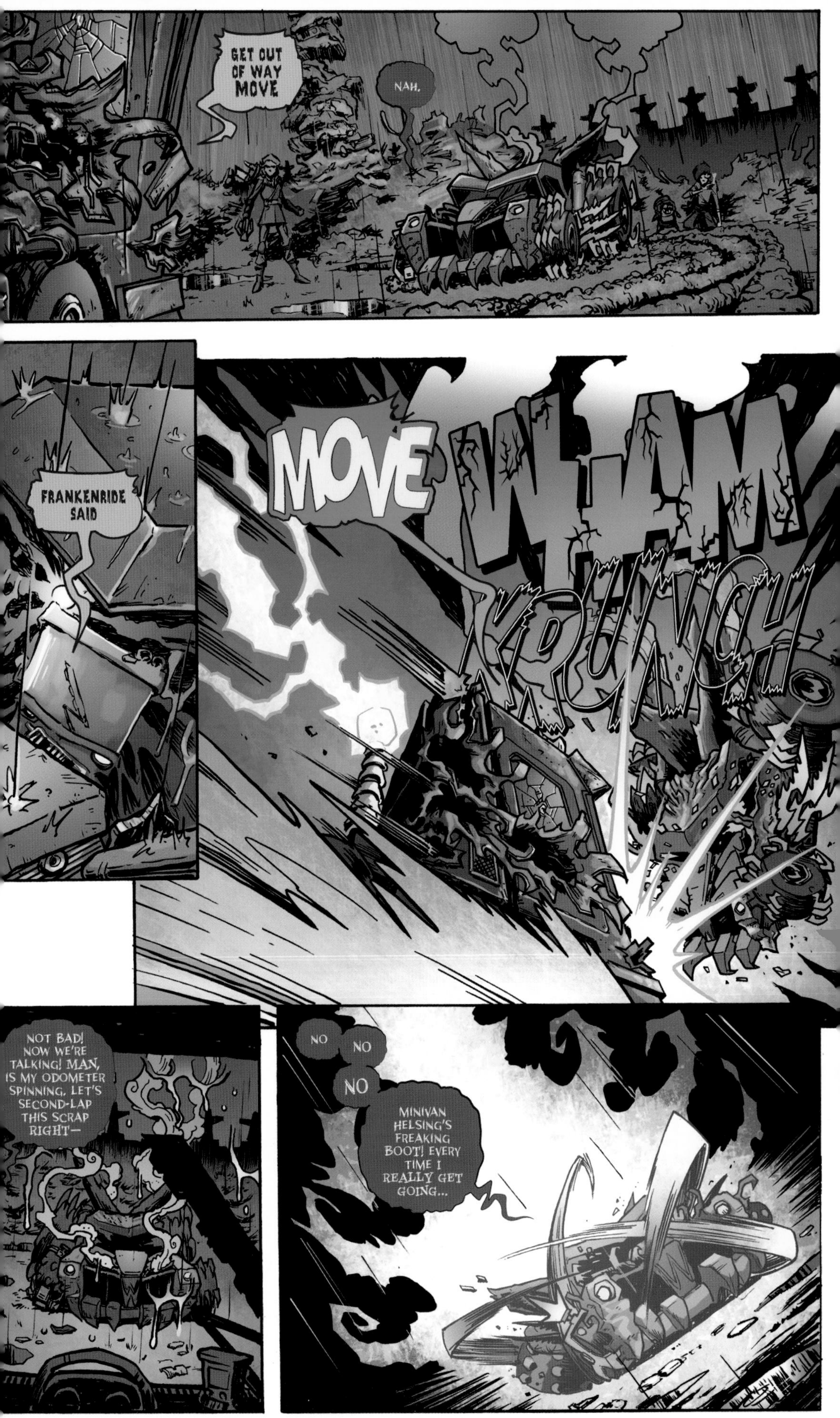
GET OUT OF WAY MOVE
NAH.
FRANKENRIDE SAID
MOVE
WHAM
KRUNCH
NOT BAD! NOW WE'RE TALKING! MAN, IS MY ODOMETER SPINNING. LET'S SECOND-LAP THIS SCRAP RIGHT—
NO
NO
NO
MINIVAN HELSING'S FREAKING BOOT! EVERY TIME I REALLY GET GOING...

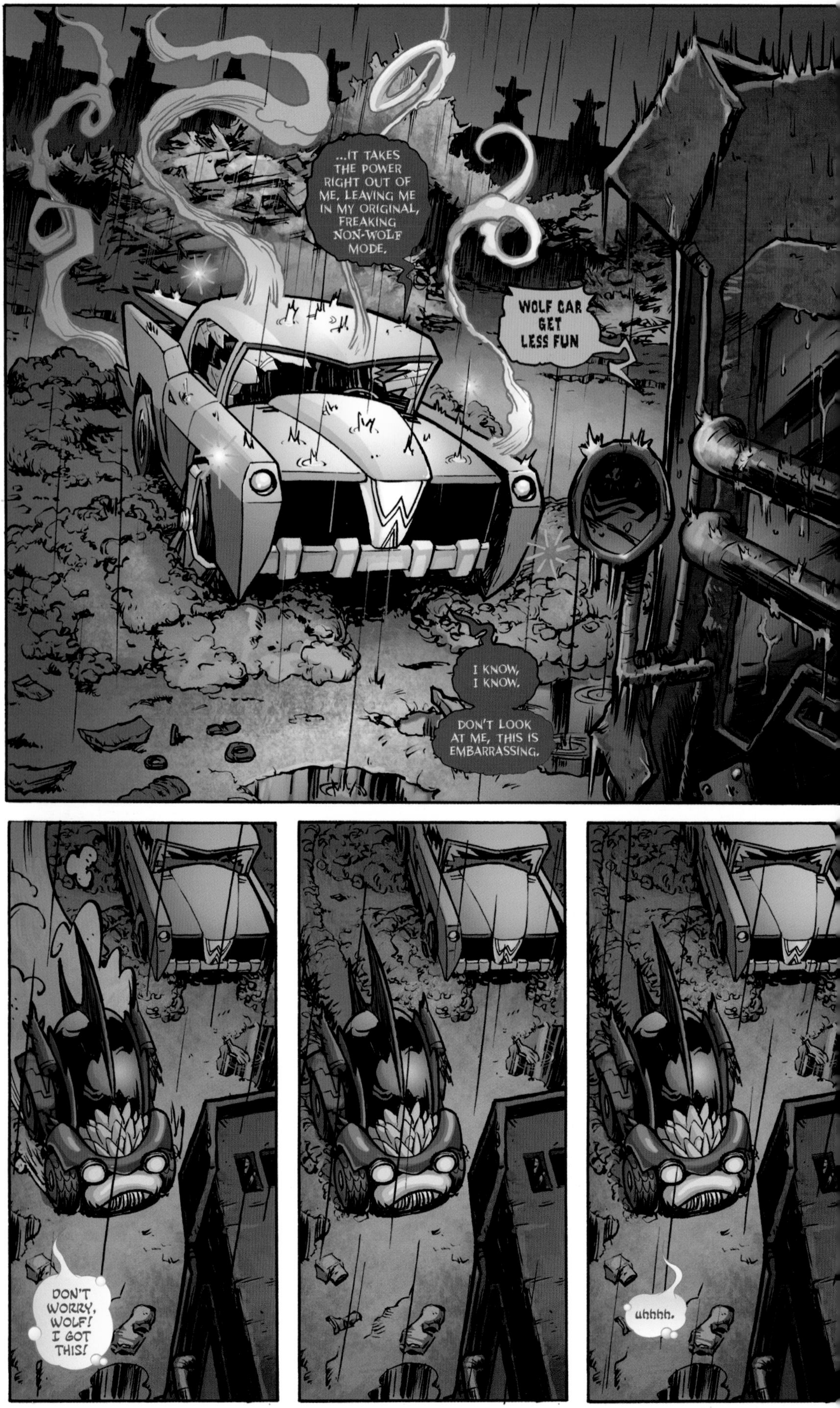
...IT TAKES THE POWER RIGHT OUT OF ME, LEAVING ME IN MY ORIGINAL, FREAKING NON-WOLF MODE.
WOLF CAR GET LESS FUN
I KNOW, I KNOW.
DON'T LOOK AT ME, THIS IS EMBARRASSING.
DON'T WORRY, WOLF! I GOT THIS!
uhhhh.

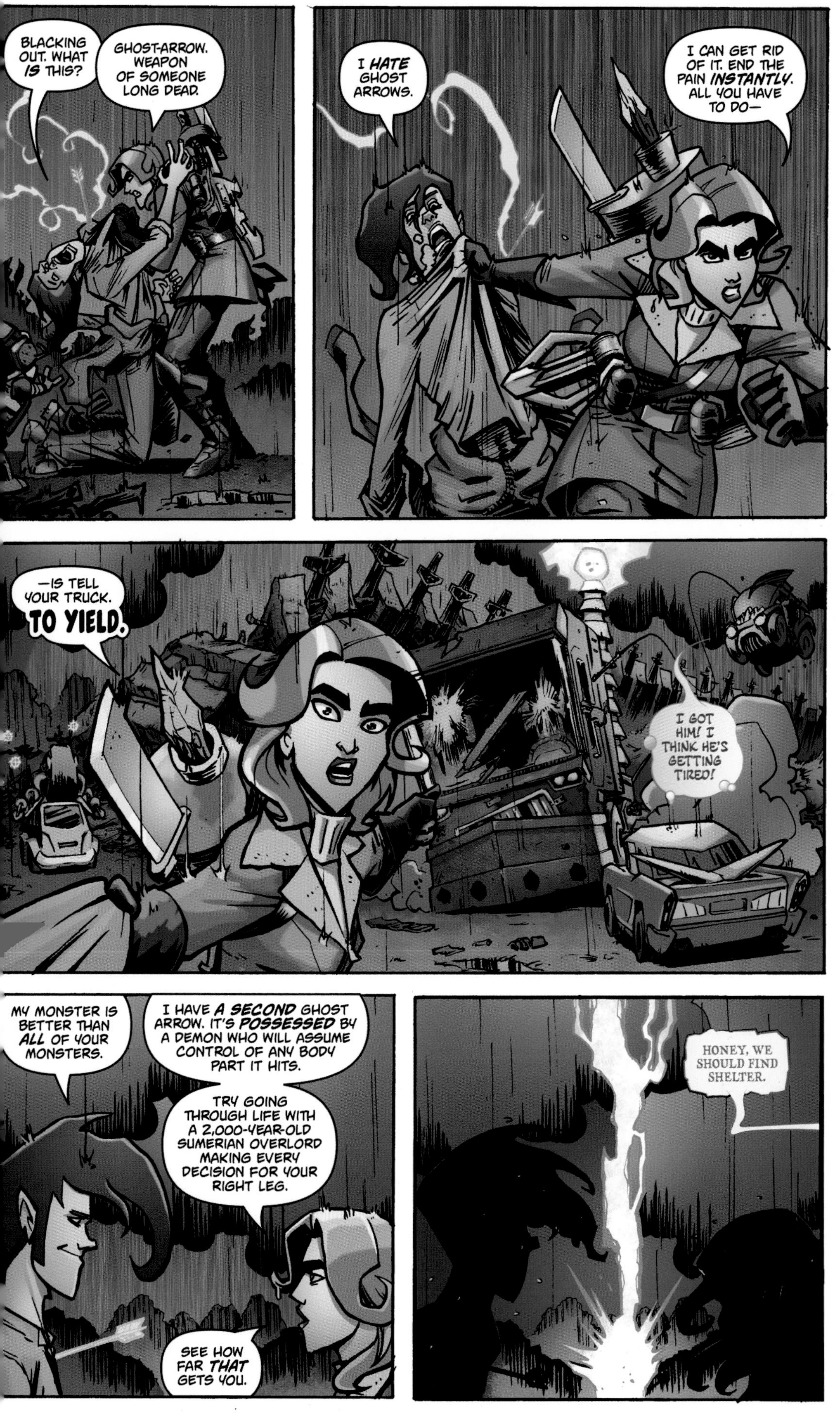
BLACKING OUT. WHAT *IS* THIS?
GHOST-ARROW. WEAPON OF SOMEONE LONG DEAD.
I *HATE* GHOST ARROWS.
I CAN GET RID OF IT. END THE PAIN *INSTANTLY*. ALL YOU HAVE TO DO—
—IS TELL YOUR TRUCK. **TO YIELD.**
I GOT HIM! I THINK HE'S GETTING TIRED!
MY MONSTER IS BETTER THAN *ALL* OF YOUR MONSTERS.
I HAVE *A SECOND* GHOST ARROW. IT'S *POSSESSED* BY A DEMON WHO WILL ASSUME CONTROL OF ANY BODY PART IT HITS.
TRY GOING THROUGH LIFE WITH A 2,000-YEAR-OLD SUMERIAN OVERLORD MAKING EVERY DECISION FOR YOUR RIGHT LEG.
SEE HOW FAR *THAT* GETS YOU.
HONEY, WE SHOULD FIND SHELTER.

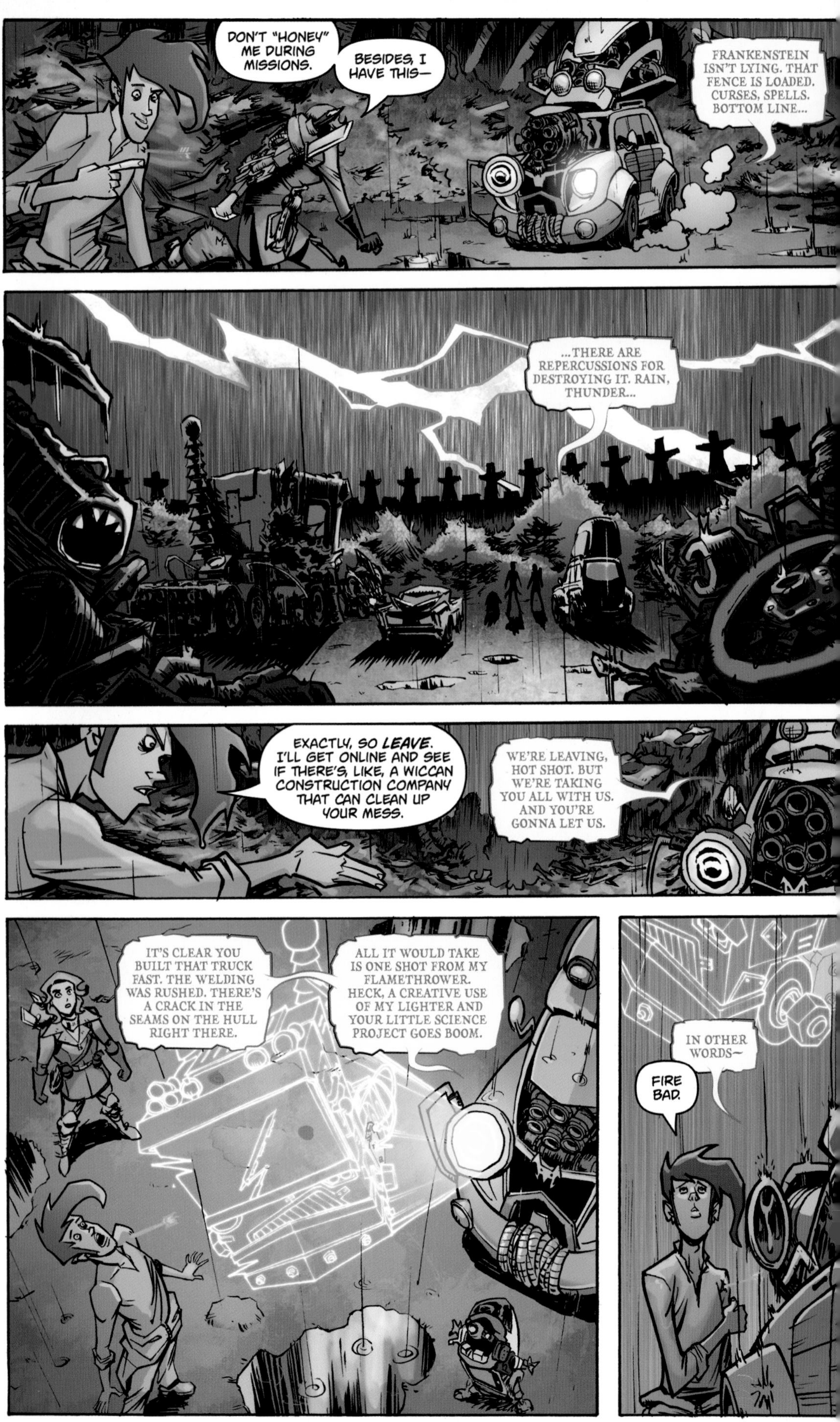
DON'T "HONEY" ME DURING MISSIONS.
BESIDES, I HAVE THIS—
FRANKENSTEIN ISN'T LYING. THAT FENCE IS LOADED. CURSES, SPELLS. BOTTOM LINE...
...THERE ARE REPERCUSSIONS FOR DESTROYING IT. RAIN, THUNDER...
EXACTLY, SO LEAVE. I'LL GET ONLINE AND SEE IF THERE'S, LIKE, A WICCAN CONSTRUCTION COMPANY THAT CAN CLEAN UP YOUR MESS.
WE'RE LEAVING, HOT SHOT. BUT WE'RE TAKING YOU ALL WITH US. AND YOU'RE GONNA LET US.
IT'S CLEAR YOU BUILT THAT TRUCK FAST. THE WELDING WAS RUSHED. THERE'S A CRACK IN THE SEAMS ON THE HULL RIGHT THERE.
ALL IT WOULD TAKE IS ONE SHOT FROM MY FLAMETHROWER. HECK, A CREATIVE USE OF MY LIGHTER AND YOUR LITTLE SCIENCE PROJECT GOES BOOM.
IN OTHER WORDS~
FIRE BAD.

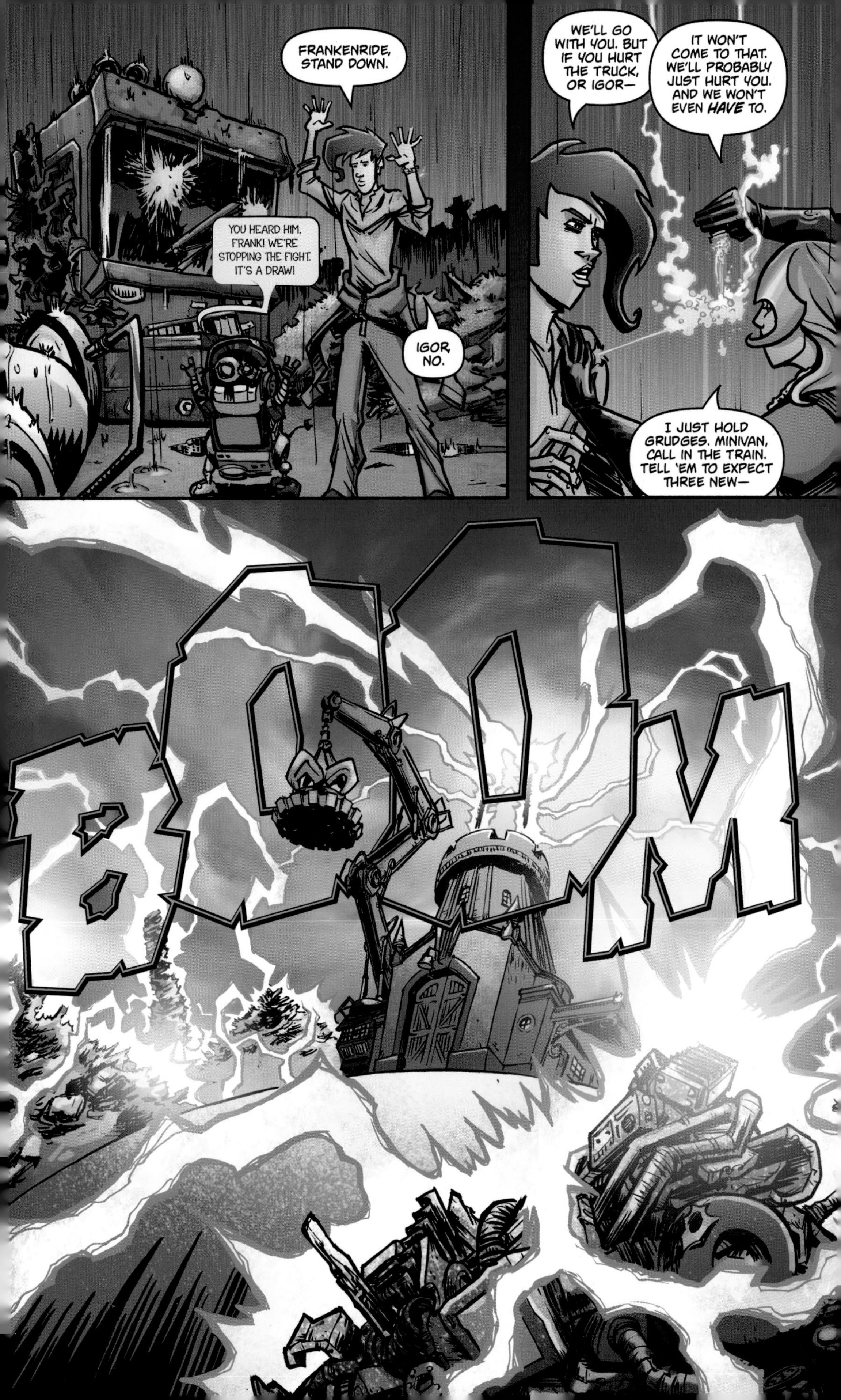
FRANKENRIDE, STAND DOWN.
YOU HEARD HIM, FRANK! WE'RE STOPPING THE FIGHT. IT'S A DRAW!
IGOR, NO.
WE'LL GO WITH YOU. BUT IF YOU HURT THE TRUCK, OR IGOR—
IT WON'T COME TO THAT. WE'LL PROBABLY JUST HURT YOU. AND WE WON'T EVEN HAVE TO.
I JUST HOLD GRUDGES. MINIVAN, CALL IN THE TRAIN. TELL 'EM TO EXPECT THREE NEW—
BOOM

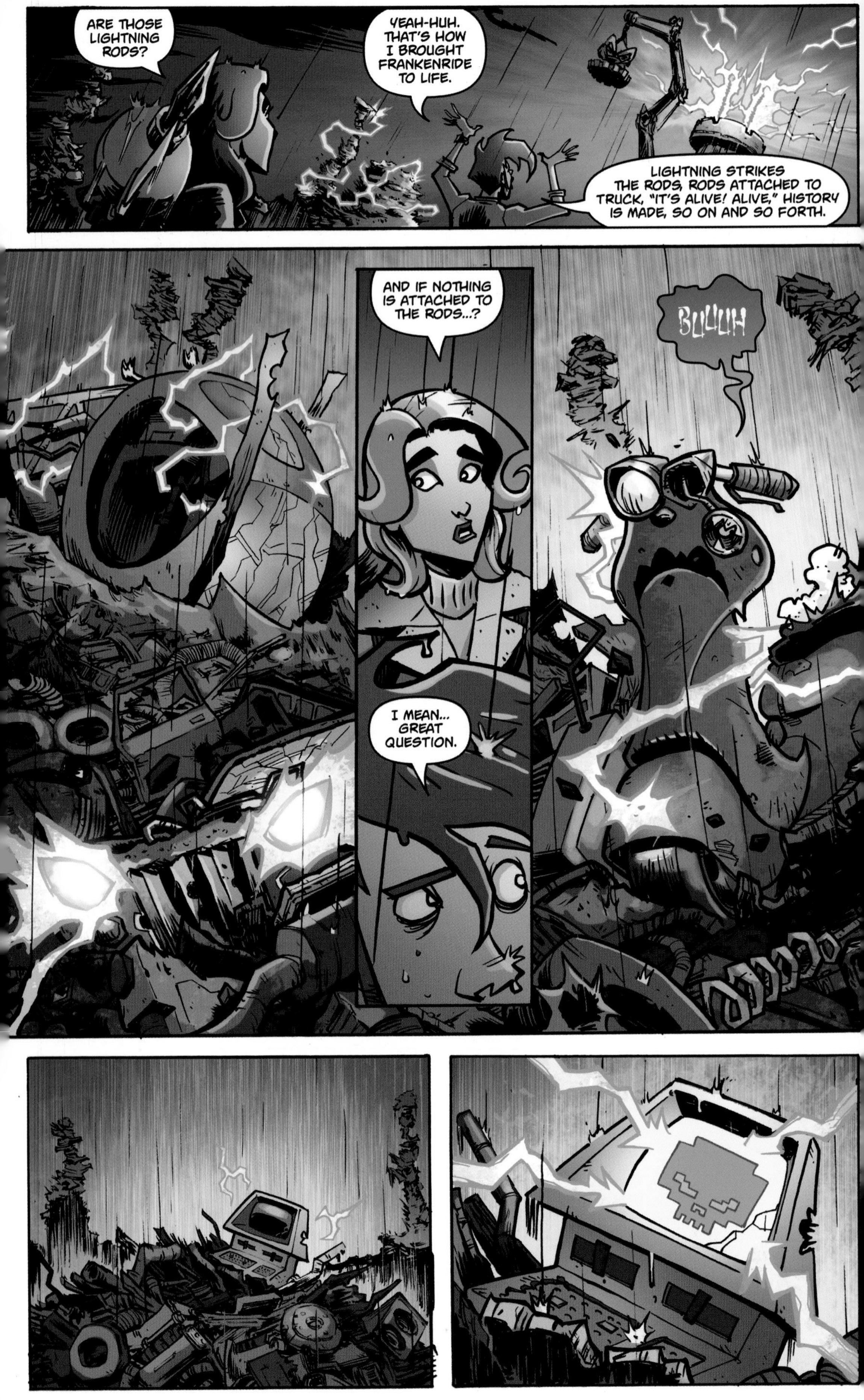
ARE THOSE LIGHTNING RODS?
YEAH-HUH. THAT'S HOW I BROUGHT FRANKENRIDE TO LIFE.
LIGHTNING STRIKES THE RODS, RODS ATTACHED TO TRUCK, "IT'S ALIVE! ALIVE," HISTORY IS MADE, SO ON AND SO FORTH.
AND IF NOTHING IS ATTACHED TO THE RODS...?
BLUUH
I MEAN... GREAT QUESTION.

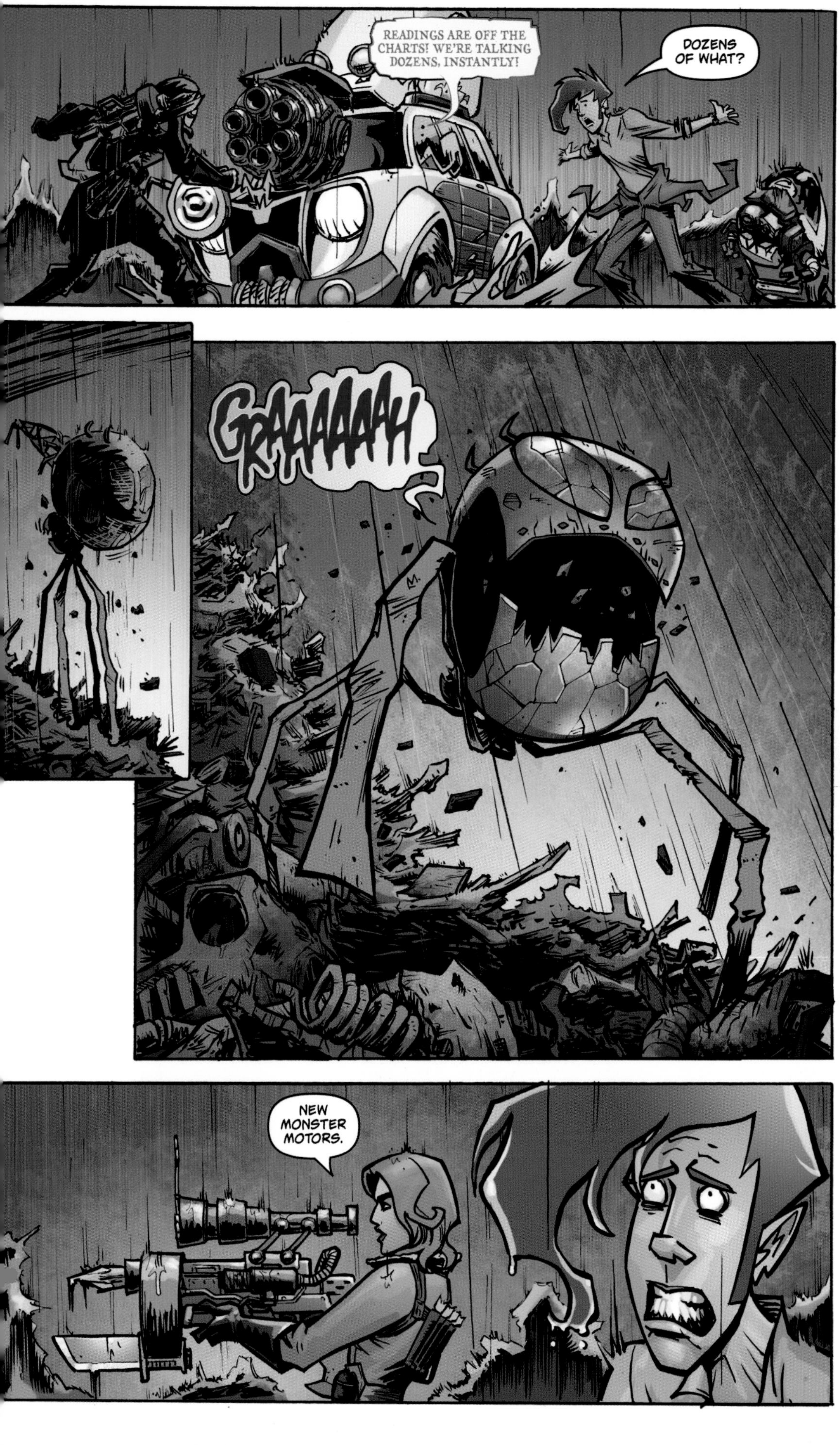
READINGS ARE OFF THE CHARTS! WE'RE TALKING DOZENS, INSTANTLY!
DOZENS OF WHAT?
GRAAAAAAH
NEW MONSTER MOTORS.

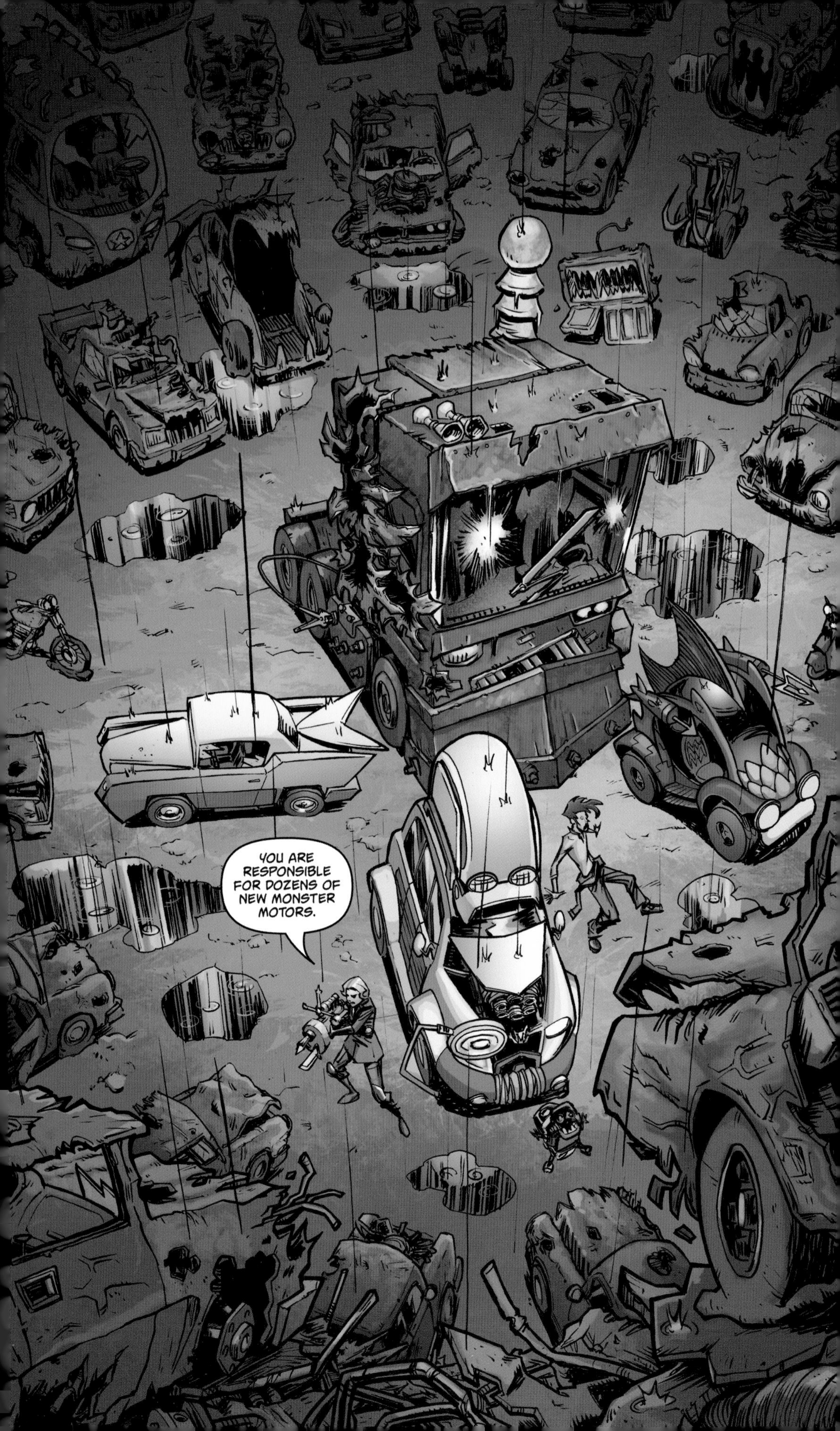
YOU ARE RESPONSIBLE FOR DOZENS OF NEW MONSTER MOTORS.

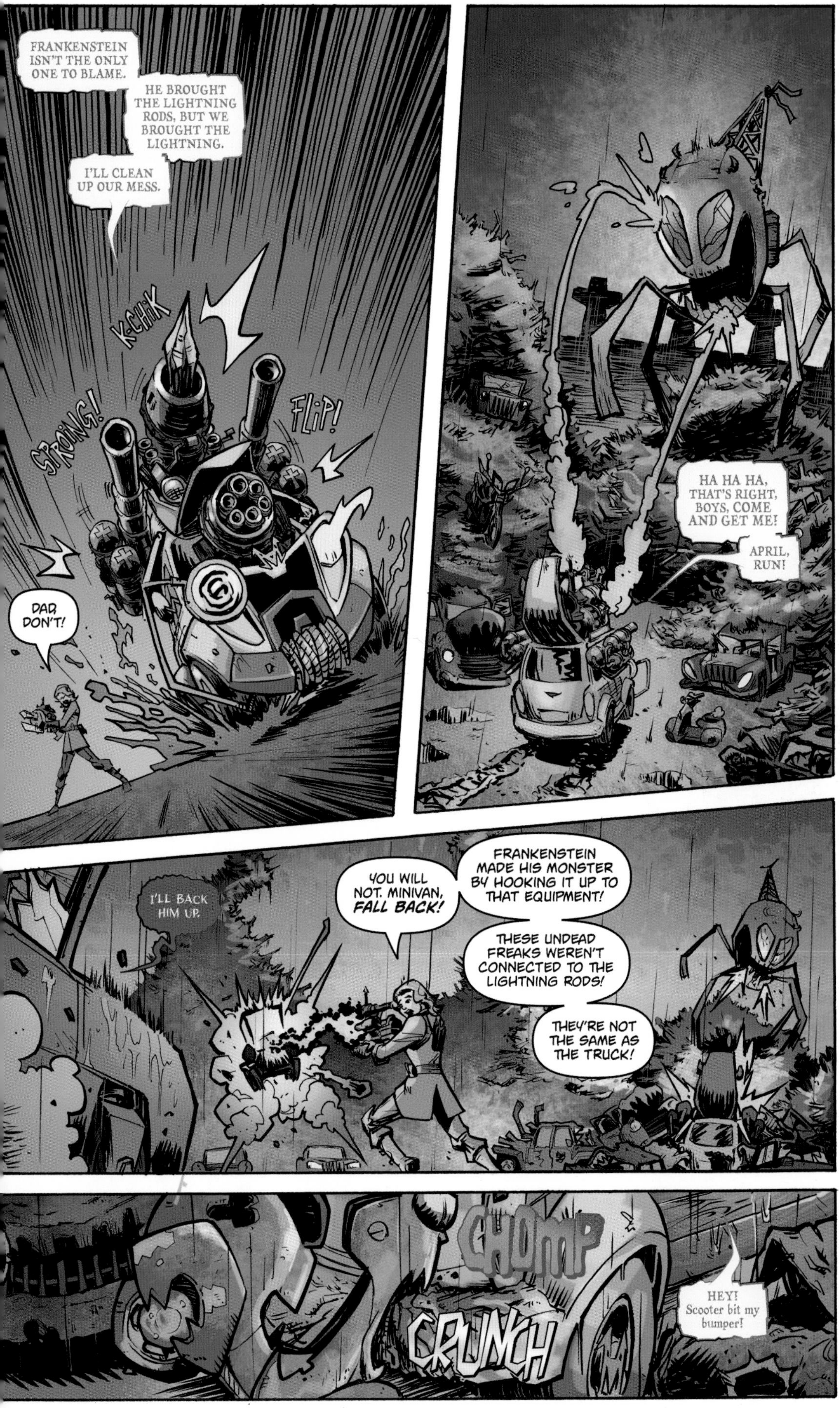
FRANKENSTEIN ISN'T THE ONLY ONE TO BLAME.
HE BROUGHT THE LIGHTNING RODS, BUT WE BROUGHT THE LIGHTNING.
I'LL CLEAN UP OUR MESS.
K-CHIK
SPROING!
FLIP!
DAD, DON'T!
HA HA HA, THAT'S RIGHT, BOYS, COME AND GET ME!
APRIL, RUN!
I'LL BACK HIM UP.
YOU WILL NOT. MINIVAN, FALL BACK!
FRANKENSTEIN MADE HIS MONSTER BY HOOKING IT UP TO THAT EQUIPMENT!
THESE UNDEAD FREAKS WEREN'T CONNECTED TO THE LIGHTNING RODS!
THEY'RE NOT THE SAME AS THE TRUCK!
CHOMP
CRUNCH
HEY! Scooter bit my bumper!

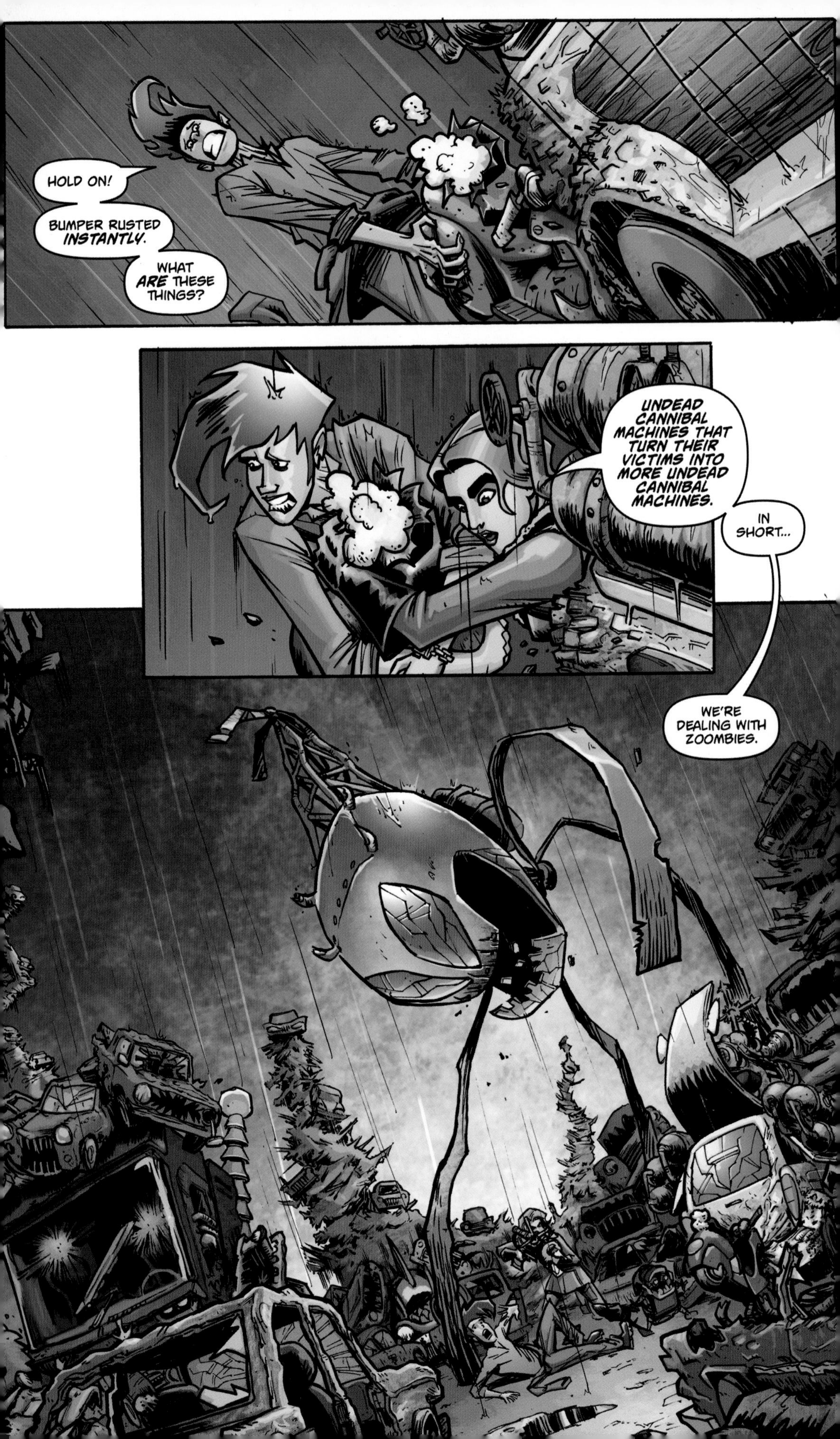
HOLD ON!
BUMPER RUSTED *INSTANTLY*.
WHAT *ARE* THESE THINGS?
UNDEAD CANNIBAL MACHINES THAT TURN THEIR VICTIMS INTO MORE UNDEAD CANNIBAL MACHINES.
IN SHORT...
WE'RE DEALING WITH ZOOMBIES.

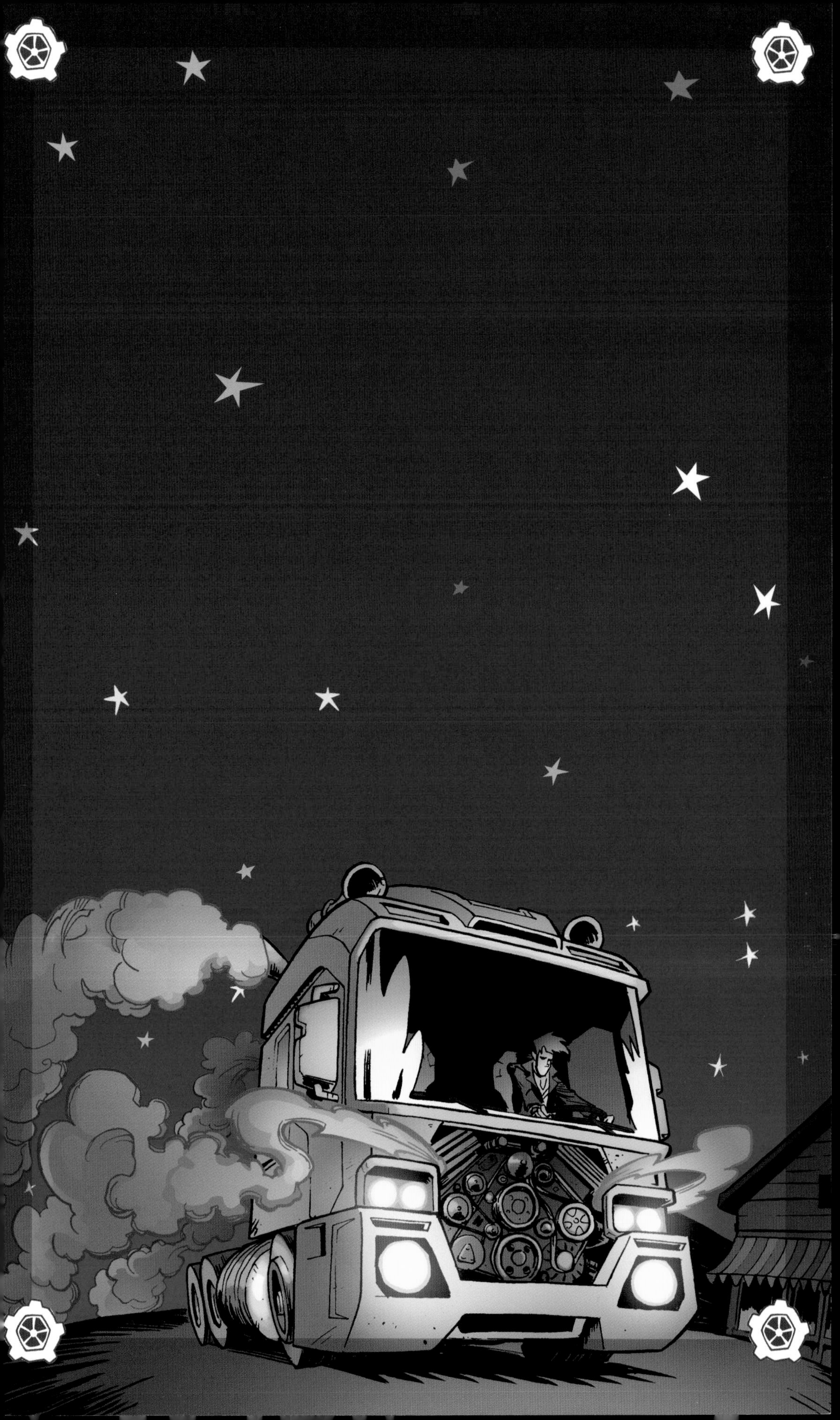

THE CURSE *of* MINIVAN HELSING, PART 2

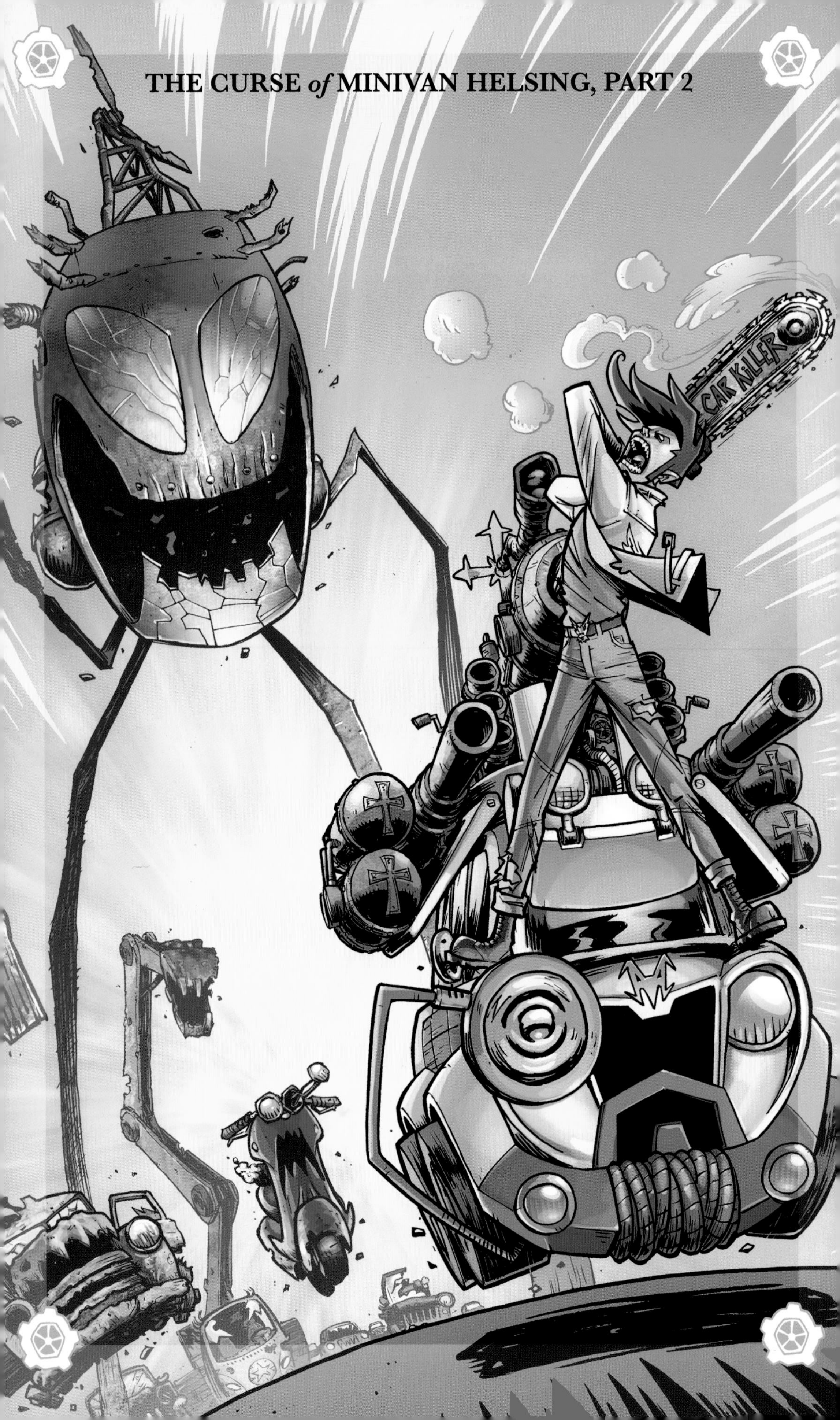
CAR KILLER

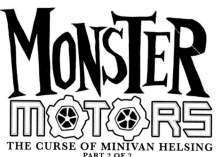

MONSTER MOTORS

THE CURSE OF MINIVAN HELSING

PART 2 OF 2

BY BRIAN LYNCH, NICK ROCHE, LEN O'GRADY AND TOM B. LONG

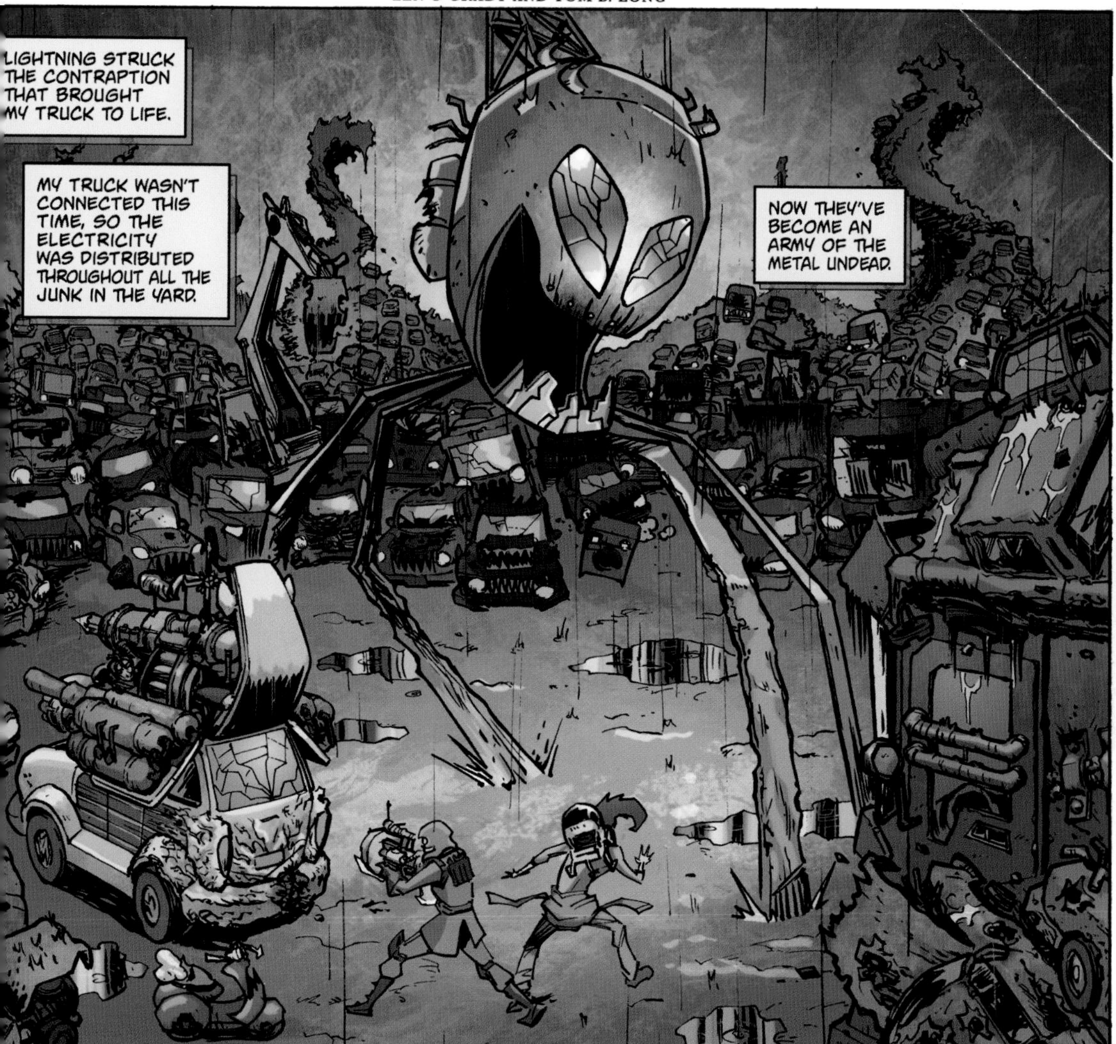
LIGHTNING STRUCK THE CONTRAPTION THAT BROUGHT MY TRUCK TO LIFE.
MY TRUCK WASN'T CONNECTED THIS TIME, SO THE ELECTRICITY WAS DISTRIBUTED THROUGHOUT ALL THE JUNK IN THE YARD.
NOW THEY'VE BECOME AN ARMY OF THE METAL UNDEAD.

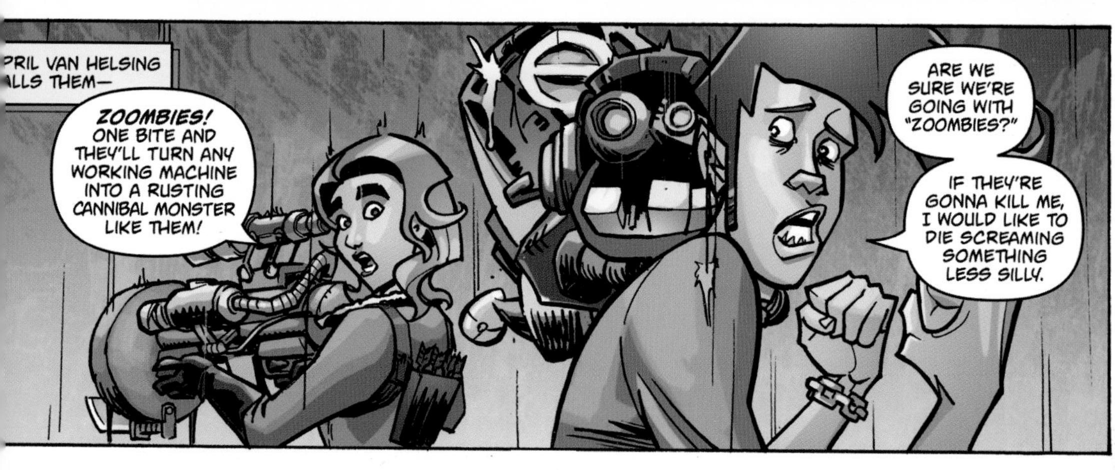
PRIL VAN HELSING LLS THEM—
ZOOMBIES! ONE BITE AND THEY'LL TURN ANY WORKING MACHINE INTO A RUSTING CANNIBAL MONSTER LIKE THEM!
ARE WE SURE WE'RE GOING WITH "ZOOMBIES?"
IF THEY'RE GONNA KILL ME, I WOULD LIKE TO DIE SCREAMING SOMETHING LESS SILLY.

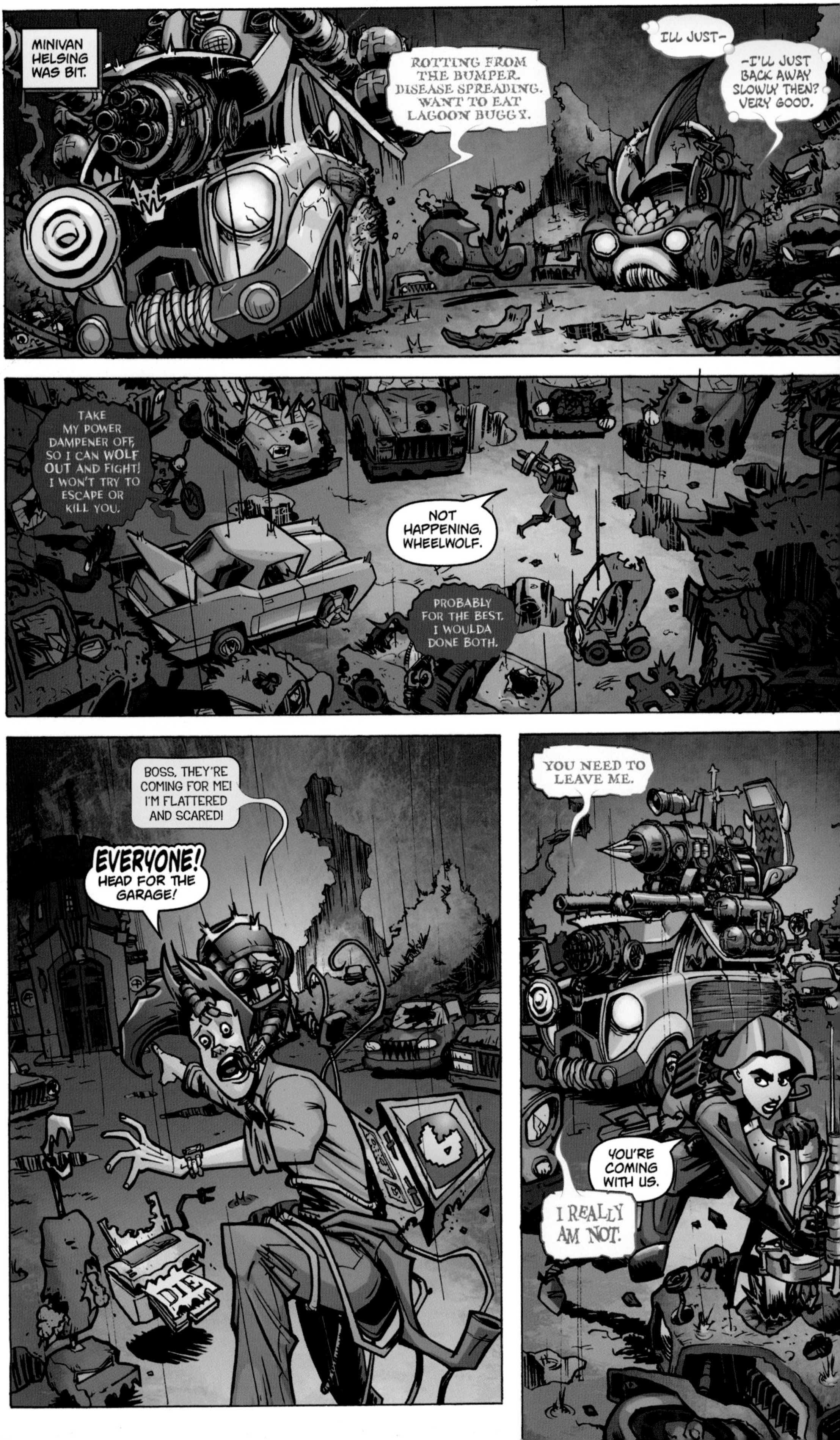
MINIVAN HELSING WAS BIT.
ROTTING FROM THE BUMPER. DISEASE SPREADING. WANT TO EAT LAGOON BUGGY.
I'LL JUST-
-I'LL JUST BACK AWAY SLOWLY THEN? VERY GOOD.
TAKE MY POWER DAMPENER OFF, SO I CAN WOLF OUT AND FIGHT! I WON'T TRY TO ESCAPE OR KILL YOU.
NOT HAPPENING, WHEELWOLF.
PROBABLY FOR THE BEST. I WOULDA DONE BOTH.
BOSS, THEY'RE COMING FOR ME! I'M FLATTERED AND SCARED!
EVERYONE! HEAD FOR THE GARAGE!
DIE
YOU NEED TO LEAVE ME.
YOU'RE COMING WITH US.
I REALLY AM NOT.

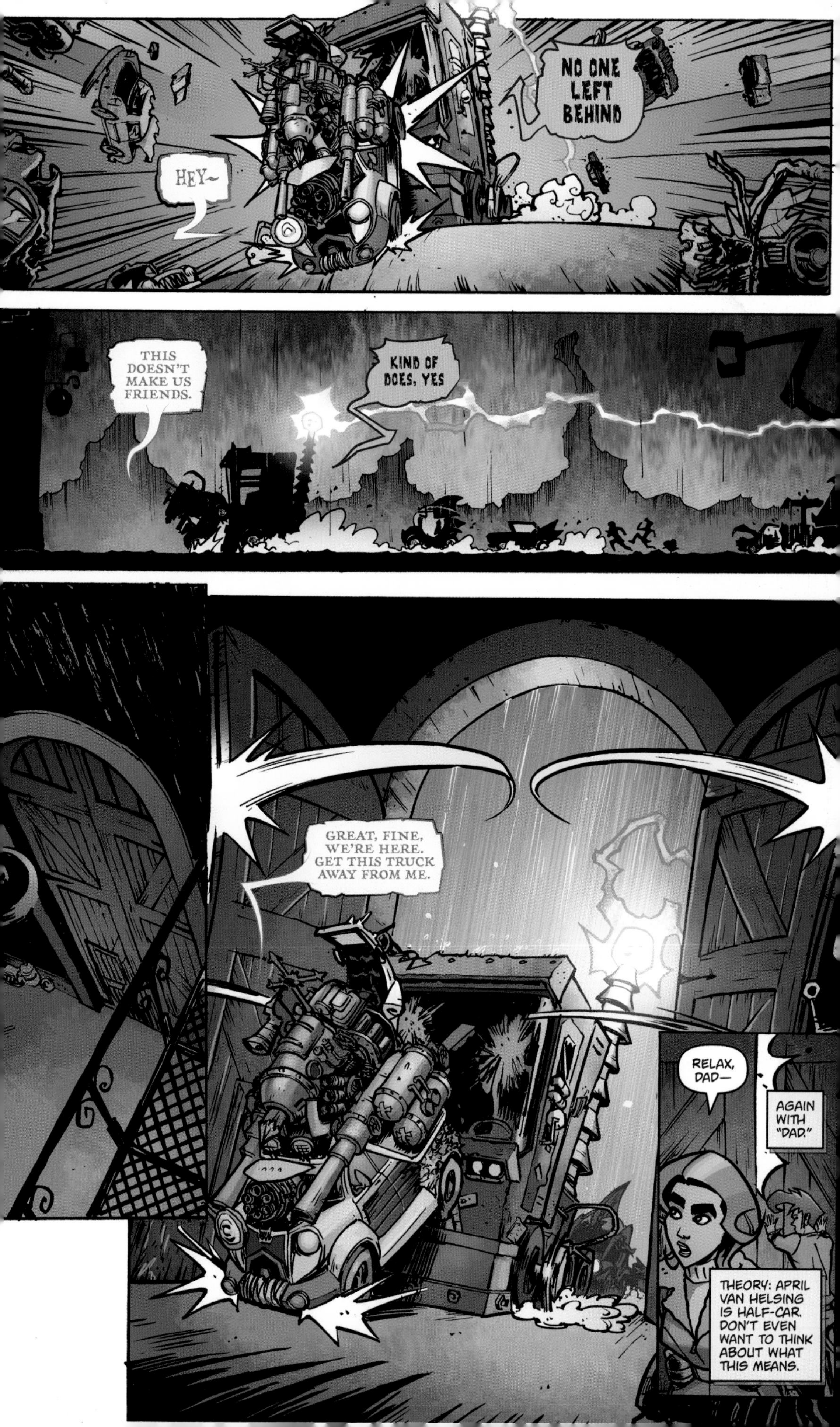
NO ONE LEFT BEHIND
HEY~
THIS DOESN'T MAKE US FRIENDS.
KIND OF DOES, YES
GREAT, FINE, WE'RE HERE. GET THIS TRUCK AWAY FROM ME.
RELAX, DAD—
AGAIN WITH "DAD."
THEORY: APRIL VAN HELSING IS HALF-CAR. DON'T EVEN WANT TO THINK ABOUT WHAT THIS MEANS.

AAAAAAND THERE ARE MORE ZOOMBIES IN HERE. GEARHEADS *NEVER* THROW AWAY THEIR JUNK.

I'M A MECHANIC. THESE ARE WORKS IN PROGRESS.

IF IT'S ALL RIGHT WITH YOU, I WOULD VERY MUCH LIKE TO HALT THEIR PROGRESS.

LISTEN UP! THERE ARE PLENTY OF WAYS TO *MAKE* ZOMBIES: COMET. WITCH DOCTOR CURSE. BITE FROM A SUMERIAN RAT GO-KART.

BUT AS FAR AS WE KNOW, THERE ARE ONLY *TWO* WAYS TO TAKE THEM DOWN: VIOLENTLY REMOVE THEIR POWER SUPPLY...

...OR VIOLENTLY REMOVE *THEM* FROM THE EARTH.

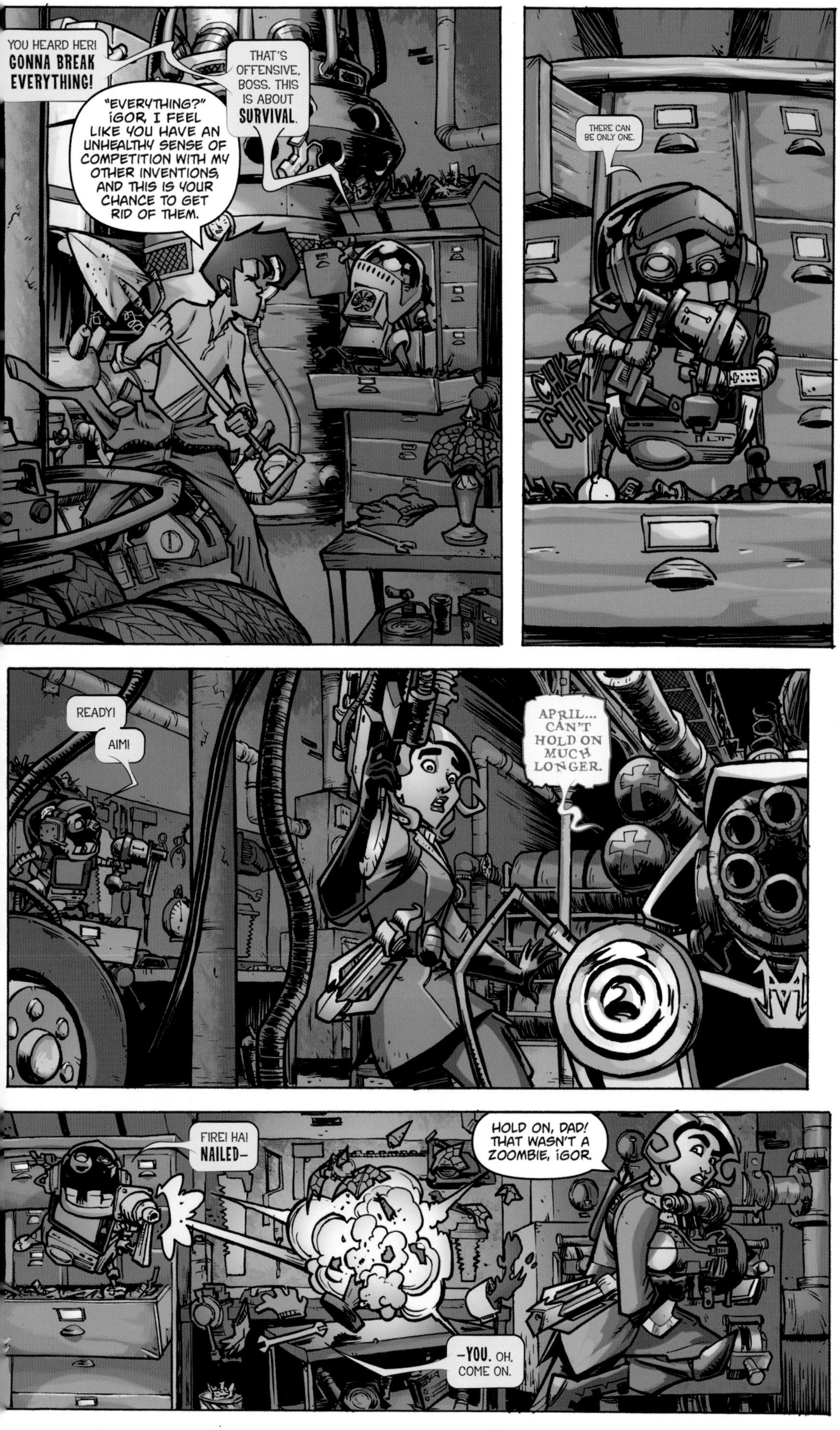

YOU HEARD HER! GONNA BREAK EVERYTHING!
THAT'S OFFENSIVE, BOSS. THIS IS ABOUT SURVIVAL.
"EVERYTHING?" IGOR, I FEEL LIKE YOU HAVE AN UNHEALTHY SENSE OF COMPETITION WITH MY OTHER INVENTIONS, AND THIS IS YOUR CHANCE TO GET RID OF THEM.
THERE CAN BE ONLY ONE.
CHK CHK
READY!
AIM!
APRIL... CAN'T HOLD ON MUCH LONGER.
FIRE! HA! NAILED-
HOLD ON, DAD! THAT WASN'T A ZOOMBIE, IGOR.
-YOU. OH, COME ON.

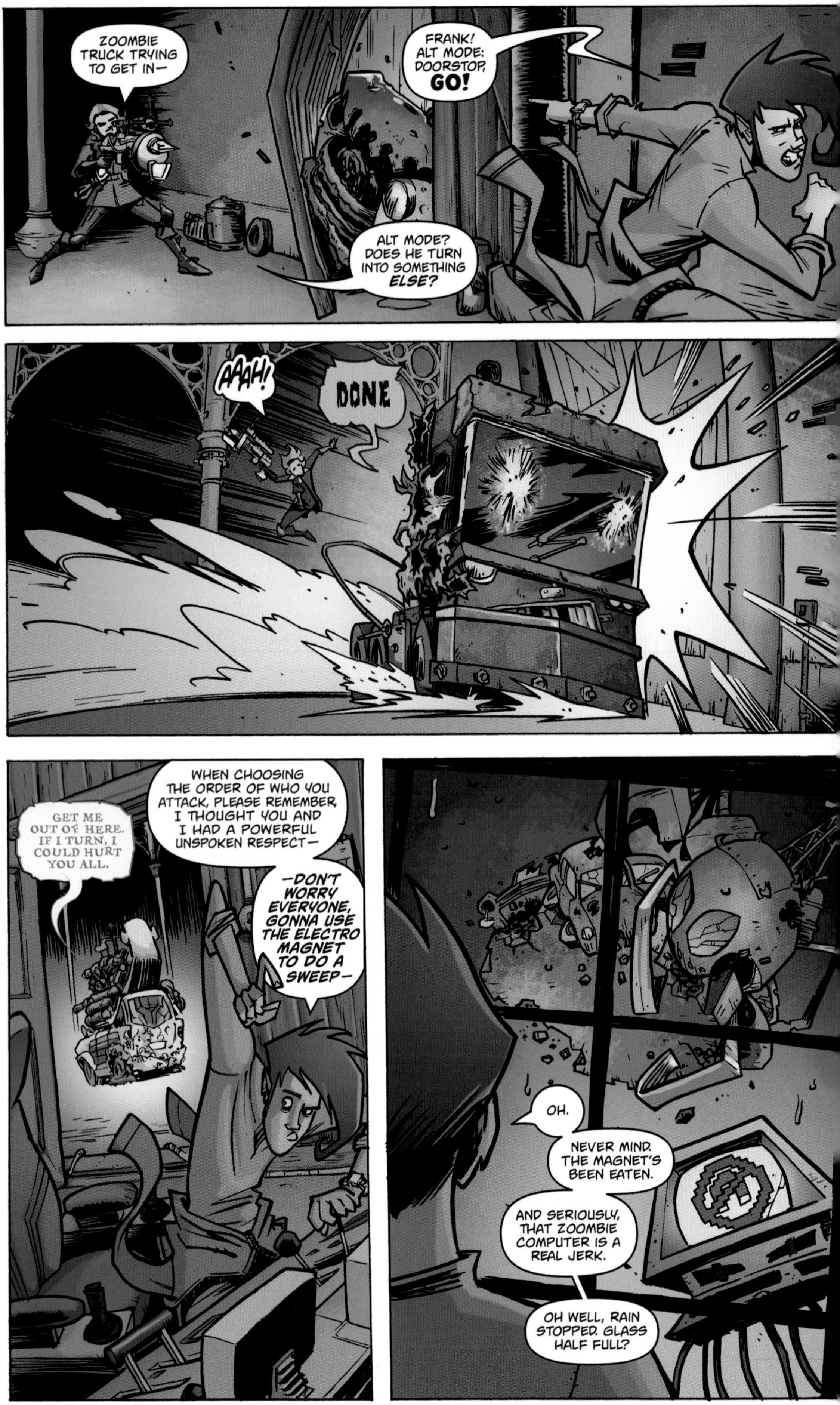
ZOOMBIE TRUCK TRYING TO GET IN—
FRANK! ALT MODE: DOORSTOP, GO!
ALT MODE? DOES HE TURN INTO SOMETHING ELSE?
AAAH!
DONE
GET ME OUT OF HERE. IF I TURN, I COULD HURT YOU ALL.
WHEN CHOOSING THE ORDER OF WHO YOU ATTACK, PLEASE REMEMBER, I THOUGHT YOU AND I HAD A POWERFUL UNSPOKEN RESPECT—
—DON'T WORRY EVERYONE, GONNA USE THE ELECTRO MAGNET TO DO A SWEEP—
OH.
NEVER MIND. THE MAGNET'S BEEN EATEN.
AND SERIOUSLY, THAT ZOOMBIE COMPUTER IS A REAL JERK.
OH WELL, RAIN STOPPED. GLASS HALF FULL?

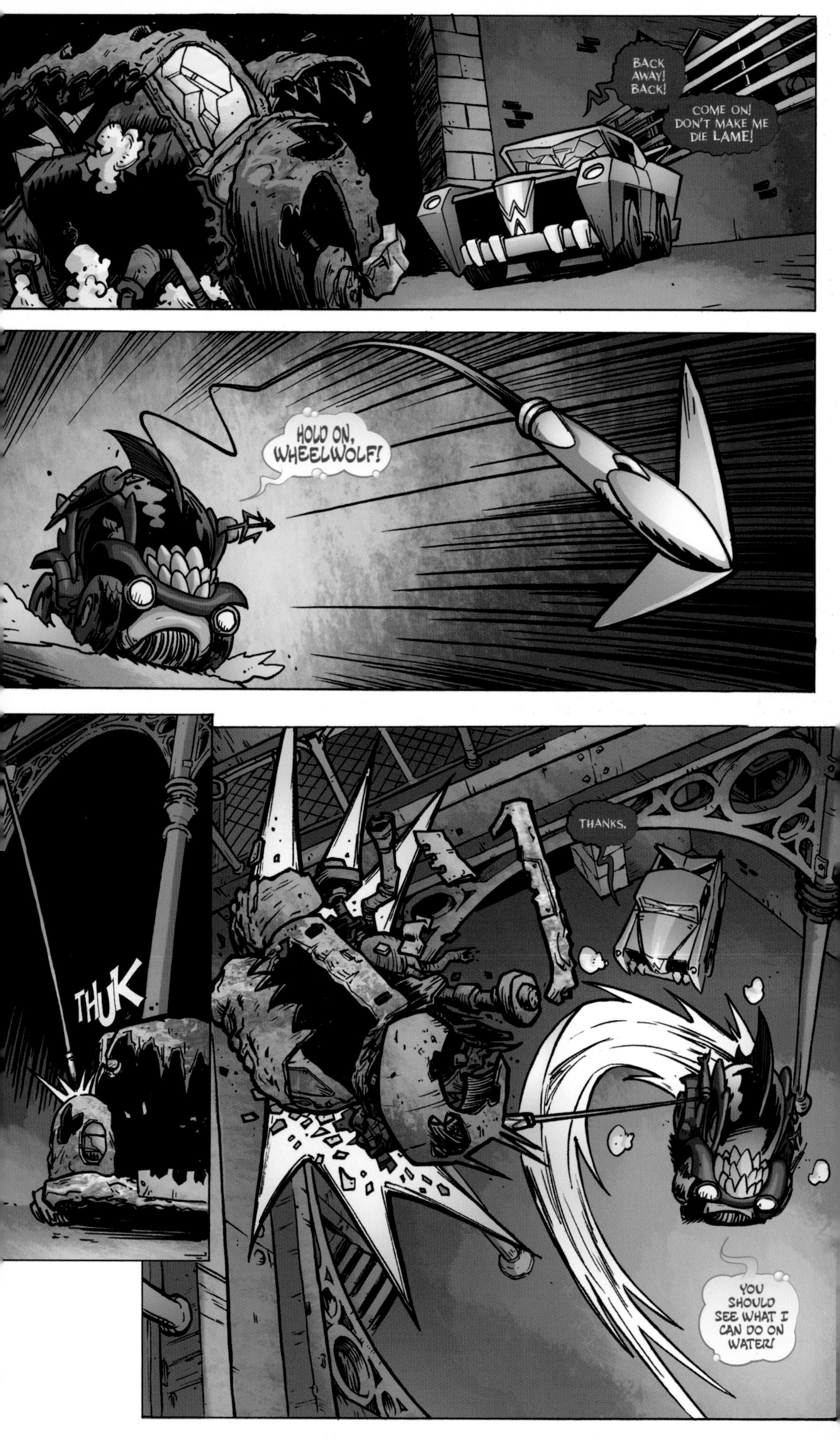
BACK AWAY! BACK!
COME ON! DON'T MAKE ME DIE LAME!
HOLD ON, WHEELWOLF!
THUK
THANKS.
YOU SHOULD SEE WHAT I CAN DO ON WATER!

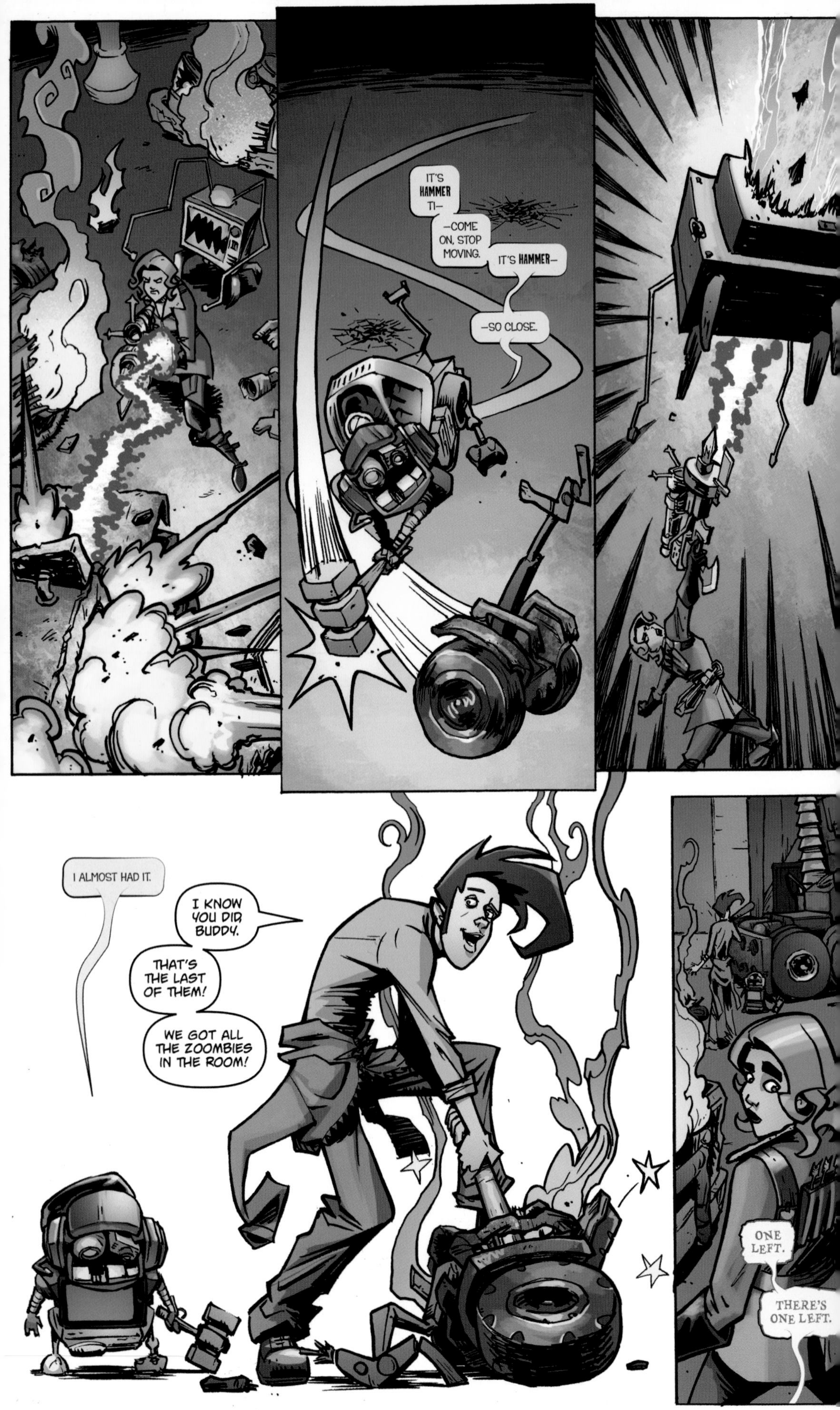
IT'S HAMMER TI—
—COME ON, STOP MOVING.
IT'S HAMMER—
—SO CLOSE.
I ALMOST HAD IT.
I KNOW YOU DID, BUDDY.
THAT'S THE LAST OF THEM!
WE GOT ALL THE ZOOMBIES IN THE ROOM!
ONE LEFT.
THERE'S ONE LEFT.

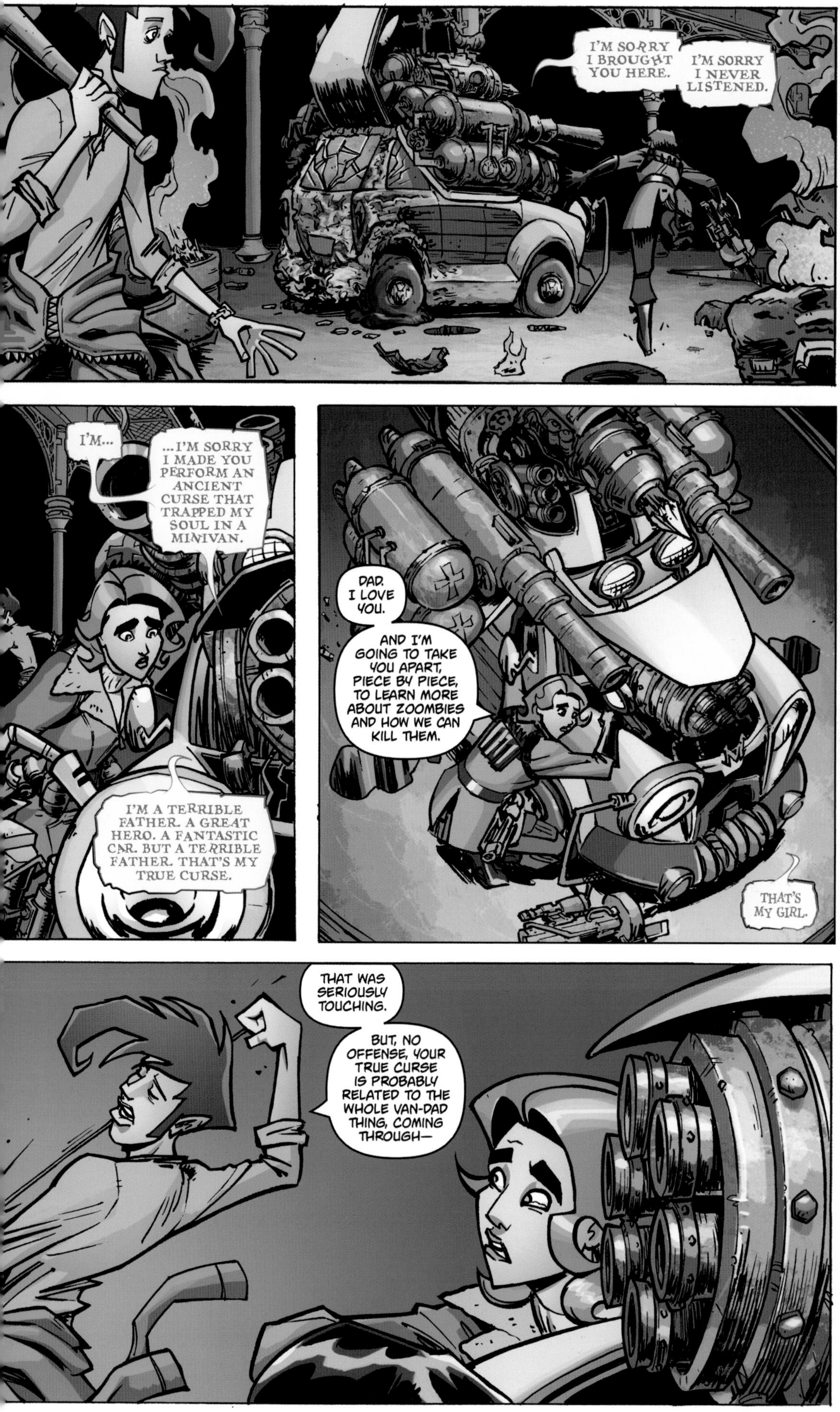
I'M SORRY I BROUGHT YOU HERE.
I'M SORRY I NEVER LISTENED.
I'M...
...I'M SORRY I MADE YOU PERFORM AN ANCIENT CURSE THAT TRAPPED MY SOUL IN A MINIVAN.
I'M A TERRIBLE FATHER. A GREAT HERO. A FANTASTIC CAR. BUT A TERRIBLE FATHER. THAT'S MY TRUE CURSE.
DAD. I LOVE YOU.
AND I'M GOING TO TAKE YOU APART, PIECE BY PIECE, TO LEARN MORE ABOUT ZOOMBIES AND HOW WE CAN KILL THEM.
THAT'S MY GIRL.
THAT WAS SERIOUSLY TOUCHING.
BUT, NO OFFENSE, YOUR TRUE CURSE IS PROBABLY RELATED TO THE WHOLE VAN-DAD THING, COMING THROUGH—

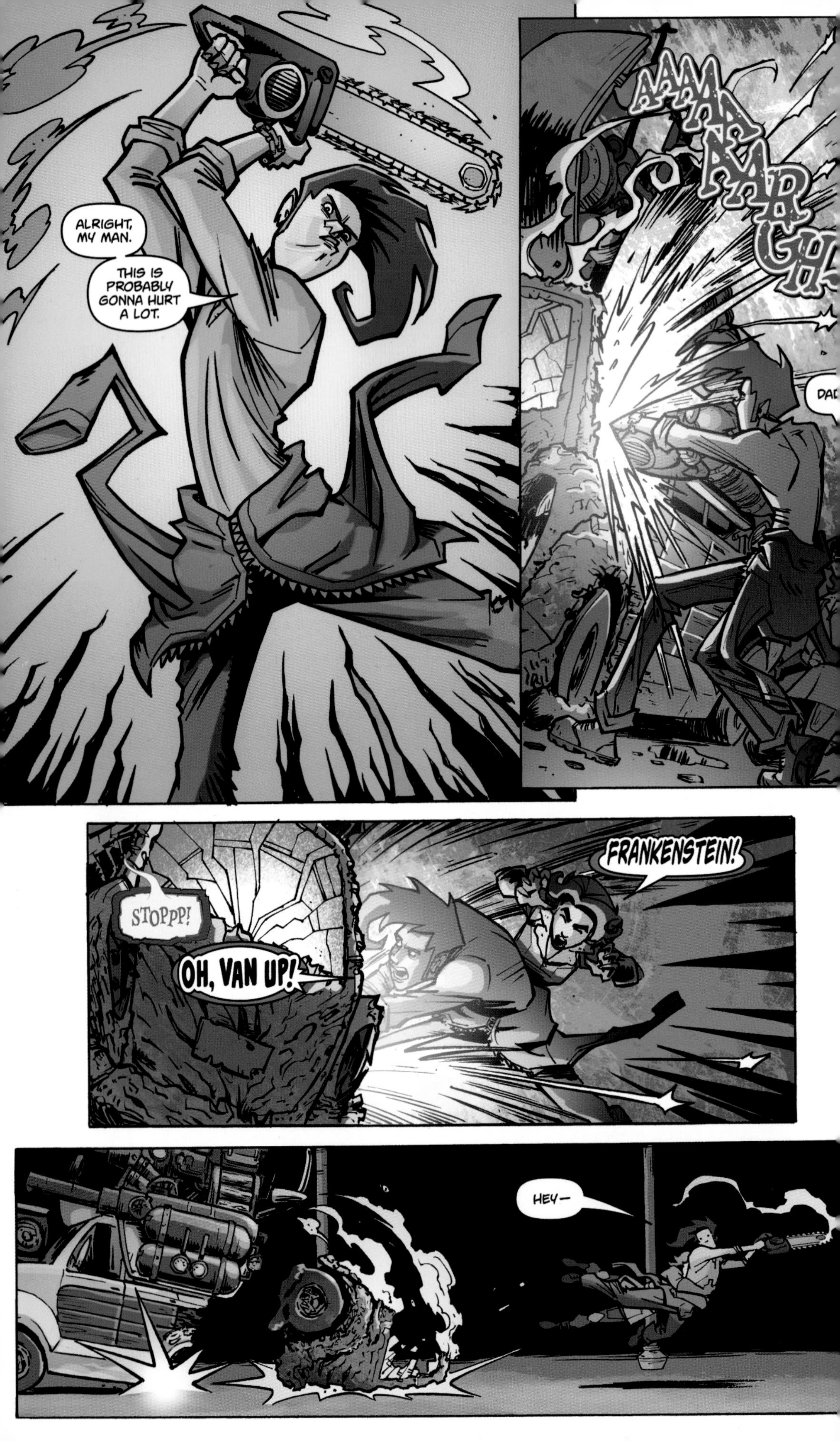

ALRIGHT, MY MAN.
THIS IS PROBABLY GONNA HURT A LOT.
AAAAARARGH
DAD
FRANKENSTEIN!
STOPPP!
OH, VAN UP!
HEY—

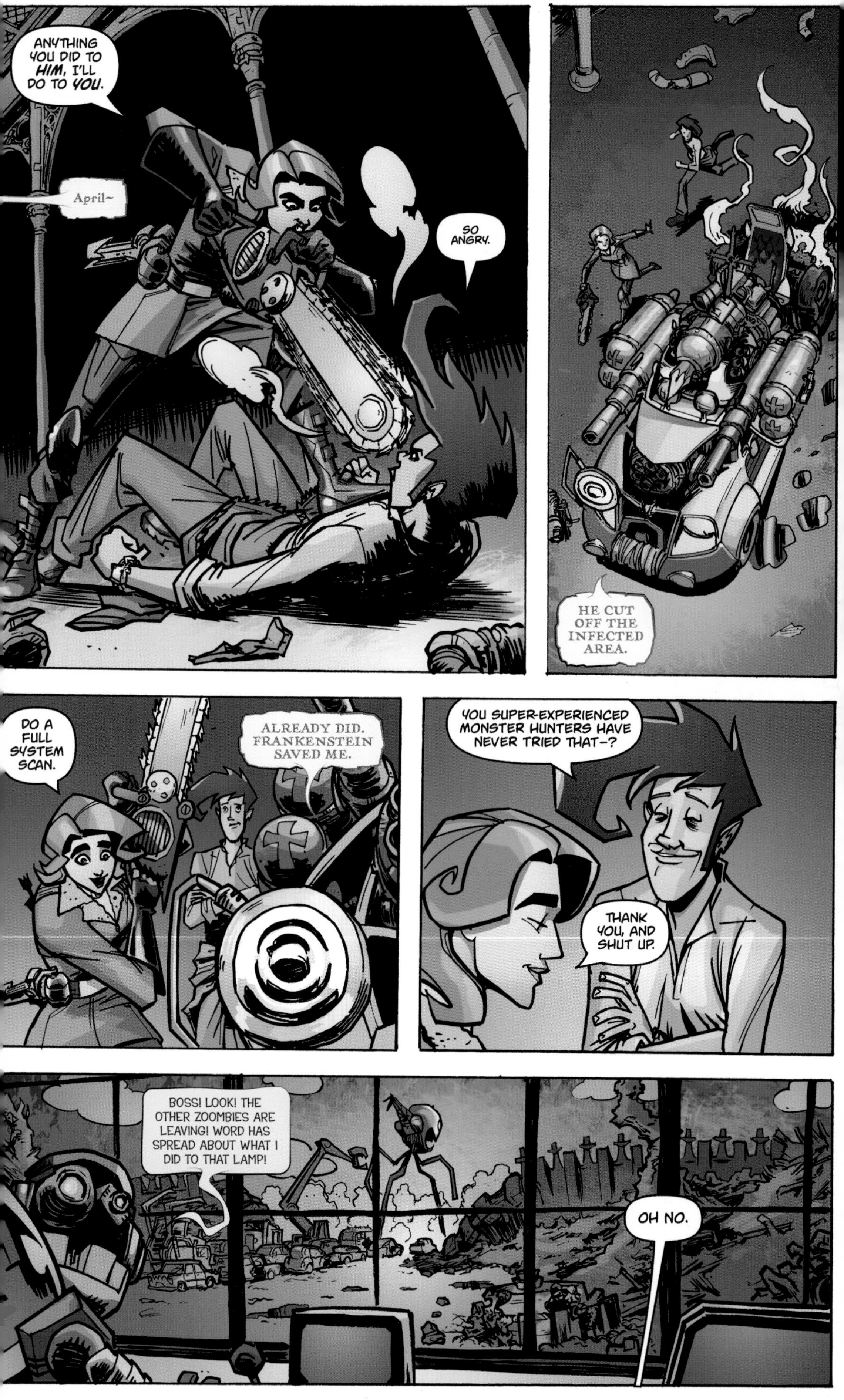
ANYTHING YOU DID TO HIM, I'LL DO TO YOU.
April~
SO ANGRY.
HE CUT OFF THE INFECTED AREA.
DO A FULL SYSTEM SCAN.
ALREADY DID. FRANKENSTEIN SAVED ME.
YOU SUPER-EXPERIENCED MONSTER HUNTERS HAVE NEVER TRIED THAT-?
THANK YOU, AND SHUT UP.
BOSS! LOOK! THE OTHER ZOOMBIES ARE LEAVING! WORD HAS SPREAD ABOUT WHAT I DID TO THAT LAMP!
OH NO.

"WITH NO ZOOMBIE BRETHREN LEFT IN HERE, THEY'RE HEADING FOR A BIGGER SCORE."

BUH BUH BUH

TRANSYLVANIA.

BINGO BANGO.

"THEY'LL BITE EVERY VEHICLE.

"EVERY ELECTRONIC DEVICE.

"WE'LL BE DEALING WITH THOUSANDS OF ZOOMBIES."

AND THEN THEY'LL TRAVEL TO THE NEXT TOWN AND DO IT ALL OVER.

LIKE A BUNCH OF GIANT, METAL, POORLY-NAMED LOCUSTS.

DAD, WE'RE GOING TO NEED TO SEE A MAP OF EVERYTHING BETWEEN FRANKENSTEIN'S GARAGE AND TRANSYLVANIA.

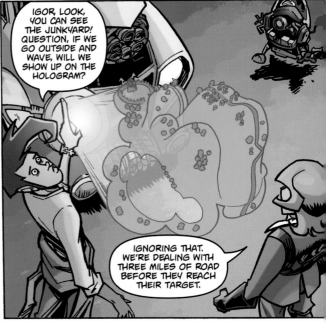

IGOR, LOOK, YOU CAN SEE THE JUNKYARD! QUESTION, IF WE GO OUTSIDE AND WAVE, WILL WE SHOW UP ON THE HOLOGRAM?

IGNORING THAT. WE'RE DEALING WITH THREE MILES OF ROAD BEFORE THEY REACH THEIR TARGET.

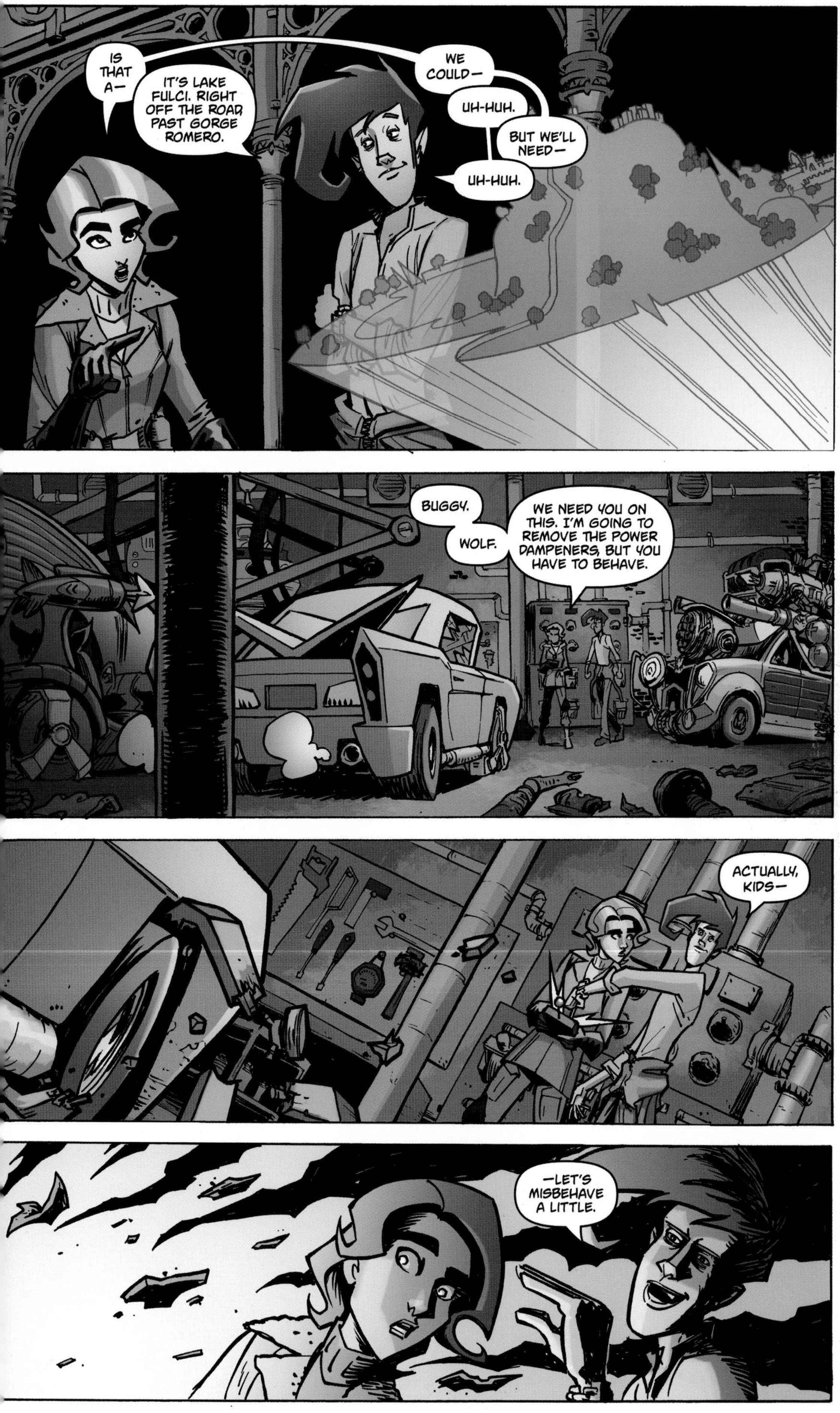

IS THAT A—
IT'S LAKE FULCI. RIGHT OFF THE ROAD PAST GORGE ROMERO.
WE COULD—
UH-HUH.
BUT WE'LL NEED—
UH-HUH.
BUGGY.
WOLF.
WE NEED YOU ON THIS. I'M GOING TO REMOVE THE POWER DAMPENERS, BUT YOU HAVE TO BEHAVE.
ACTUALLY, KIDS—
—LET'S MISBEHAVE A LITTLE.

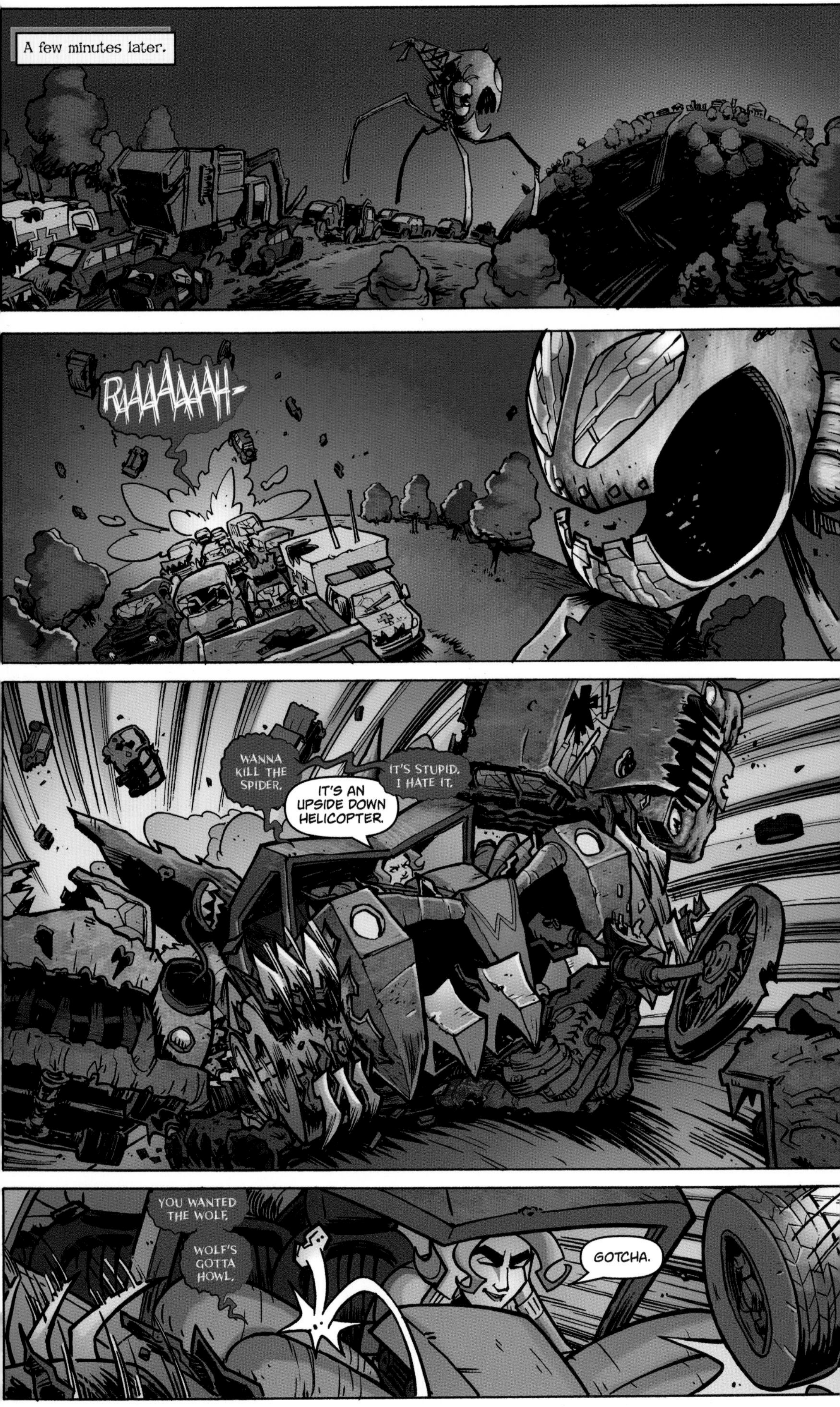
A few minutes later.
RAAAAAAAH-
WANNA KILL THE SPIDER.
IT'S STUPID. I HATE IT.
IT'S AN UPSIDE DOWN HELICOPTER.
YOU WANTED THE WOLF.
WOLF'S GOTTA HOWL.
GOTCHA.

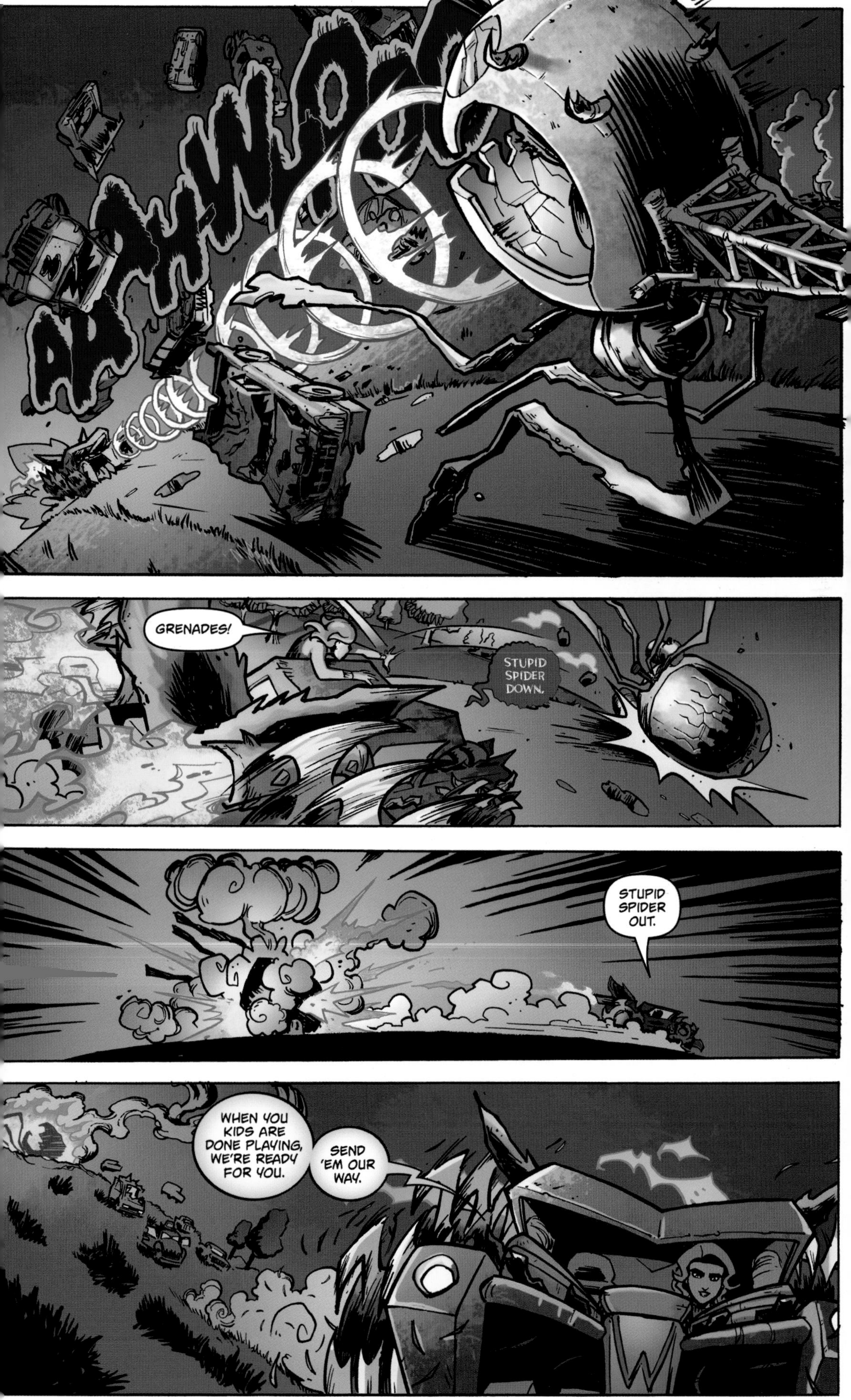
GRENADES!
STUPID SPIDER DOWN.
STUPID SPIDER OUT.
WHEN YOU KIDS ARE DONE PLAYING, WE'RE READY FOR YOU.
SEND 'EM OUR WAY.

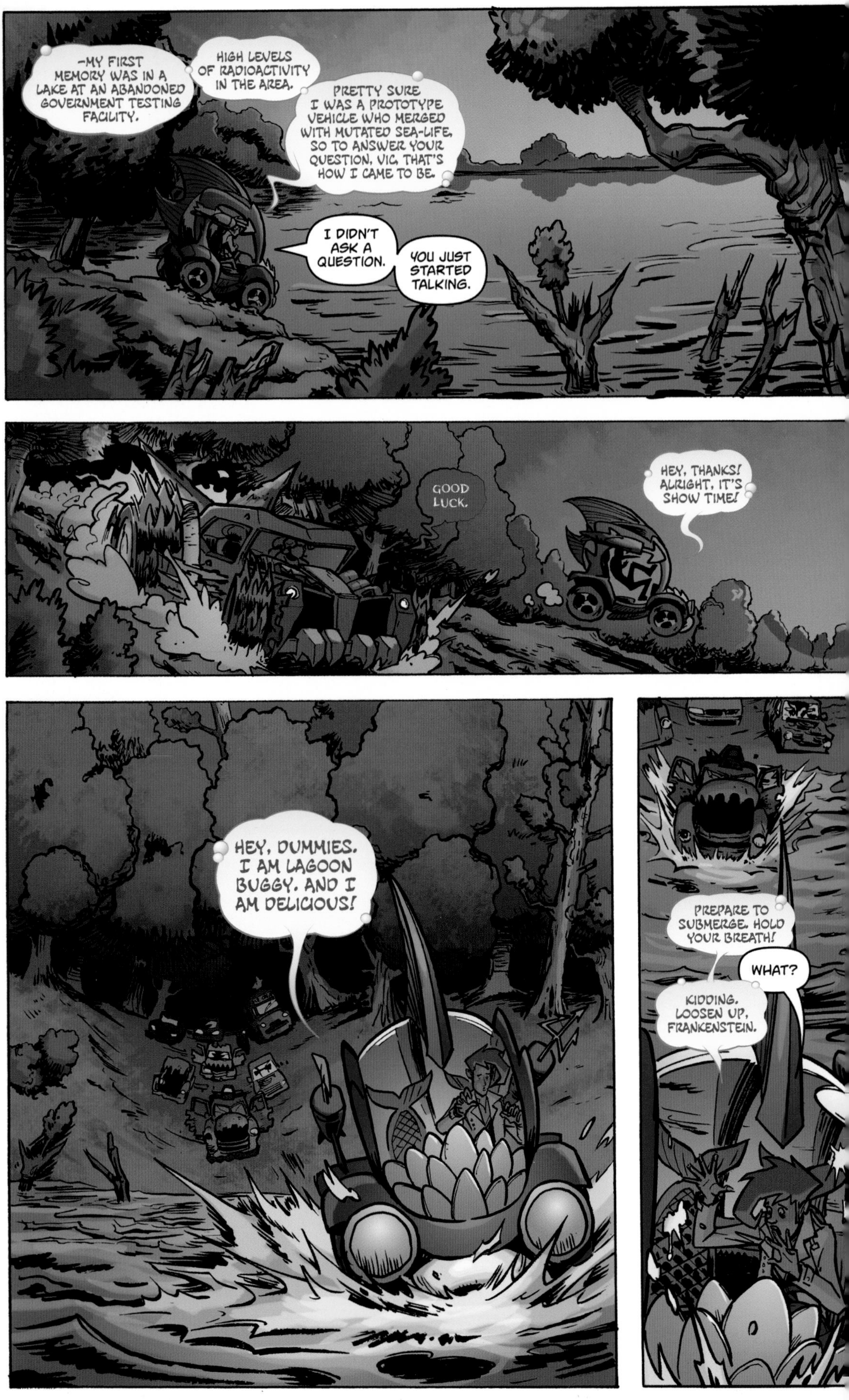
–MY FIRST MEMORY WAS IN A LAKE AT AN ABANDONED GOVERNMENT TESTING FACILITY.
HIGH LEVELS OF RADIOACTIVITY IN THE AREA.
PRETTY SURE I WAS A PROTOTYPE VEHICLE WHO MERGED WITH MUTATED SEA-LIFE, SO TO ANSWER YOUR QUESTION, VIC, THAT'S HOW I CAME TO BE.
I DIDN'T ASK A QUESTION.
YOU JUST STARTED TALKING.
GOOD LUCK.
HEY, THANKS! ALRIGHT, IT'S SHOW TIME!
HEY, DUMMIES. I AM LAGOON BUGGY. AND I AM DELICIOUS!
PREPARE TO SUBMERGE. HOLD YOUR BREATH!
WHAT?
KIDDING. LOOSEN UP, FRANKENSTEIN.

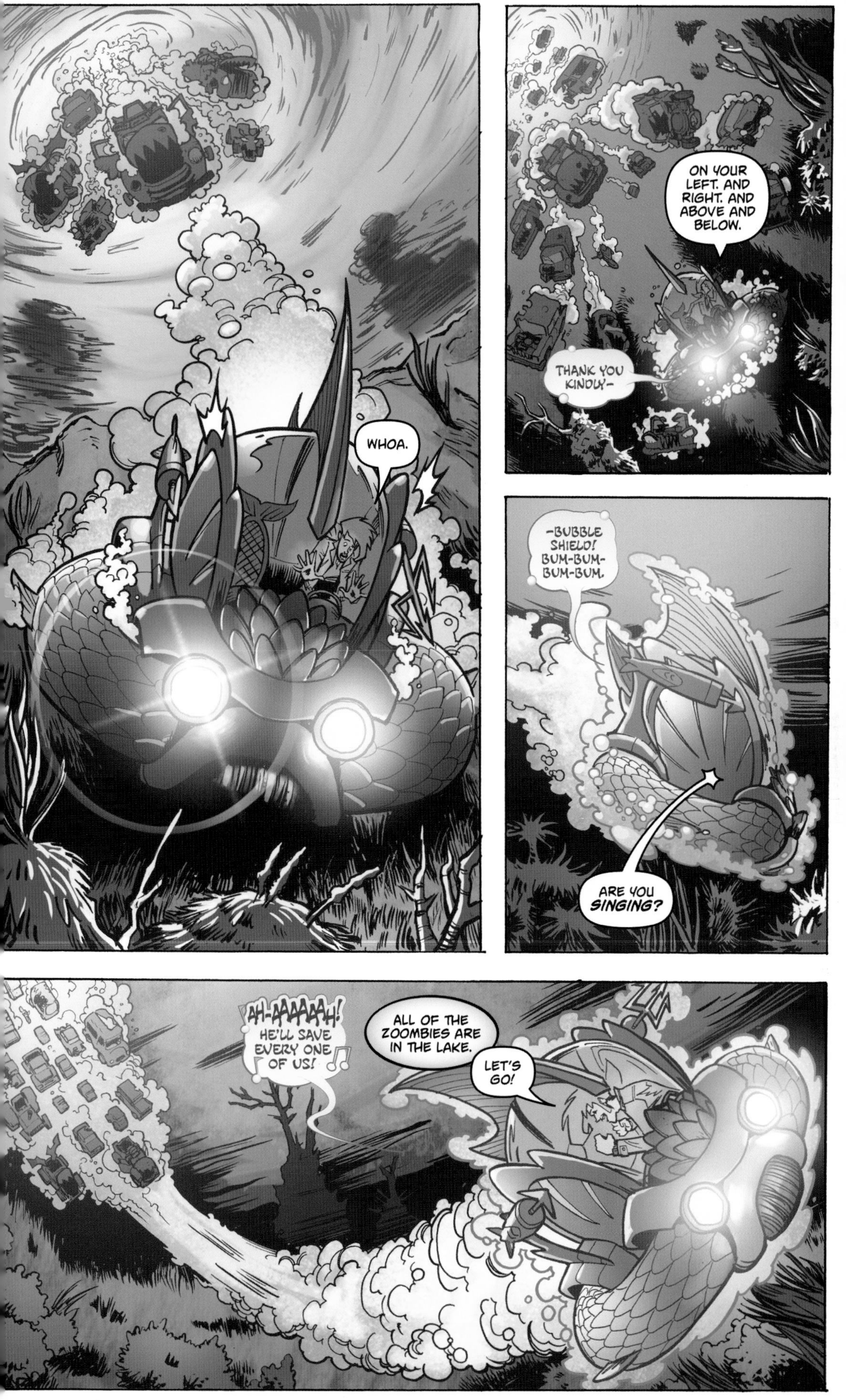
WHOA.
ON YOUR LEFT. AND RIGHT. AND ABOVE AND BELOW.
THANK YOU KINDLY–
–BUBBLE SHIELD! BUM-BUM-BUM-BUM.
ARE YOU *SINGING?*
AH-AAAAAAH! HE'LL SAVE EVERY ONE OF US!
ALL OF THE ZOOMBIES ARE IN THE LAKE.
LET'S GO!

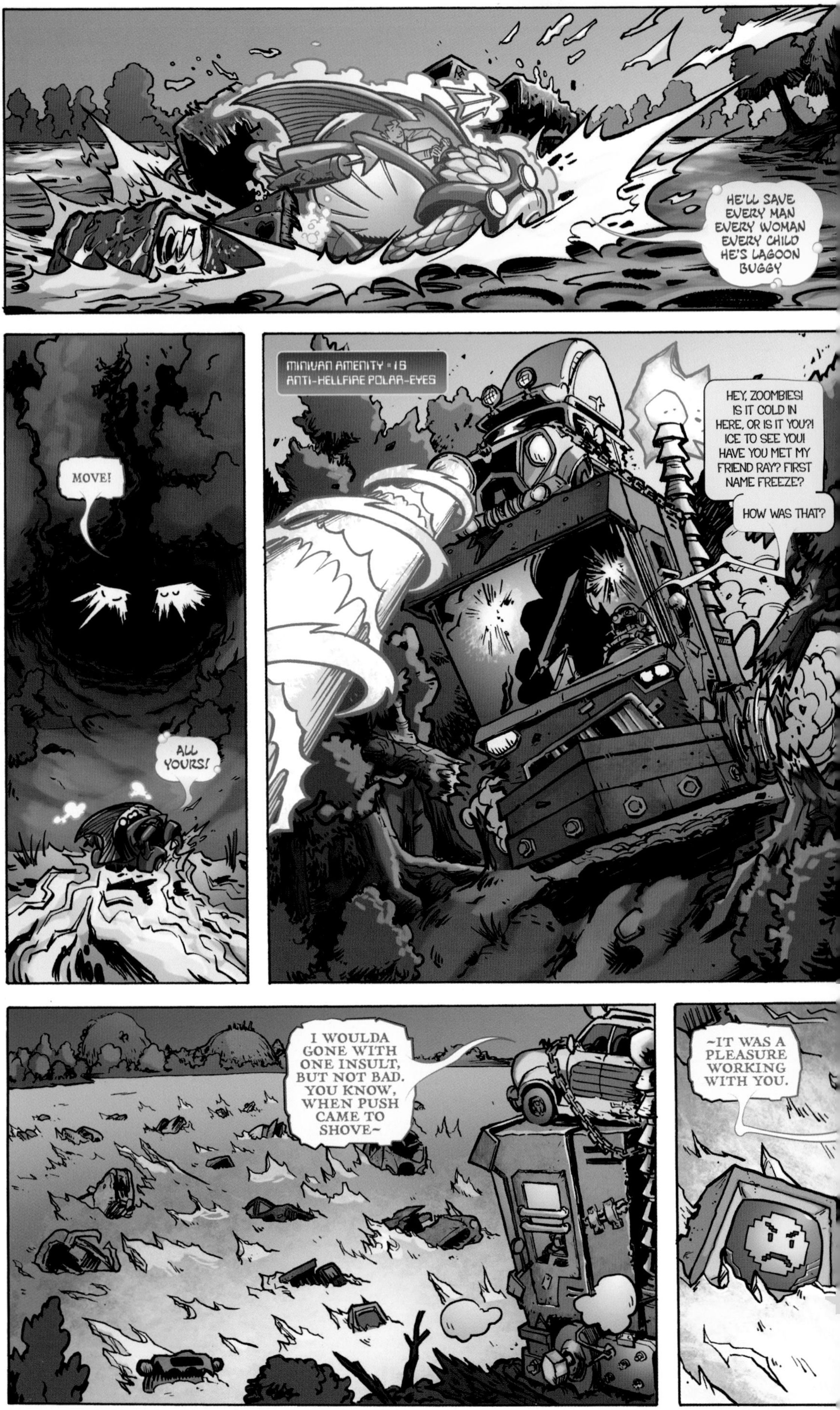
HE'LL SAVE EVERY MAN EVERY WOMAN EVERY CHILD HE'S LAGOON BUGGY
MOVE!
ALL YOURS!
MINIVAN AMENITY #16
ANTI-HELLFIRE POLAR-EYES
HEY, ZOOMBIES! IS IT COLD IN HERE, OR IS IT YOU?! ICE TO SEE YOU! HAVE YOU MET MY FRIEND RAY? FIRST NAME FREEZE?
HOW WAS THAT?
I WOULDA GONE WITH ONE INSULT, BUT NOT BAD. YOU KNOW, WHEN PUSH CAME TO SHOVE~
~IT WAS A PLEASURE WORKING WITH YOU.

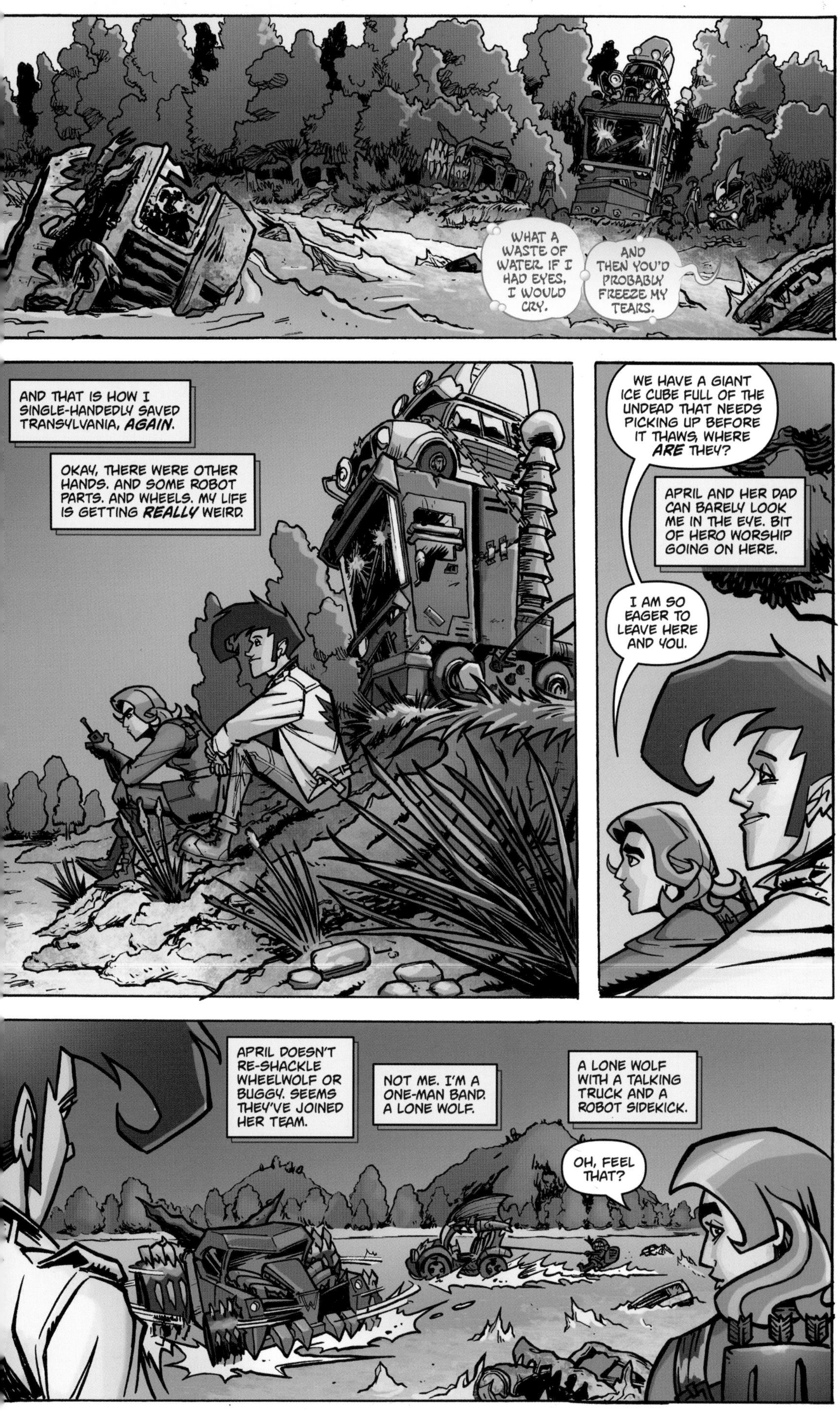
WHAT A WASTE OF WATER IF I HAD EYES, I WOULD CRY.
AND THEN YOU'D PROBABLY FREEZE MY TEARS.
AND THAT IS HOW I SINGLE-HANDEDLY SAVED TRANSYLVANIA, *AGAIN*.
OKAY, THERE WERE OTHER HANDS. AND SOME ROBOT PARTS. AND WHEELS. MY LIFE IS GETTING *REALLY* WEIRD.
WE HAVE A GIANT ICE CUBE FULL OF THE UNDEAD THAT NEEDS PICKING UP BEFORE IT THAWS, WHERE *ARE* THEY?
APRIL AND HER DAD CAN BARELY LOOK ME IN THE EYE. BIT OF HERO WORSHIP GOING ON HERE.
I AM SO EAGER TO LEAVE HERE AND YOU.
APRIL DOESN'T RE-SHACKLE WHEELWOLF OR BUGGY. SEEMS THEY'VE JOINED HER TEAM.
NOT ME. I'M A ONE-MAN BAND. A LONE WOLF.
A LONE WOLF WITH A TALKING TRUCK AND A ROBOT SIDEKICK.
OH, FEEL THAT?

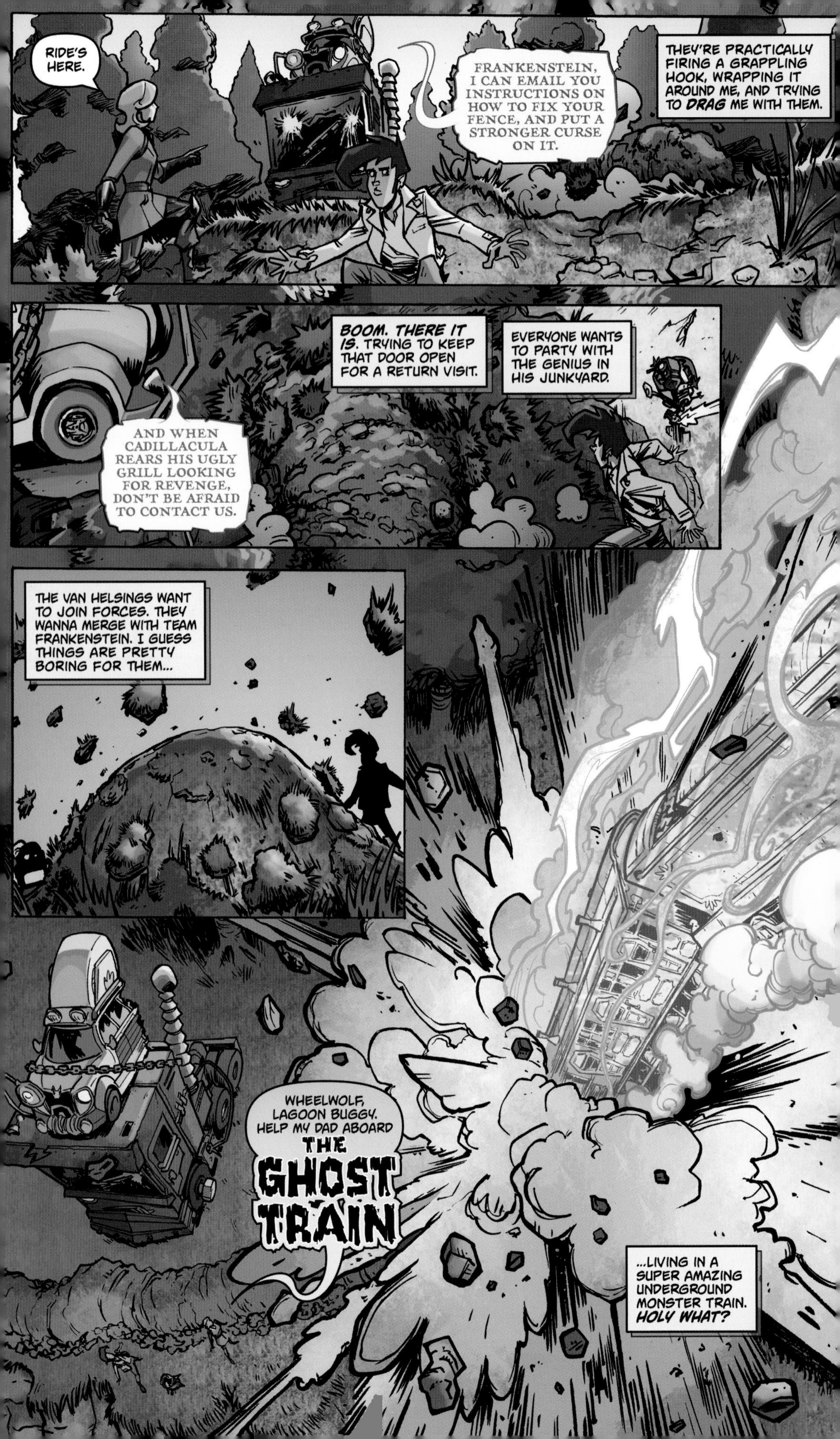
RIDE'S HERE.
FRANKENSTEIN, I CAN EMAIL YOU INSTRUCTIONS ON HOW TO FIX YOUR FENCE, AND PUT A STRONGER CURSE ON IT.
THEY'RE PRACTICALLY FIRING A GRAPPLING HOOK, WRAPPING IT AROUND ME, AND TRYING TO DRAG ME WITH THEM.
AND WHEN CADILLACULA REARS HIS UGLY GRILL LOOKING FOR REVENGE, DON'T BE AFRAID TO CONTACT US.
BOOM. THERE IT IS. TRYING TO KEEP THAT DOOR OPEN FOR A RETURN VISIT.
EVERYONE WANTS TO PARTY WITH THE GENIUS IN HIS JUNKYARD.
THE VAN HELSINGS WANT TO JOIN FORCES. THEY WANNA MERGE WITH TEAM FRANKENSTEIN. I GUESS THINGS ARE PRETTY BORING FOR THEM...
WHEELWOLF, LAGOON BUGGY. HELP MY DAD ABOARD THE GHOST TRAIN
...LIVING IN A SUPER AMAZING UNDERGROUND MONSTER TRAIN. HOLY WHAT?

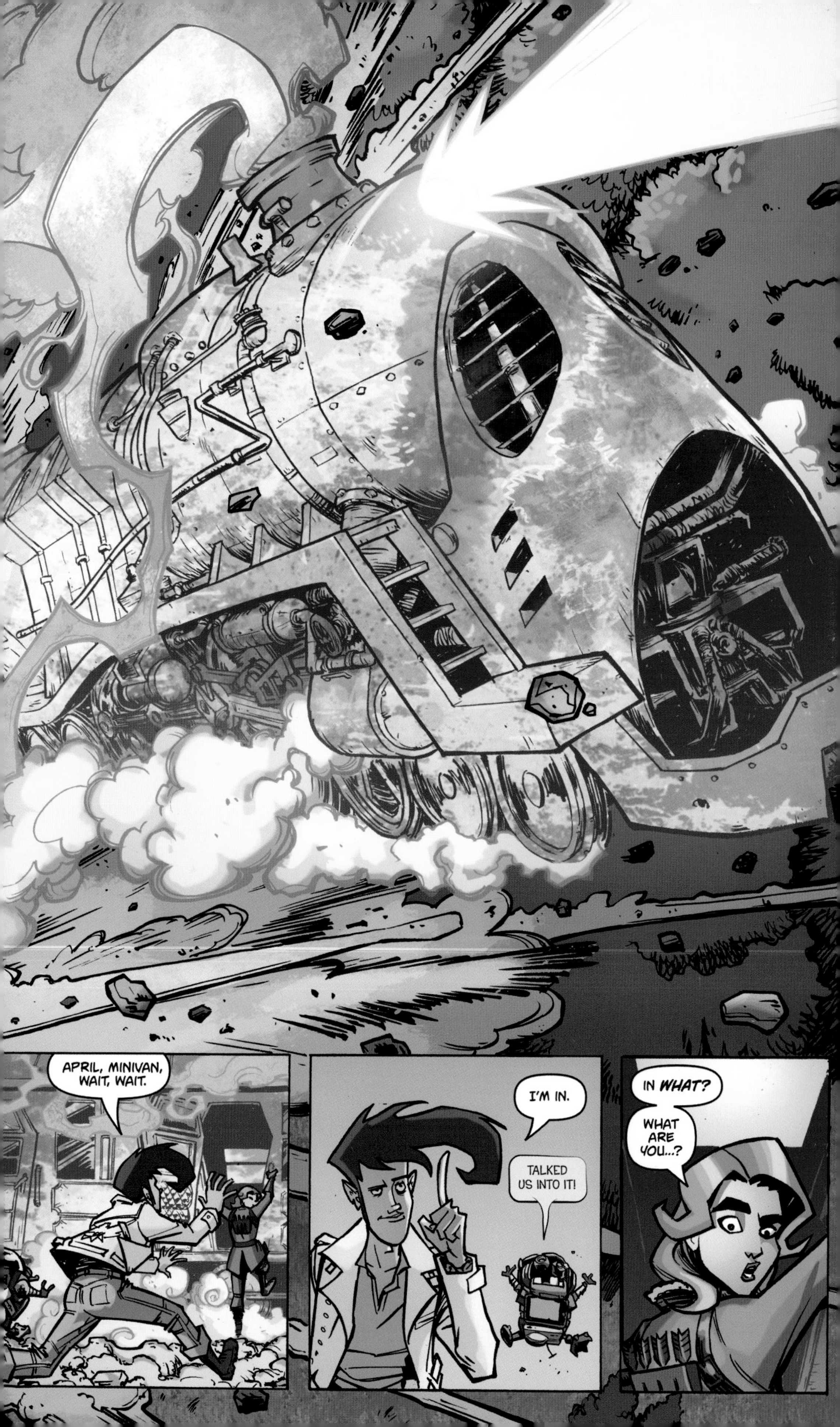
APRIL, MINIVAN, WAIT, WAIT.
I'M IN.
TALKED US INTO IT!
IN WHAT?
WHAT ARE YOU...?

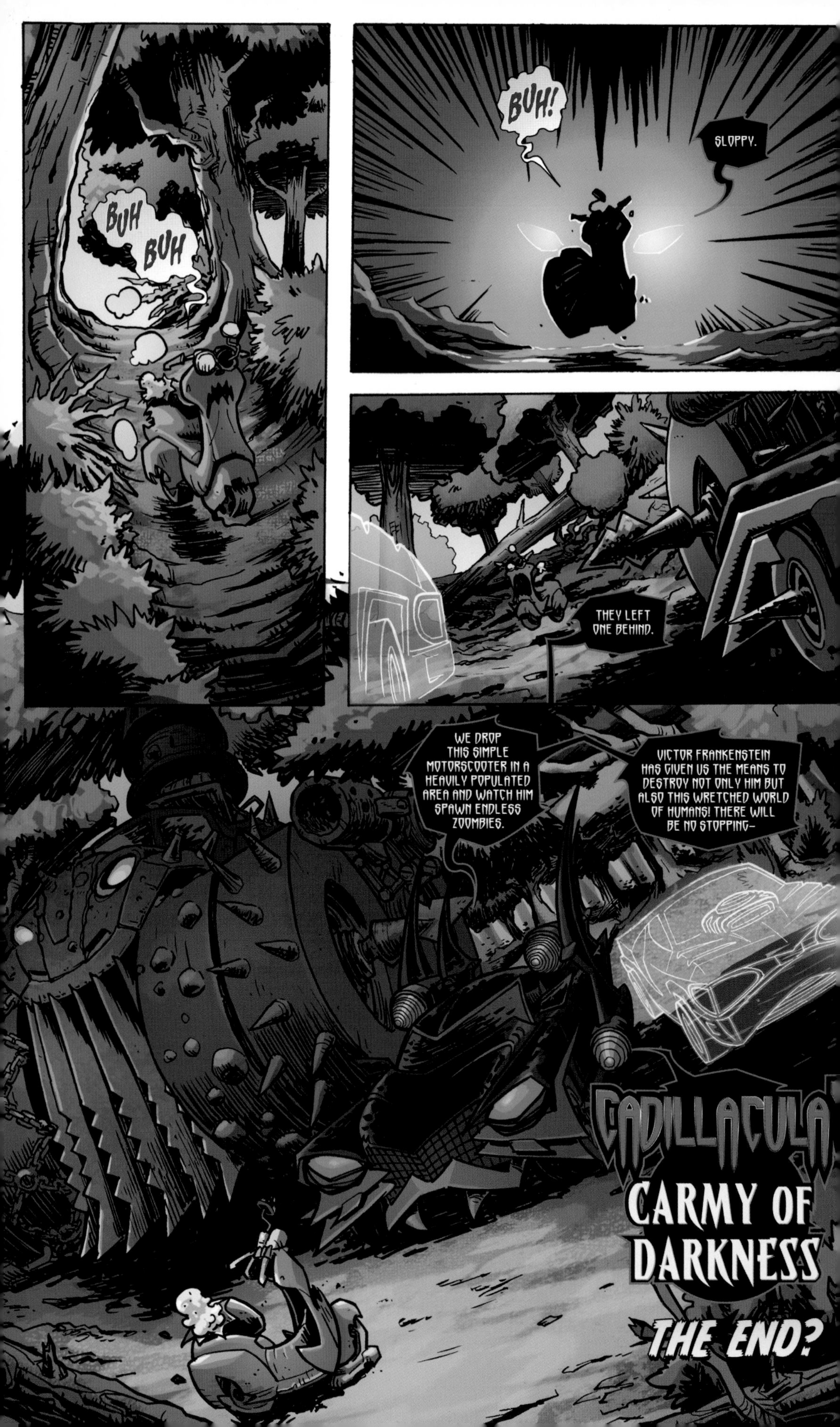
BUH
BUH
BUH!
SLOPPY.
THEY LEFT ONE BEHIND.
WE DROP THIS SIMPLE MOTORSCOOTER IN A HEAVILY POPULATED AREA AND WATCH HIM SPAWN ENDLESS ZOOMBIES.
VICTOR FRANKENSTEIN HAS GIVEN US THE MEANS TO DESTROY NOT ONLY HIM BUT ALSO THIS WRETCHED WORLD OF HUMANS! THERE WILL BE NO STOPPING–
CADILLACULA
CARMY OF DARKNESS
THE END?

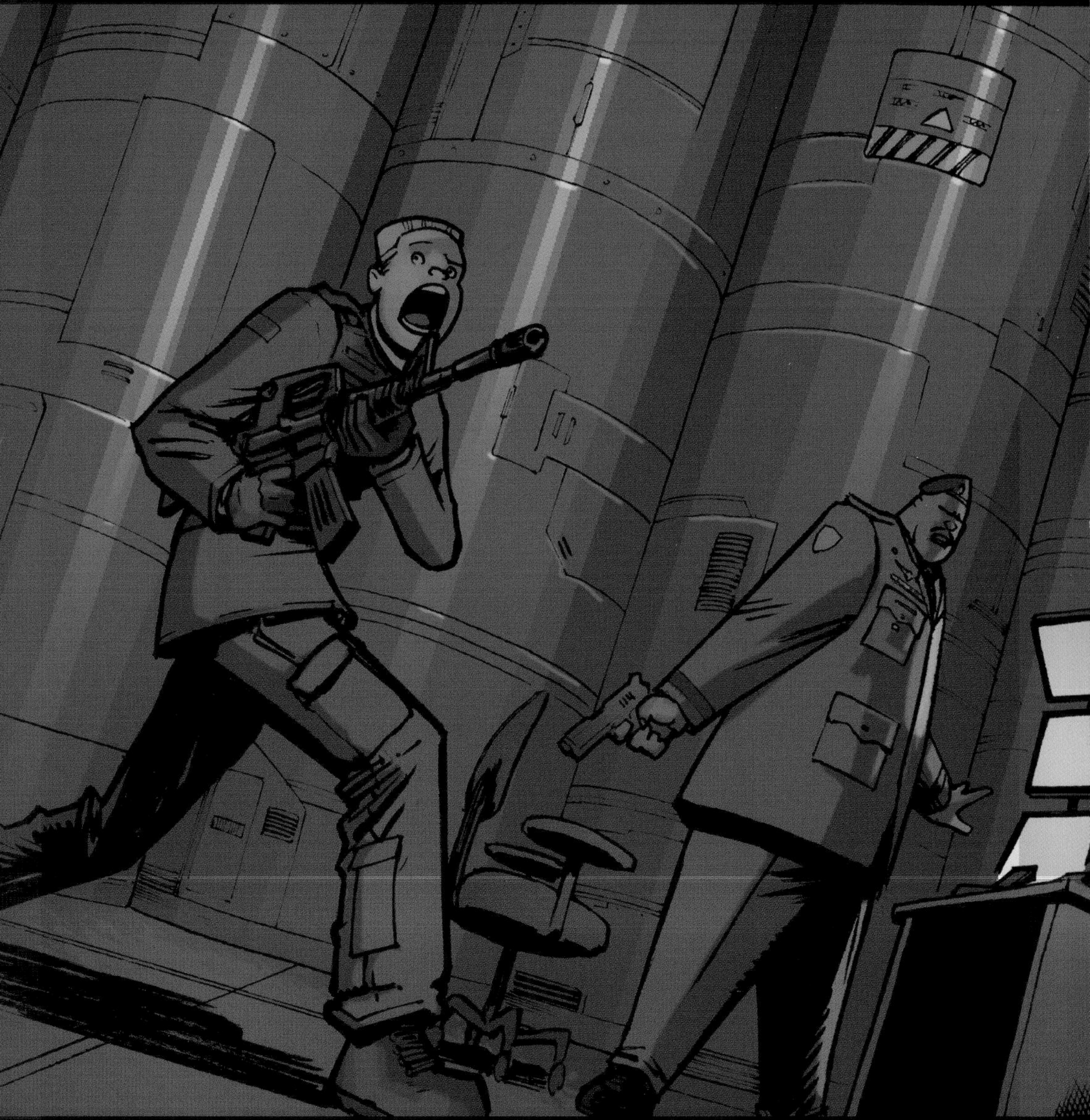

EPILOGUE: WITCH IS NEXT

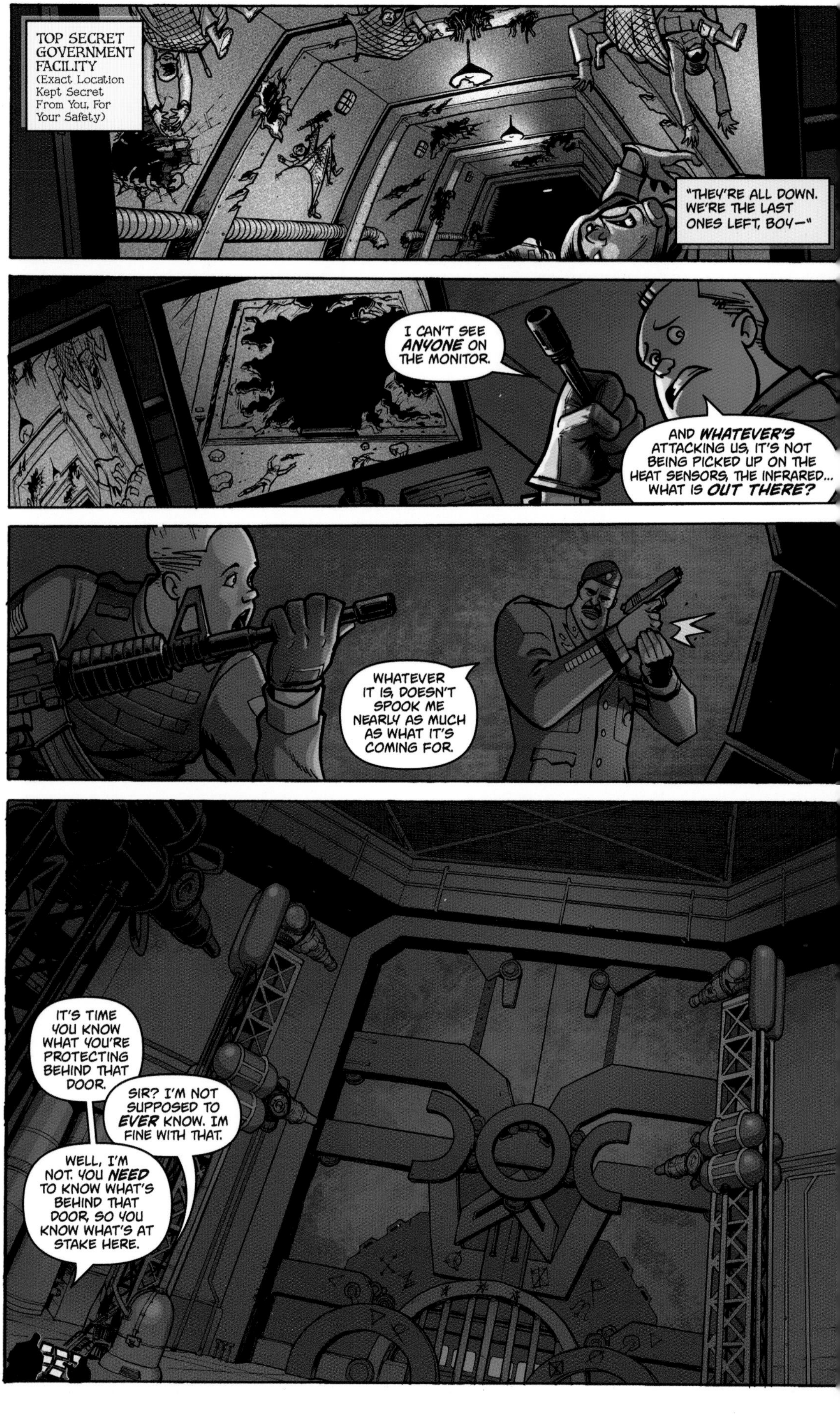
TOP SECRET GOVERNMENT FACILITY (Exact Location Kept Secret From You, For Your Safety)
"THEY'RE ALL DOWN. WE'RE THE LAST ONES LEFT, BOY—"
I CAN'T SEE ANYONE ON THE MONITOR.
AND WHATEVER'S ATTACKING US, IT'S NOT BEING PICKED UP ON THE HEAT SENSORS, THE INFRARED... WHAT IS OUT THERE?
WHATEVER IT IS, DOESN'T SPOOK ME NEARLY AS MUCH AS WHAT IT'S COMING FOR.
IT'S TIME YOU KNOW WHAT YOU'RE PROTECTING BEHIND THAT DOOR.
SIR? I'M NOT SUPPOSED TO EVER KNOW. IM FINE WITH THAT.
WELL, I'M NOT. YOU NEED TO KNOW WHAT'S BEHIND THAT DOOR, SO YOU KNOW WHAT'S AT STAKE HERE.

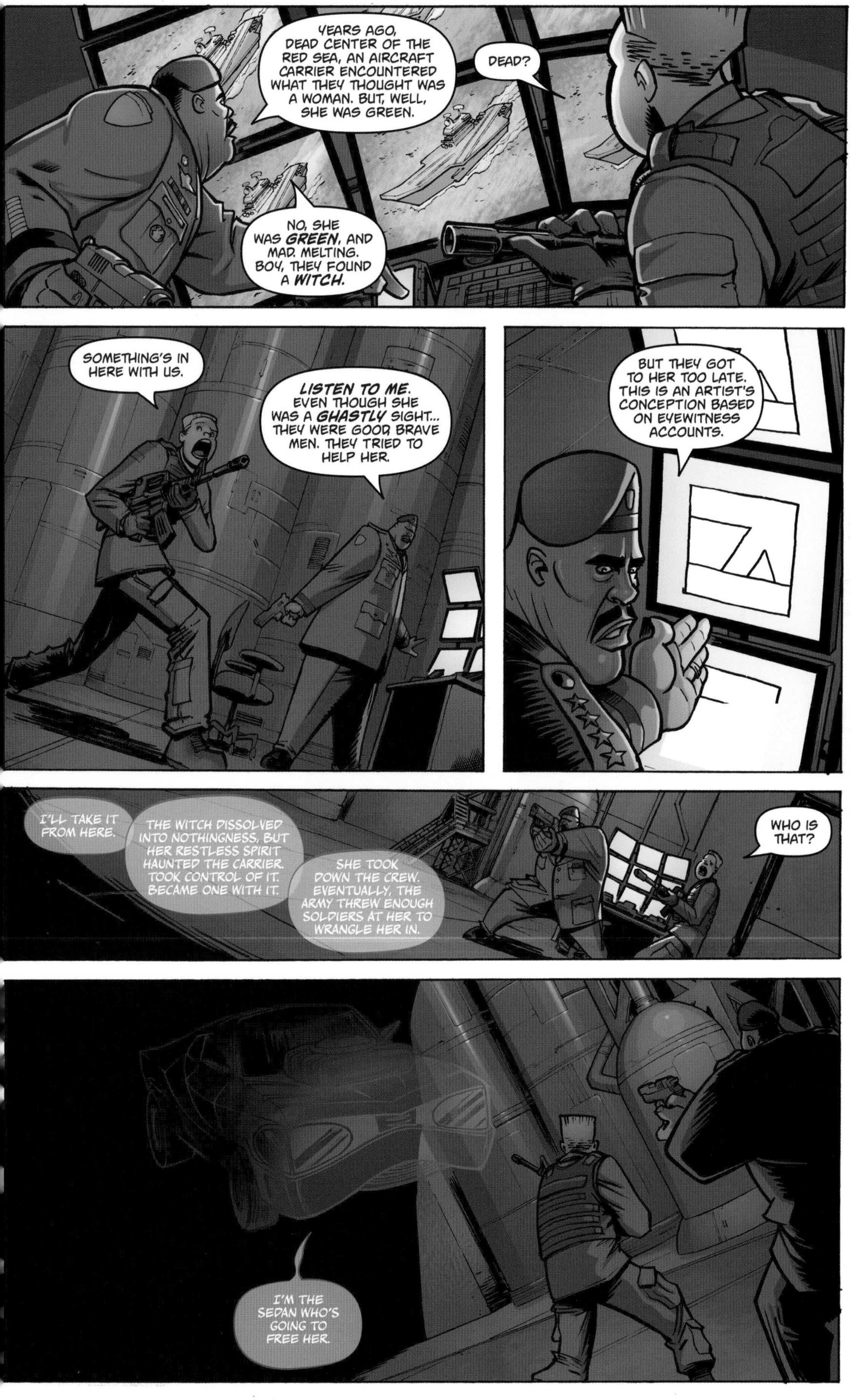

YEARS AGO, DEAD CENTER OF THE RED SEA, AN AIRCRAFT CARRIER ENCOUNTERED WHAT THEY THOUGHT WAS A WOMAN. BUT, WELL, SHE WAS GREEN.
DEAD?
NO, SHE WAS GREEN, AND MAD. MELTING. BOY, THEY FOUND A WITCH.
SOMETHING'S IN HERE WITH US.
LISTEN TO ME. EVEN THOUGH SHE WAS A GHASTLY SIGHT... THEY WERE GOOD, BRAVE MEN. THEY TRIED TO HELP HER.
BUT THEY GOT TO HER TOO LATE. THIS IS AN ARTIST'S CONCEPTION BASED ON EYEWITNESS ACCOUNTS.
I'LL TAKE IT FROM HERE.
THE WITCH DISSOLVED INTO NOTHINGNESS, BUT HER RESTLESS SPIRIT HAUNTED THE CARRIER. TOOK CONTROL OF IT. BECAME ONE WITH IT.
SHE TOOK DOWN THE CREW. EVENTUALLY, THE ARMY THREW ENOUGH SOLDIERS AT HER TO WRANGLE HER IN.
WHO IS THAT?
I'M THE SEDAN WHO'S GOING TO FREE HER.

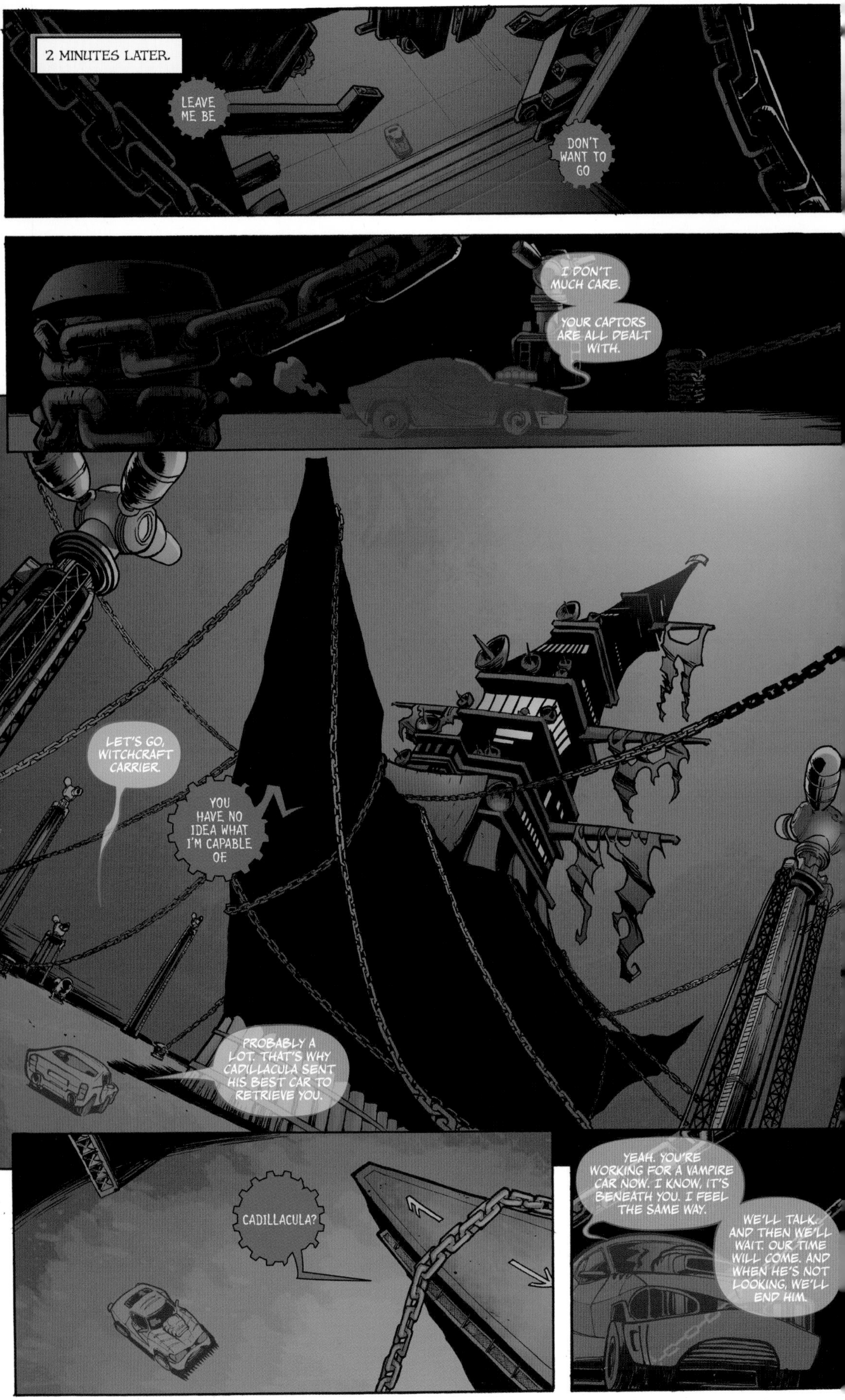

2 MINUTES LATER.
LEAVE ME BE
DON'T WANT TO GO
I DON'T MUCH CARE.
YOUR CAPTORS ARE ALL DEALT WITH.
LET'S GO, WITCHCRAFT CARRIER.
YOU HAVE NO IDEA WHAT I'M CAPABLE OF
PROBABLY A LOT. THAT'S WHY CADILLACULA SENT HIS BEST CAR TO RETRIEVE YOU.
CADILLACULA?
YEAH. YOU'RE WORKING FOR A VAMPIRE CAR NOW. I KNOW, IT'S BENEATH YOU. I FEEL THE SAME WAY.
WE'LL TALK. AND THEN WE'LL WAIT. OUR TIME WILL COME. AND WHEN HE'S NOT LOOKING, WE'LL END HIM.

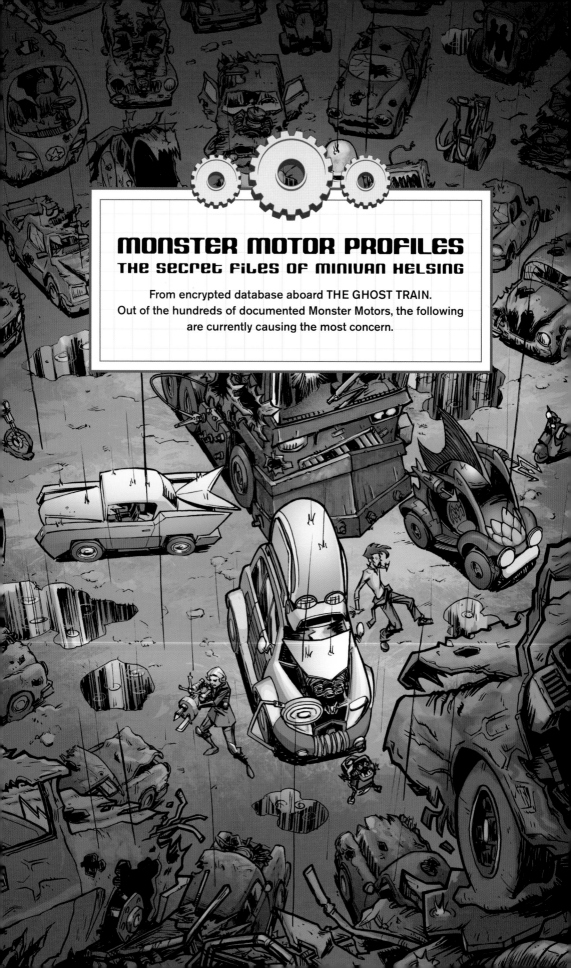

MONSTER MOTOR PROFILES
THE SECRET FILES OF MINIVAN HELSING

From encrypted database aboard THE GHOST TRAIN.
Out of the hundreds of documented Monster Motors, the following
are currently causing the most concern.

TITLE: **THE ABOMINABLE SNOWMOBILE**

VEHICLE CLASS:
Snowmobile

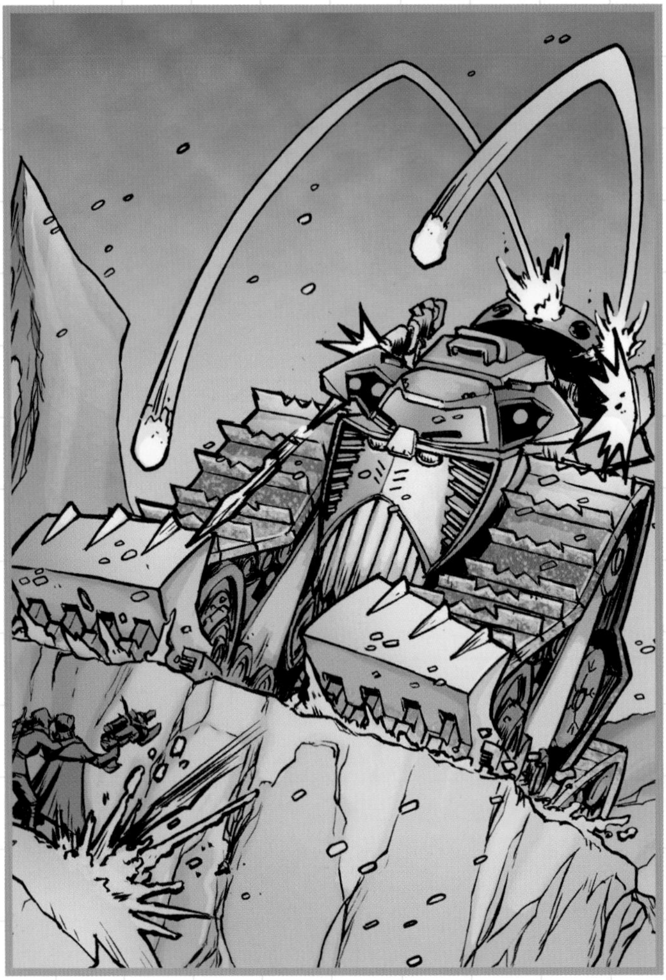

Artist's conception based on eyewitness accounts by Nick Roche

DESCRIPTION:

The Abominable Snowmobile is somewhat of a white whale. A massive snow mobile/tank creeping about the Himalayas, it was one of the first Monster Motors the Van Helsings encountered. As such, they were ill prepared to deal with it. It wounded Abraham Van Helsing and made a quick exit. The Van Helsings have been back to sweep the area numerous times. Unfortunately, aside from a few snowmobile tread tracks and eyewitness reports from frightened villagers, they have come back empty-handed.

ABILITIES:

The Abominable Snowmobile ha a variety of cold-based weapons Underside claw-scoops pick up the snow, douse it with a gust of sub-sub-sub arctic blasts, formin incredibly dangerous snowballs, that are then catapulted at frightening speed. The Snowmobile can instantly freeze water in torpedo molds and fire them in rapid succession. High-range freeze-hoses put any opponent on ice in seconds.

The Snowmobile's pelt is made c incredibly durable body armor, can stand up to most attacks, an survive in the coldest of temperatures. Also appears to b able to camouflage itself in the snow, which aids in getaways.

Finally, The Abominable Snowmobile has a winch and spiked treads for mountain climbing.

WEAKNESSES:

Very slow. He trudges along on treads, so even turning takes time. And while The Abominabl Snowmobile definitely has the advantage in arctic conditions, remove him from his natural habitat and you've won the battle.

CURRENT STATUS:

AT LARGE

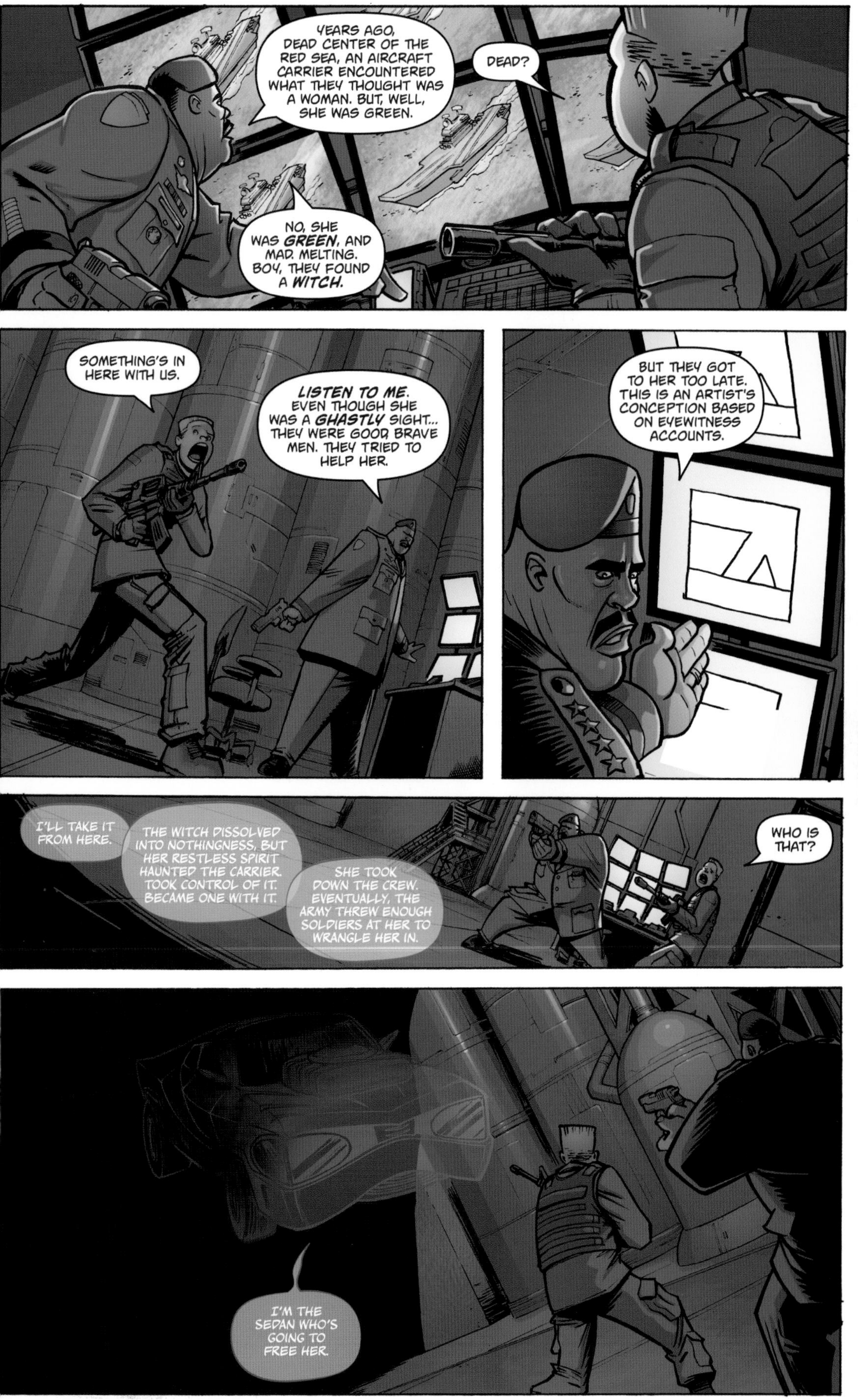

YEARS AGO, DEAD CENTER OF THE RED SEA, AN AIRCRAFT CARRIER ENCOUNTERED WHAT THEY THOUGHT WAS A WOMAN. BUT, WELL, SHE WAS GREEN.
DEAD?
NO, SHE WAS GREEN, AND MAD. MELTING. BOY, THEY FOUND A WITCH.
SOMETHING'S IN HERE WITH US.
LISTEN TO ME. EVEN THOUGH SHE WAS A GHASTLY SIGHT... THEY WERE GOOD BRAVE MEN. THEY TRIED TO HELP HER.
BUT THEY GOT TO HER TOO LATE. THIS IS AN ARTIST'S CONCEPTION BASED ON EYEWITNESS ACCOUNTS.
I'LL TAKE IT FROM HERE.
THE WITCH DISSOLVED INTO NOTHINGNESS, BUT HER RESTLESS SPIRIT HAUNTED THE CARRIER. TOOK CONTROL OF IT. BECAME ONE WITH IT.
SHE TOOK DOWN THE CREW. EVENTUALLY, THE ARMY THREW ENOUGH SOLDIERS AT HER TO WRANGLE HER IN.
WHO IS THAT?
I'M THE SEDAN WHO'S GOING TO FREE HER.

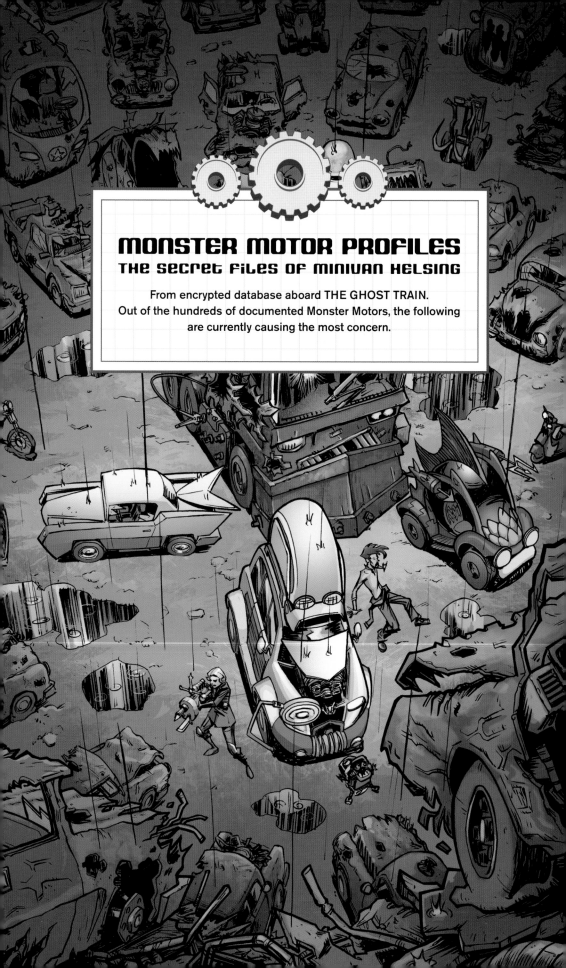

MONSTER MOTOR PROFILES
THE SECRET FILES OF MINIVAN HELSING

From encrypted database aboard THE GHOST TRAIN.
Out of the hundreds of documented Monster Motors, the following
are currently causing the most concern.

TITLE: THE ABOMINABLE SNOWMOBILE

VEHICLE CLASS:
Snowmobile

Artist's conception based on eyewitness accounts by Nick Roche

DESCRIPTION:

The Abominable Snowmobile is somewhat of a white whale. A massive snow mobile/tank creeping about the Himalayas, it was one of the first Monster Motors the Van Helsings encountered. As such, they were ill prepared to deal with it. It wounded Abraham Van Helsing and made a quick exit. The Van Helsings have been back to sweep the area numerous times. Unfortunately, aside from a few snowmobile tread tracks and eyewitness reports from frightened villagers, they have come back empty-handed.

ABILITIES:

The Abominable Snowmobile has a variety of cold-based weapons. Underside claw-scoops pick up the snow, douse it with a gust of sub-sub-sub arctic blasts, forming incredibly dangerous snowballs, that are then catapulted at frightening speed. The Snowmobile can instantly freeze water in torpedo molds and fire them in rapid succession. High-range freeze-hoses put any opponent on ice in seconds.

The Snowmobile's pelt is made of incredibly durable body armor, can stand up to most attacks, and survive in the coldest of temperatures. Also appears to be able to camouflage itself in the snow, which aids in getaways.

Finally, The Abominable Snowmobile has a winch and spiked treads for mountain climbing.

WEAKNESSES:

Very slow. He trudges along on treads, so even turning takes time. And while The Abominable Snowmobile definitely has the advantage in arctic conditions, remove him from his natural habitat and you've won the battle.

CURRENT STATUS:

AT LARGE

TITLE: **CADILLACULA** *"Gas is life. And yours shall be mine."*

VEHICLE CLASS:
Classic American Automobile

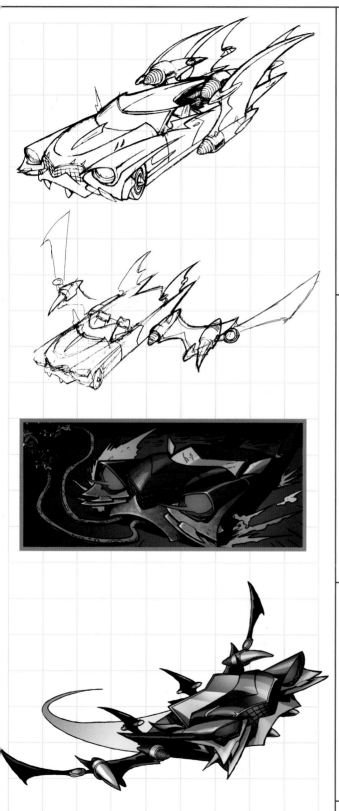

DESCRIPTION:

Cadillacula has been around for centuries, long before the first appearance of any other Monster Motor. Given enough power, he can completely change his make and model. As such, he's been a horse-drawn buggy, one of the first motorcars ever, even an Impala for a long stretch (although then, he was simply known as Vlad).

Cadillacula is the most evil Monster Motor on this planet. Sees every machine as a means to an end: you're either a minion or a meal. Has a severe hatred for humans. The more people he can run down while carrying out his nefarious schemes, the better. Ideally, he'd like to exist in a world WITHOUT humans. And while he's at it, he'd really like to rule that world.

ABILITIES:

Metal "teeth" in grill allow Cadillacula to suck the fuel (life) out of other vehicles. That vehicle dies and can never return (or so we thought, see: FRANKENRIDE). With each victim he claims, Cadillacula grows more and more powerful. Capable of complete self-repair. If he steals enough fuel, he can engage in complete vehicular regeneration.

Cadillacula has an array of weapons: gatling guns, missiles, torpedoes. Also has collapsible metal wings and turbine jets, allowing for flight.

Even in weakened states, Cadillacula can control any machine via Hypnotic Headlights. As long as Cadillacula can see it, he can control it.

WEAKNESSES:

Recently tried to syphon electrical energy instead of fuel and nearly did himself in. Earlier models of this Monster Motor had a real weakness to sunlight. This is untested on the current incarnation, would be very fun to see what happens.

Artist's conception based on eyewitness accounts by Nick Roche

CURRENT STATUS:

AT LARGE

TITLE: **DR. JEKYLL/MR. HYBRID**

"They call me Jekyll. But I am more infamous, down certain dark streets, by my other name."

VEHICLE CLASS:

Smart car/heavily armored, impossibly armed hybrid truck

SPARE TYRE
ROOF RACK
JEK

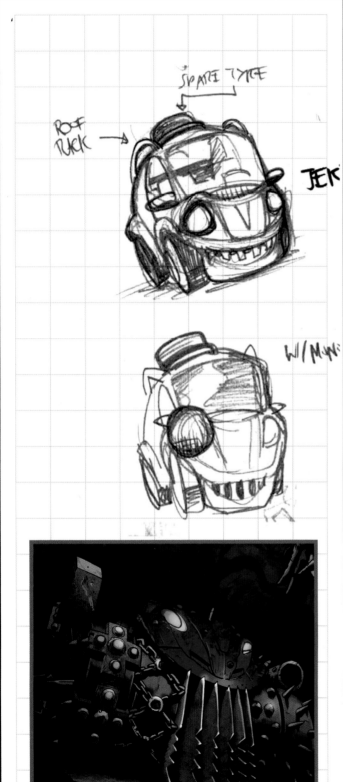

Artist's conception based on eyewitness accounts by Nick Roche

DESCRIPTION:

At first blush, Jekyll is your average smart car. But don't underestimate him, he's the world's SMARTEST car. He even enrolled in an online medical school, receiving his doctorate in six months.

Jekyll wanted a body to match his mind, so he started experimenting on himself, gaining a scary amount of upgrades and weapons. Jekyll can grow, expand, and transform into something altogether different. He becomes a completely different car... with a completely different personality: savage and brutal. This is Mr. Hybrid. No need for gas, he is literally fueled by the rage that he normally suppresses. Jekyll likes having a master. He doesn't have to rule, he prefers to drive alongside or behind a stronger Monster Motor. So far no one has been worthy, any attempts at finding a master have resulted in Mr. Hybrid coming out and destroying him or her.

ABILITIES:

As Dr. Jekyll, not many weapons but he is THE smartest of the Monster Motors. As Mr Hybrid, a nearly indestructible, heavily armed truck. Newer, deadlier features every time we encounter him: spikes, chains, bladed battering rams, plasma cannons. Hybrid is a big blunt weapon of raging destruction.

WEAKNESSES:

Jekyll has a few tricks up his sleeve, but for the most part his shell is that of a normal car. Easily defeated, IF you're fast enough to take him down before he transforms.

Mr. Hybrid is slow moving, which is helpful if/when you have to make a quick getaway. But his primary weakness is mental. He loses intelligence once he grows bigger. Can possibly be outsmarted. That said, not looking forward to rolling into battle against him.

CURRENT STATUS:

AT LARGE

TITLE: **FRANKENRIDE** *"Buckle up for safety. Where do you want to go?"*

VEHICLE CLASS:

Fully electric big rig truck, assembled from remains of other vehicles.

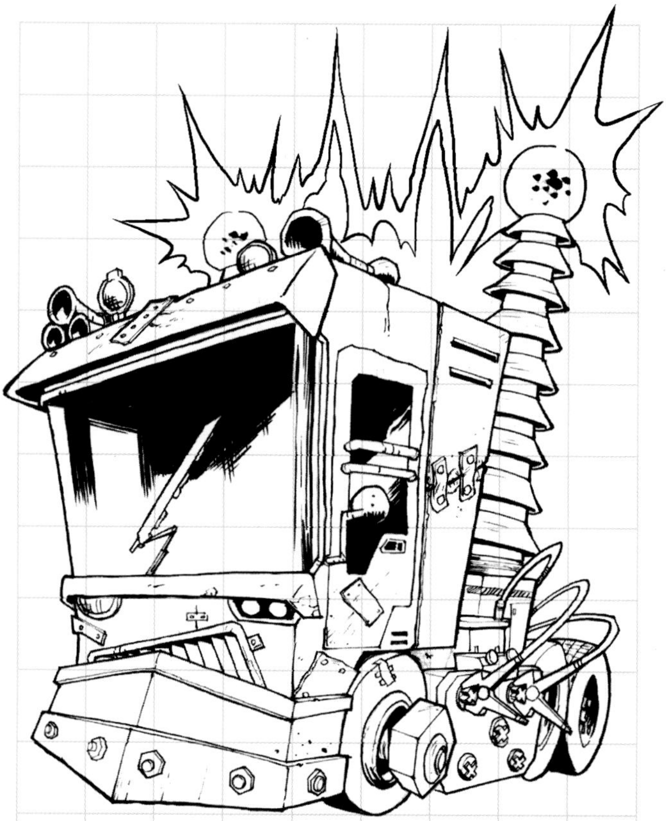

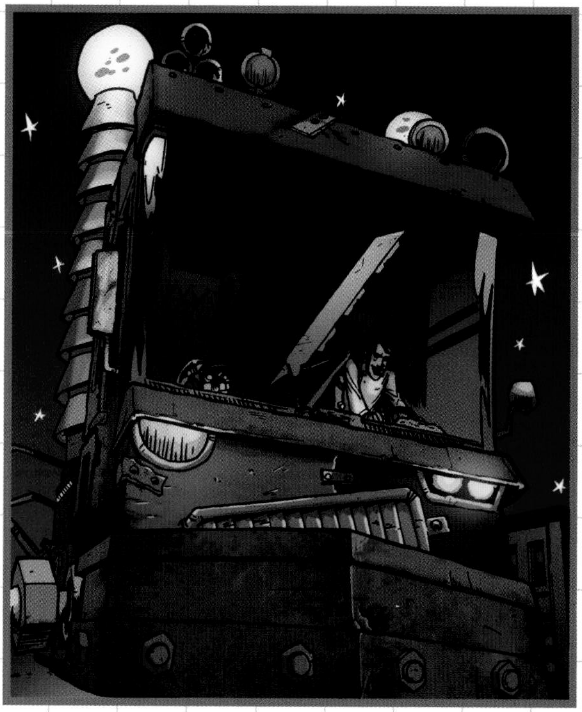

Artist's conception based on eyewitness accounts by Nick Roche

DESCRIPTION:

Frankenride is the creation of Vic Frankenstein (see: FRANKENSTEIN, VICTOR). The truck remains very loyal to his creator, like a dim-witted, three-ton dog.

We have no idea HOW this thing can think for itself. Frankenstein pulled off artificial intelligence once before with his robot assistant, but there's no evidence he tried that with the truck. It just... happened. That's scary. There are enough Monster Motors on this planet without some deluded mechanic running around making more.

That said, Frankenride has proven a valuable ally. He's dependable, he's good in a fight, and he is STRONG. Not saying he's on our team just yet, but he can think he is, all the easier to keep a headlight on him.

ABILITIES:

Recharged via lightning rod/slab in Frankenstein's Garage, the truck runs 100% on electricity, making it immune to Cadillacula's fuel-sucking attacks. Furthermore, Cadillacula's Hypnotic Headlights have no effect on Frankenride.

Frankenride is pure brute force. Front bumper battering ram. Smokestacks have been converted into lightning rods. Frankenride can rotate the stacks, allowing him to fire electricity at opponents.

WEAKNESSES:

At first glance, none. Frankenride seems indestructible. But Cadillacula did a number on him with missiles and gunfire. Also, a quick scan has provided us with a possible Achilles Wheel: a small crack in the vehicle's patchwork stitching means if this thing comes near fire, it's over.

CURRENT STATUS:

Housed at Frankenstein's Garage in Transylvania, Kentucky.

TITLE:
FRANKENSTEIN, VICTOR

"Genius. Loner. Heartthrob. These are just a few of the things I assume people call me when I'm not there."

SPECIES:
Human

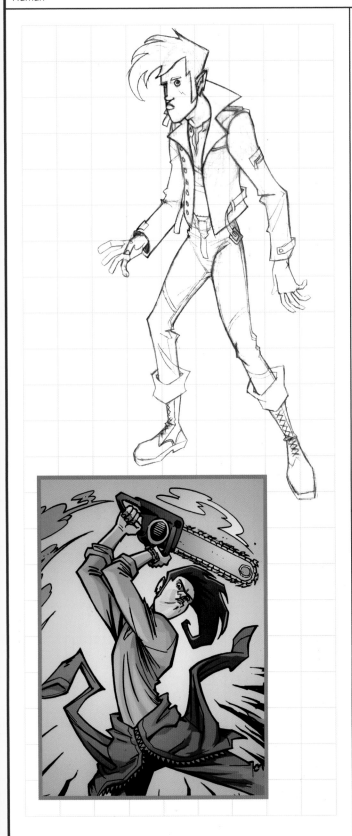

Artist's conception based on eyewitness accounts by Nick Roche

DESCRIPTION:

Frankenstein's parents abandoned him at an early age. From there he bounced around from foster home to foster home. This sounds like a sad story, until you meet him. About five minutes in, you kinda get it. Most people don't like him, and he doesn't like most people. He DOES, however, really get along with machines. Vic Frankenstein is, technically, a mechanic. But it goes beyond that. I would never say this to his face, but he's a genius. Frankenstein graduated top of his class at Ingolstadt School for Automotive Repair. Completing all his assignments in a few weeks, he killed time by building a truck from scratch. He followed THAT up by building a robot with artificial intelligence (see: iGOR).

These actions do not worry us. It's what he did NEXT that makes him a person of interest. Victor Frankenstein is the only human of record to intentionally BUILD a Monster Motor (see: FRANKENRIDE). That would be bad enough, but the same device then spawned a legion of Zoombies.

Frankenstein survived an attack from Cadillacula. Survived is an understatement, in fact he DEFEATED the evil vampire car. He also helped take down the aforementioned legion of zoombies that he created. Vic Frankenstein might just be the deciding factor in the war between good and evil Monster Motor. That thought should keep any sane person or vehicle up at night.

ABILITIES:

His intelligence is off the charts. He creates mechanical life (too much). He's also an excellent driver. Frankenstein is extremely brave. His confidence level is off the charts. Can take a hit quite well. Claims to know various forms of kung fu, but his technique in battle has proven this a lie.

WEAKNESSES:

His overwhelming confidence might in fact be a front. Nobody loves themselves this much. I mean, certain rock stars or Internet celebrities, maybe.

As stated above, Frankenstein is a terrible fighter. And his social skills are, to say the least, lacking.

CURRENT STATUS:

Living in Transylvania, Kentucky.

TITLE:

THE GHOST TRAIN

VEHICLE CLASS:

Haunted Steam Train

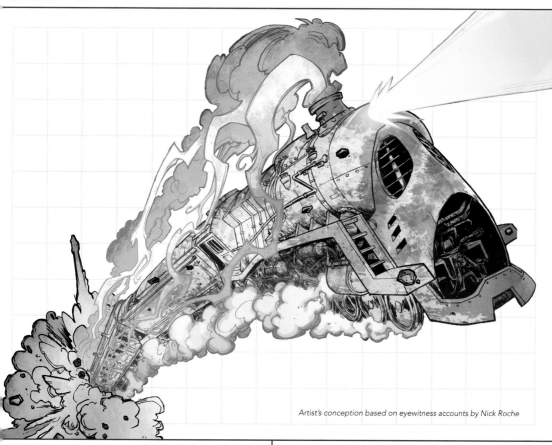

Artist's conception based on eyewitness accounts by Nick Roche

DESCRIPTION:

The Ghost Train began, as Monster Motors often do, as a typical run of the mill vehicle. Classic steam/passenger/cargo train. But during an unscheduled midnight trip, the train was in a crash that killed the only person on board: the conductor. A new conductor was hired, but after one trip, the train was decommissioned. Official reason: the accident had damaged the train more than the owners had originally thought.

But now we know the truth. The train was haunted by the ghost of The Conductor. He didn't want anyone on his train ever again. Truth be told, he didn't trust himself, he just didn't want anyone else hurt.

The Van Helsings helped him make peace with his past and soon after recruited him as part of the team.

The Ghost Train doesn't ride on tracks, the mere sight of it would raise too many questions, and it lets out a bit of a ghostly moan as it travels that would freak out the normals. But April Van Helsing had a solution: the train could burrow underground to reach its destination.

ABILITIES:

The Ghost Train is a moving fortress. It has your typical passenger cars, sleeping compartments, dining car, etc. But it's also outfitted with holding cells for problem Monster Motors, a meeting room that can fit all manners of vehicles, an armory, training room, the works.

The Ghost Train can also go intangible (along with it's cargo, human or metal) for limited amounts of time, can fly, and can reach speeds that would leave a normal, boring train in the dust.

WEAKNESSES:

The Ghost Train is manned/controlled by the mysterious figure known only as The Conductor. He can't leave his vehicle (and doesn't want to). He and the train are bonded. That means the behavior of the train is tied directly to The Conductor's emotions. Get him excited, the train goes faster. If he's depressed, the train mopes along. And if he's angry, it's... let's just say it makes for a bumpy ride.

If one were to find a way to remove The Conductor (and there are certainly any number of spells or amulets that can take out a ghost) The Ghost Train would cease being supernatural, and would have to be re-named simply "The Train."

CURRENT STATUS:

Ally of Minivan Helsing.

TITLE: **iGOR** *"Boss, they're coming for me! I'm flattered and scared!"*

SPECIES:
Robot

CHK
CHK

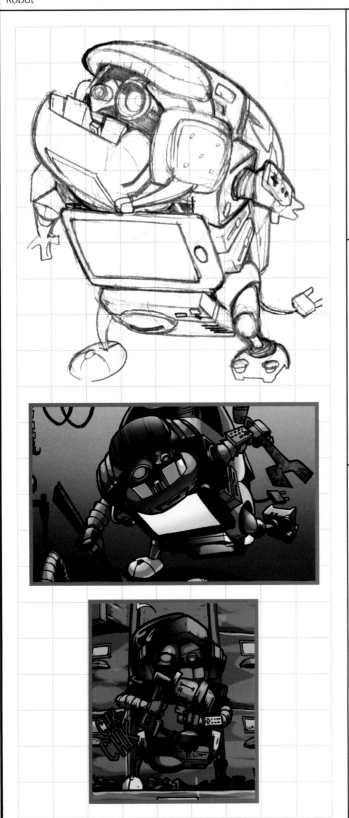

Artist's conception based on eyewitness accounts by Nick Roche

DESCRIPTION:

When Victor Frankenstein attended Ingolstadt School for Automotive Repair, his instructors often made the students pair off with one another for assignments. Frankenstein didn't think any of the other students were at his level (probably true) so he built someone to partner with. Sneaking in afterhours and taking apart the other students' computers, game consoles, and tablets, Frankenstein assembled iGOR (interactive Garage Operations Robot). iGOR is Frankenstein's assistant, best friend, and right-hand-bot.

ABILITIES:

iGOR is fluent in 12 languages. Has memorized over 2,000 vehicle owner's manuals. He packs 15 terabytes to store Frankenstein's MP3s, and can make incredible playlists to fit the mood of any situation.

iGOR was built to last. He's taken bumps and kicks and came out just fine. He's smart loyal, and quite frankly, nicer to deal with than Frankenstein. Easily the most advanced manmade artificial life form we've encountered.

WEAKNESSES:

iGOR tends to get over-excited, causing extreme clumsiness which more often than not leads to carnage. Very hard to run on those stubby joystick legs and very hard to get up if he falls backwards due to the computer monitor hump on his back. The more that is asked of him, the quicker his battery expires, requiring an overnight charging. And iGOR frequently forgets to close out his applications, which leads to an even more limited battery life.

iGOR can't drive, but that's not a big deal as most of the vehicles he encounters can drive themselves.

His biggest weakness, however, is that iGOR was MADE to do whatever Frankenstein says. He worships him, responds to his every command, and thinks the sun rises and sets on Victor Frankenstein. His POV is very skewed, and quite frankly, very wrong.

CURRENT STATUS:

Assistant to Victor Frankenstein.

THE INVISIBLE SEDAN

*"You're working for a vampire car now.
I know, it's beneath you. I feel the same way."*

VEHICLE CLASS:
Altered classic '70s street machine

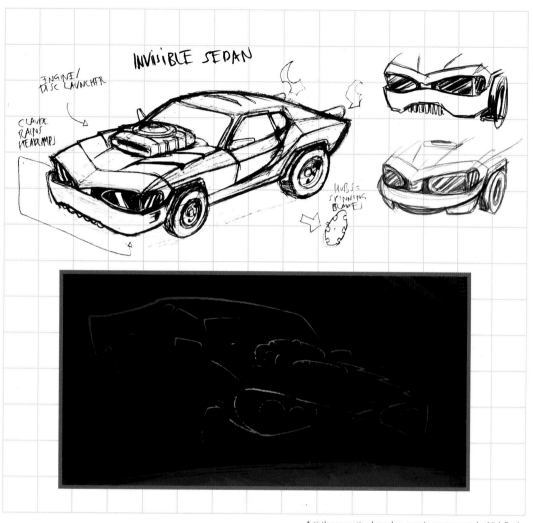

INVISIBLE SEDAN

ENGINE/
DISC LAUNCHER

CLAUDE
RAINS
HEADLAMPS

HUBS=
SPINNING
BLADES

Artist's conception based on eyewitness accounts by Nick Roche

DESCRIPTION:

Not much is known about the vile creature known only as The Invisible Sedan. Very few have encountered him and lived to tell about it. A more perfect vehicular assassin you won't find... quite literally: this Sedan has the ability to blend in with his surroundings.

Invisible Sedan is a sneak and a liar, not even trusted by his allies. Just because you're on Invisible Sedan's side doesn't mean you're safe; he'll sell you out and take you down without a second thought. And you'll never see it coming. Has destroyed just as many allies as he has enemies.

ABILITIES:

When he doesn't care about being detected, Invisible Sedan wears ridged protective armor. But for stealth missions, Invisible Sedan pops off the shell, leaving a transparent automobile that is virtually undetectable.

Invisible Sedan has a great number of strobe weapons, via headlights and side arms, that can disorient or blind human and machine alike. Capable of firing spinning blades that can slice through metal. Unlimited supply of NOS makes him a blur on the streets.

WEAKNESSES:

The Invisible Sedan loses his armor to enter stealth mode. That's when he's most vulnerable... but good luck finding him.

TITLE: **LAGOON BUGGY** *"When we're not helping on missions, we get to sleep in cages!"*

VEHICLE CLASS:

Dune Buggy with Hovercraft Capabilities

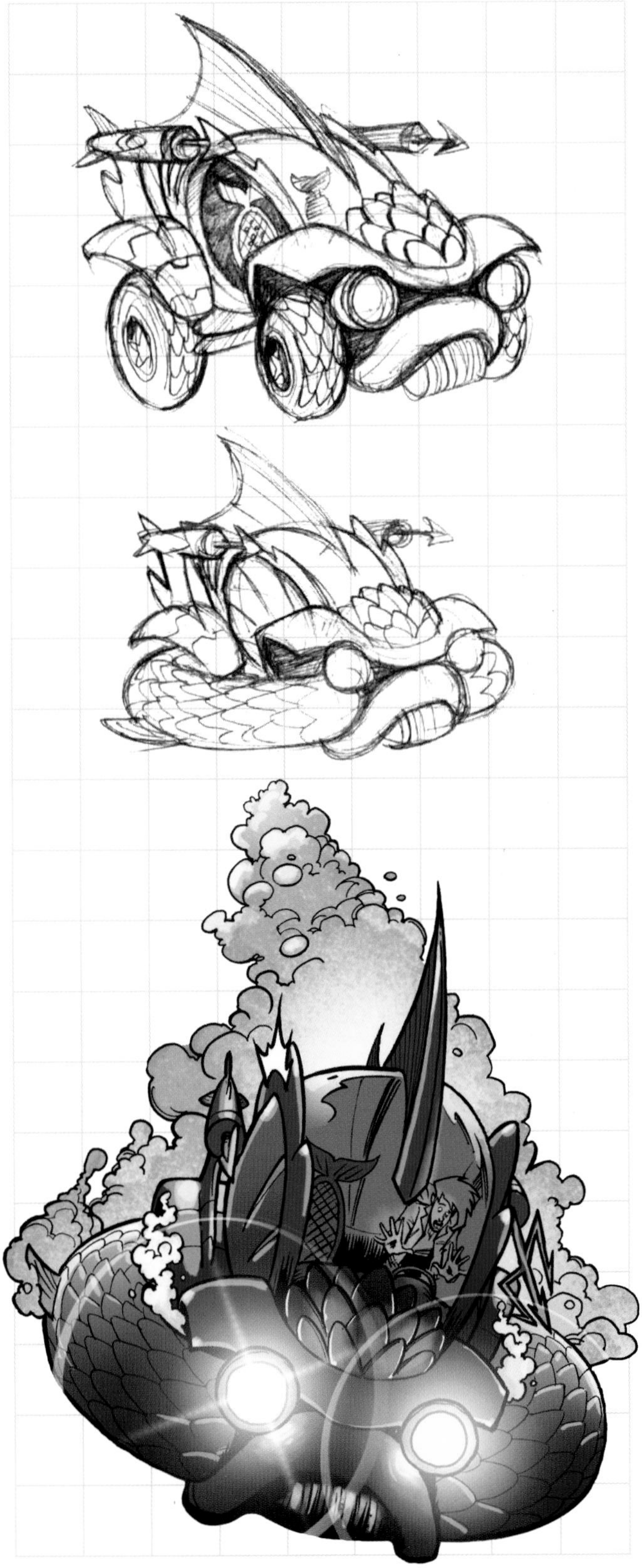

Artist's conception based on eyewitness accounts by Nick Roche

DESCRIPTION:

We pulled Lagoon Buggy out of a top-secret government facility that was used for training and experiments. Heavy radioactivity in the area, our nearest guess is this caused a merging of military vehicle and mutated sea creature.

Buggy was an easy capture and so far rehabilitation has gone (pardon the pun) swimmingly. Lagoon Buggy is docile, and, oddly enough, happy… as long as we keep his tank nice and murky, and populated with snakes, fish, and frogs to keep him company. Lagoon Buggy especially likes Wheelwolf, but that admiration is not returned.

ABILITIES:

High speed dune buggy. Green, scaled armor provides surprisingly formidable protection. Torpedoes, pitchfork projectiles, Lagoon Buggy's not bad on land…

…but on water, he's unbeatable. Inflatable hovercraft bottom. Incredible speed on the surface, even faster UNDER water. Has chameleon-like capabilities, able to change outer shell color. Domed top is sealed and 100% waterproof. Can create a surprisingly durable bubble-shield.

WEAKNESSES:

The longer Lagoon Buggy is on land, the weaker and slower he gets. He needs to submerge in water every couple of hours to recharge. And while there is no other Monster Motor better in the water, on land he is vulnerable. Lagoon Buggy is no pushover, mind you, but it is a weakness that can easily be exploited. Also, very talkative (can be annoying) and easily distracted (once drove off to chase a dragonfly in the middle of field training).

CURRENT STATUS:

Ally of Minivan Helsing.

MINIVAN HELSING

"I'm a great hero. A fantastic car. But I'm a terrible father."

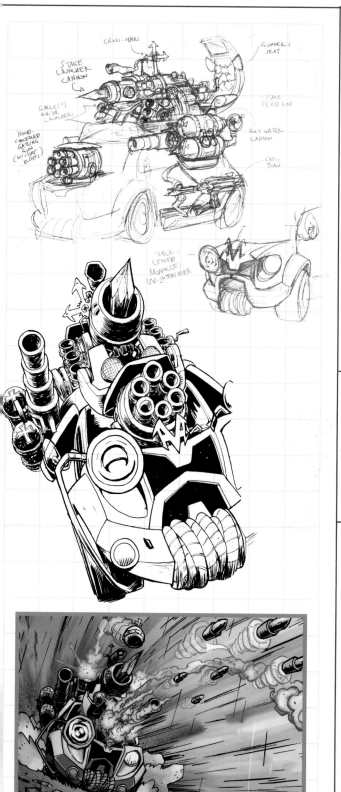

Labels on illustration: CROSS-HAIRS, GUNNERS SEAT, STAKE LAUNCHER CANNON, STAKE FEED LINE, GARLIC(?) MORTAR LAUNCHER, HOLY WATER CANNON, HOOD-CONCEALED GATLING GUN (W/SILVER BULLETS), CROSS BOW, THICK LENSED MONOCLE - UV-INTENSIFIER

DESCRIPTION:

If you're reading this, you are a trusted ally of Minivan Helsing. But just the same, this is privileged information, so keep it under your hood.

Abraham Van Helsing was the greatest monster hunter of all time. When the supernatural started upping their game, shedding their flesh and becoming vehicles of mass destruction, Abraham had to act fast. He discovered a curse that would allow him to transfer his essence from his elderly human body into that of a huge armored vehicle. But, you know how curses go... something went wrong, Abraham overshot and his essence landed smack-dab in a neighbor's minivan. Abraham Van Helsing was no more, but thanks to some serious vehicular upgrades, Minivan Helsing is a force to be reckoned with.

Quite simply, Minivan Helsing, along with his still-human daughter April, remains the last and truest line of defense between human and Monster Motor.

ABILITIES:

Equipped with a weapon for ANY monster he rolls up against. Headlights fire UV light. Freeze rays. Side gun turrets that fire silver bullets. Turbines, NOS, missiles, grappling hooks, melee bombs, stakes. There are more weapons, of course. Minivan Helsing has ALL the tricks of the trade.

WEAKNESSES:

Minivan Helsing may be unbeatable, but his partner and daughter April is all-too-human. While trained in every manner of martial arts and weapons handling, she is NOT a Monster Motor. Get to her, you get to him.

Artist's conception based on eyewitness accounts by Nick Roche

CURRENT STATUS:

Saving the world.

TITLE: **APRIL VAN HELSING** *"I am so eager to leave here and you."*

SPECIES:
Human

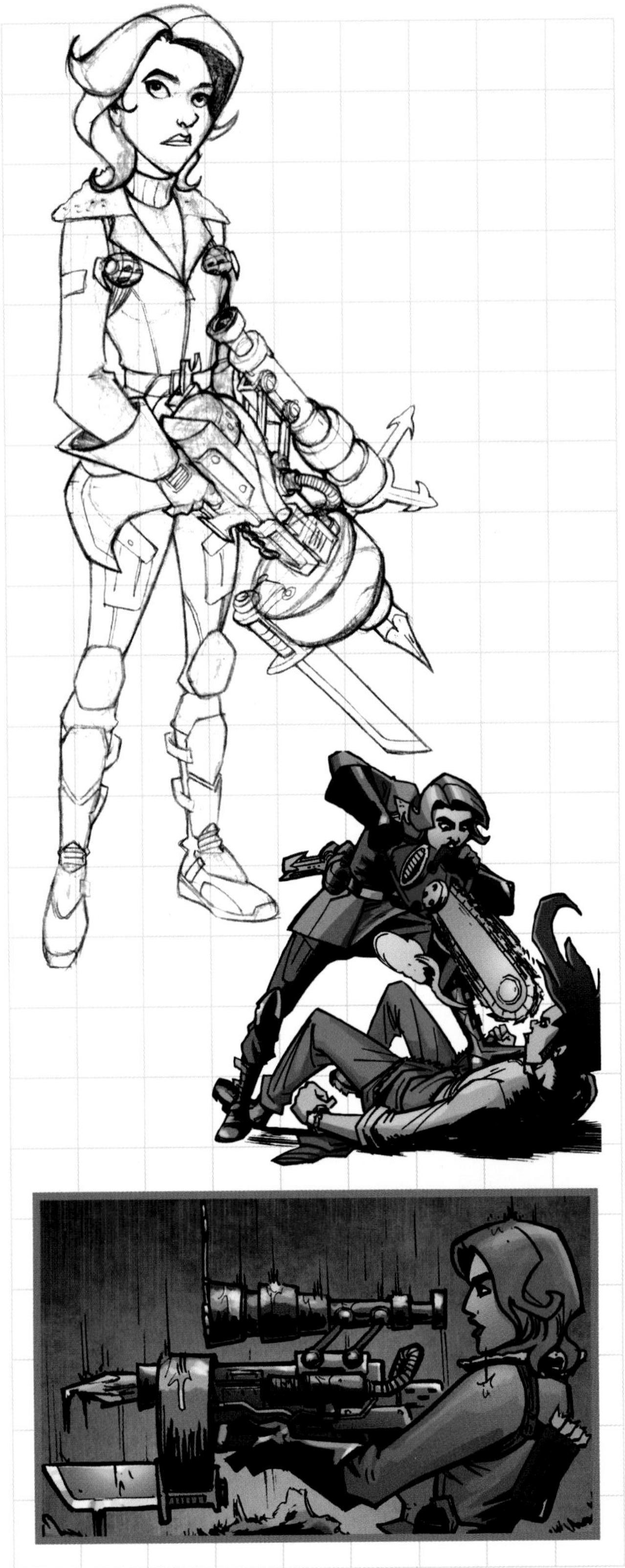

Artist's conception based on eyewitness accounts by Nick Roche

DESCRIPTION:

April Van Helsing has spent her entire life battling evil side-by-side with her father, Abraham. She truly knows no other way. She's never met her mother, in fact, Abraham is the only human she's had any kind of relationship with up to this point.

At four she was Abraham's weapons caddy, lugging a large case of supernatural gear a few steps behind Dad while he fought the forces of evil. By her early teens she started actually USING the weapons, and soon became as formidable a warrior as Abraham (though he would never admit this). As he got older, he got slower and more frail, and April had to take over. This put a strain on their relationship, but not nearly as much as when Abraham transferred his soul to that of a Minivan. Now the only human she KNEW wasn't human anymore.

ABILITIES:

Near Olympic-level athlete. Trained in countless martial arts. Incredibly strong, fast, and agile. She's a brilliant tactician. Can speak fluently in all languages. Knows the history of, and has happily used, every weapon on this and a few other plains of existence.

WEAKNESSES:

Because of how she was raised, she hasn't had to deal with many humans. As such, she has a short fuse, tends to get into a lot of unnecessary fights, and (understatement incoming) has trust issues.

Ironically, considering her career choice, April is a very bad driver.

Plus, despite her abilities, April is a human being going up against supernatural machines. Weapons or not, she's at a disadvantage.

CURRENT STATUS:

Saving the world.

WHEELWOLF

"You wanted the wolf. Wolf's gotta howl."

VEHICLE CLASS:
Classic Car/High-speed Savage Racer

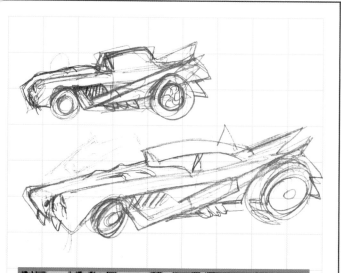

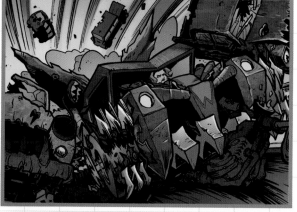

Artist's conception based on eyewitness accounts by Nick Roche

DESCRIPTION:

There are plenty of wolfcars out there. Long ago, the first wolfcar bit another car, turned him or her, they bit another vehicle, turned that, so on, so forth. We have documentation there are actual wolftrucks, wolfcycles, even a wolfjet. By day they're perfectly normal vehicles. But by night, especially during full moons, they transform into savage weaponized monsters.

Wheelwolf is the first wolf vehicle we've captured. We trapped him in the woods, the remains of Rabbits, Rams, and Broncos hanging in his nearby cave. The vehicles, not the animals. Wheelwolf doesn't hunt living things because he doesn't like being around living things. Also doesn't like being around machines. He's grouchy enough when the moon ISN'T full. When it IS full, well… we give him his space.

ABILITIES:

Daytime mode, he's your typical (talking) car. Come nighttime, when his lunar paneling is fully charged, his exterior flips and spins, whirls and clicks and he turns into an aggressive, feral beast. Bigger, faster, stronger. Weapons are of the sharp and pointy variety: metal spikes extend from wheels for extra stability on rocky landscapes. Sharp jagged rear fins, blades, anything to help rip up his opponents.

Wheelwolf is capable of extra sensory tracking via yellow headlights. Turbo boost capabilities allow him to hit the air for limited amounts of time.

Has a sonic "wolf howl" that can disorient Monster Motors, and brings humans to their knees. And he likes to use it.

WEAKNESSES:

During the day he's especially vulnerable. A typical car.

If you have to battle him at night, berserker rage could easily be exploited. Wheelwolf flies off the handle easily, doesn't think clearly and is prone to overheating.

CURRENT STATUS:

Ally of Minivan Helsing.

TITLE: **WITCHCRAFT CARRIER** *"You have NO IDEA what I'm capable of."*

VEHICLE CLASS:
Aircraft Carrier

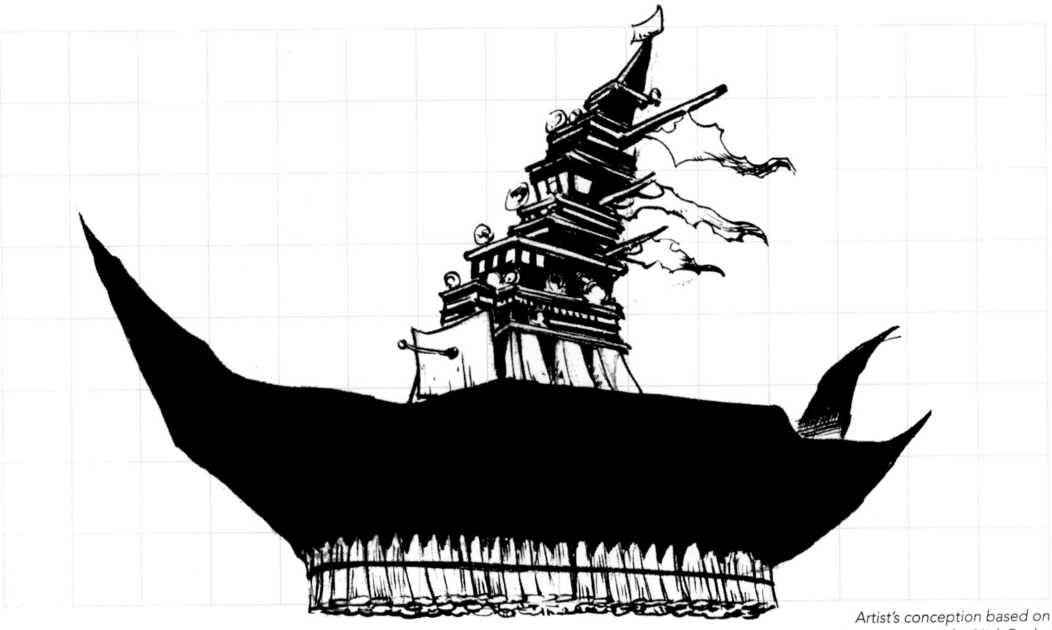

Artist's conception based on eyewitness accounts by Nick Roche

DESCRIPTION:

A fully manned aircraft carrier came across a woman drowning in the ocean. No boat, no one around, how she got there was a mystery. Among the other mysteries, why was the woman's skin green? Why was the water boiling around her? Why did contact with the water appear to be killing her? The answer, as we know now, is that she was a witch. The bad kind. Yes, there are good witches, we work with some of them, but this specific witch was most definitely not one of them. We think she was probably tricked into teleporting into the water, and if the carrier hadn't seen her, that's the last anyone would have heard from her.

But the aircraft carrier DID see her, the sailors immediately pulled her aboard. This was a decision they would soon regret. She died on the deck, literally melted away... but soon, strange things started happening on the carrier. It began to change. Not just in appearance, the aircraft carrier literally turned against its men. The lucky ones got ejected into the water, the others, well, the newly dubbed Witchcraft Carrier was powerful. Some say the men were turned into toads, forced to do her bidding as her new crew. Others say, "come on, toads? That's stupid." But hey, sometimes reality is stupid.

The army and navy were eventually able to bring down Witchcraft Carrier after days of fighting, and she was taken to a top-secret government location. Street ops have revealed she was recently freed by an operative of Cadillacula. This is bad news.

ABILITIES:

Too numerous to mention. Her abilities are off the charts. Her power, like her, is enormous. She has a full library of spells and curses at her disposal. Teleportation, camouflage, ability to turn her enemies into whatever she wants, we're just getting started. She has hundreds of brooms strapped to her underbelly, and as such, can fly. In fact, she's capable of moving at speeds unheard of for something her size. Plus her already armored shell has all sorts of force fields and protective spells surrounding her.

She's given her aircraft carrier weapons a supernatural upgrade. Her torpedoes now have a mind of their own, are actually eel-like in nature. Mean sons of guns, they lock on a target and won't relent until it's destroyed.

Oddly, the control room has been converted to a ALL CANDY INTERIOR: gingerbread walls, candy cane levers. Witches, man.

Finally, as Witchcraft Carrier is the official home of Cadillacula, he has made some changes. She now has a Cadillacula throne room (why would a car need a throne?), prison cells, and a vehicle dungeon/torture room.

WEAKNESSES:

The most ironic weakness of all for an aircraft carrier: Witchcraft Carrier CANNOT touch water. As such, she uses force fields or simply hovers above bodies of water if she HAS to. This weakness is a HUGE bonus for us: for one thing, if she sees water, she panics, but MORE IMPORTANTLY: we could, in theory, take down one of the most powerful of all Monster Motors with a well-aimed fire hose.

CURRENT STATUS:

Homebase for Cadillacula

TLE:
ZOOMBIES

EHICLE CLASS:
arious

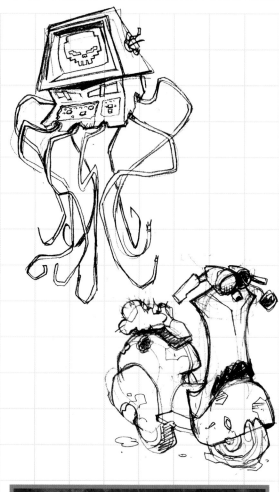

Artist's conception based on eyewitness accounts by Nick Roche

DESCRIPTION:

There are plenty of wolfcars out there. Your classic zombie is a rotting, mindless drone. Zoombies, the mechanical equivalent, aren't much different: rusting, missing parts, falling apart... and very hungry. Zoombies eat metal, but what they REALLY crave is the power supply: a battery, electrical charge of ANY kind. It keeps them going.

There are various ways to make a Zoombie: a curse, a spell, random comets, a bite from a Sumerian Rat Go-Cart, and, as of late, strategically placed lightning. It's easy to make them, and we've seen all manners of these cannibal machines: cars, trucks, helicopters, even blenders, computers. If it has a battery, it can be turned into a Zoombie.

ABILITIES:

The ability to cut through metal with what passes for their teeth. But it's what their bite DOES that's really scary: one chomp, heck, even the slightest nibble, turns a normal machine into a Zoombie as well. It's incredibly easy to make these things. If you have ONE, drop it in a used car lot, BOOM, fifteen minutes later, every single car has a bite in the hood and is trying to find it's next meal.

They are also incredibly hard to destroy. Yes, a Zoombie is typically rusting, falling apart, decomposing, making them easy to break. But just because you rip one to pieces, that doesn't mean it's taken care of. You take a Zoombie apart, and every piece will keep coming after you.

WEAKNESSES:

Incredibly dumb. Can't talk, can't really think for themselves. You can outsmart them. As they're usually falling apart and/or rusting, they're usually slow-moving, so you can outrun them.

They are driven (no pun intended, this is serious business) by ONE thing: their insatiable hunger. There's no guesswork involved with what they want, no Zoombie is trying to take over the world, they JUST want to eat. It's that simple. This can be used to trap or distract them. Once you have them, destroying them is a whole other thing. We've found two methods work: (1) destroying their power supply or (2) destroying them completely.

If a machine is bitten, Vic Frankenstein helped us discover that if we remove the infected area quickly enough, the victim CAN live.

CURRENT STATUS:

Many are prisoners of Minivan Helsing for evaluation, but at least one, a tiny red Motorscooter (nicknamed Bad Motorscooter) is unaccounted for. Last seen in the woods surrounding Transylvania, Kentucky.

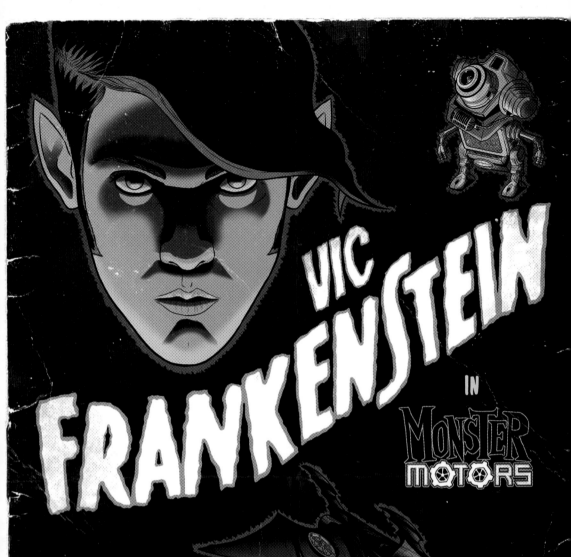

VIC FRANKENSTEIN

IN **MONSTER MOTORS**

With

BRIAN LYNCH • NICK ROCHE
LEN O'GRADY • TOM B. LONG
CHRIS RYALL • MICHAEL BENEDETTO
&
DARYL SHAW • DEE CUNNIFFE

IDW PICTURES

Pin-up by Daryl Shaw and Dee Cunniffe

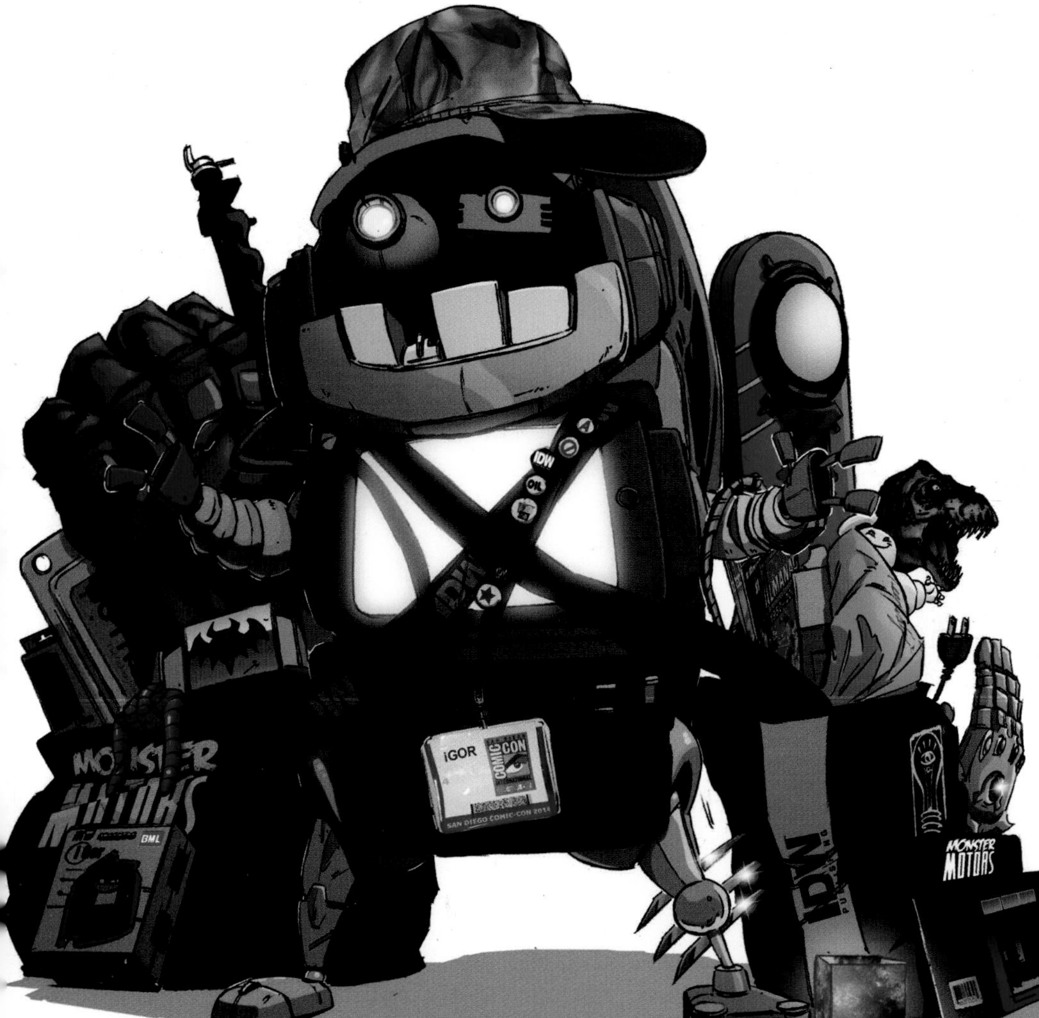

IDW
iGOR
COMIC-CON
SAN DIEGO COMIC-CON 2014
MONSTER MOTORS
MONSTER MOTORS

ART BY DAN SCHOENING, COLORS BY LUIS ANTONIO DELGADO